PATHWAYS

To our mentor and friend Ole Nørgaard

PATHWAYS

– A STUDY OF SIX POST-COMMUNIST COUNTRIES

Edited by Lars Johannsen & Karin Hilmer Pedersen

AARHUS UNIVERSITY PRESS

Pathways – a study of six post-communist countries
© The authors and Aarhus University Press 2009
Cover: Jørgen Sparre
Typeface: Minion Pro
Printed by Narayana Press, Gylling

Printed in Denmark 2009

ISBN 978 87 7934 434 1

Published with the financial support of
Aarhus Universitets Forskningsfond

Aarhus University Press
Langelandsgade 177
DK-8200 Århus N
www.unipress.dk

White Cross Mills
Hightown, Lancaster, LA1 4XS
United Kingdom
www.gazellebookservices.co.uk

PO Box 511
Oakwille, CT 06779
USA
www.oxbowbooks.com

541-562
Svanemærket tryksag

Mixed Sources

Product group from well-managed
forests and other controlled sources
www.fsc.org Cert no. SW-COC-003428
© 1996 Forest Stewardship Council

FSC

Contents

Preface

The working title of this volume was: *Comparing the incomparable*, and as such this book has made a long journey. In keeping with the Tocquevillian tradition, Professor Ole Nørgaard initiated a research series under the heading 'Understanding Politics in X-country'. The authors were asked to write articles containing fundamental insights into the logic of the current workings of the polity of a country of which they had comprehensive knowledge. Moreover, and again following the Tocquevillian tradition, the articles were to be written in the light of each country's uniqueness compared to other countries in the region, and in particular to the country of a West European reader. The result was a series of 15 country research papers published at the Department of Political Science, Aarhus University.

Regrettably, this volume had to be compiled without Ole Nørgaard. Shortly before his death he envisioned a volume that was to combine methodological boldness with solid unique analysis. Ole was fond of saying that 'good research has a success rate of 50 per cent'. A good researcher should venture into uncharted waters; otherwise we would be doomed to repeat the mistakes of those who came before us. To honour his memory we took this task upon ourselves.

From the original 15 country studies we chose six countries, each of which contains a key feature decisive for the initial institutional choices that frame the capability or incapability of governments to produce policies – and thus to stabilise the political system as such. We thereby refrain from looking only at the process of democratisation and democratic consolidation. Instead we look at stabilising and de-stabilising features in democratic as well as authoritarian regimes.

The initial institutional choices are based upon the elite preferences engendered by the different impacts of the quadruple transition process in which nation building and state building intertwine with marketisation and political regime change. Moreover, we look at how the international context enhances or constrains elite preferences within these four interconnected transformations.

Comparing the incomparable was part of a larger project investigating *Democracy, the State and Administrative Reform* in former communist countries. We want to thank the Danish Social Science Research Council and the University of Aarhus Research Foundation for their generous financial support. We also want to thank Else Løvdal for her attempts to mend our linguistic incapacities and for all her good humour and support throughout the lifetime of this project.

With this volume we and the authors wish to express our special thanks to Ole Nørgaard, but alas this has to be done in memoriam. He was a driving force behind this and many other projects. His kindness, support, foresight and friendship will be most fondly remembered.

January 2009
Lars Johannsen & Karin Hilmer Pedersen

CHAPTER 1

After the Wall:

Political development trajectories in selected post-communist countries

Lars Johannsen and Karin Hilmer Pedersen

Since The Wall was demolished, the event that symbolised freedom from the Soviet empire and catalysed the implosion of the Soviet Union itself, political developments in what we now call former communist countries have taken various paths. Power has changed hands peacefully by the ballot in Central and Eastern Europe, and the economies have resumed growth after initial contractions. The Baltic States stood out as shining miracles, in stark contrast to several former Soviet republics that plunged into war, civil strife, poverty and outright dictatorship. Harold Macmillan's 1960 'wind of change' jumped continents, but only Slovenia took the fast track to membership of the European Union after narrowly escaping the atrocities in the wake of the dissolution of Yugoslavia.

In order to trace these various paths of development we build on insights gained during the last fifteen years of studies of transition, democratisation and political development, asking why a feature is decisive for change in one context while not in another; and why one context accords particular incentives and preferences among elites in some countries but not in others. Important though it is in view of the many theoretical debates that revolve around it, democracy should not be seen as the dependent variable. We look instead for the feature that was decisive for the political development in each country in question. We thereby change the focus from the content of the outcome (democracy or not) to the paths chosen by elites. An alternative formulation is: 'what is the *key* to understanding the political development of the said country?'

In methodological terms we offer a foundation for (re)constructing an alternative view of transition trajectories in the post-communist space. We do so by deconstructing the 'keys' to development into combinations of four interlinked transformation areas: political institutions, economic liberalisation, nation building and state building. Adding to this web of interconnected transformation areas, we discuss how the international context may either reinforce elite positions or constrain decision making.

Tracing the different trajectories of political development in post-communist countries requires a choice of cases from within the post-communist region that exhibit maximum variation in independent variables. We have accordingly selected six countries – Kazakhstan, Georgia, Estonia, Slovenia, the Czech Republic and Poland. The agenda and the cases echo the depths of Valerie Bunce's comment that post-communist development encompasses virtually 'all the fundamental issues in politics' (Bunce 2001, 793), namely [re-]construction of economic and political regimes, decisions about national composition and affiliation of populations, and the state and its capacity to command compliance (to govern) and extract resources. The cases presented here thus truly reflect the 'comparable cases strategy' (Landman 2000; Lijphart 1975), in which the outcome is the product of multiple causal factors acting in concert. In strict methodological terms the choice of maximum variation in the constituent independent variables should be followed by a parallel similarity between the outcome and the explanatory factors. However, among our cases Kazakhstan and Georgia are examples of autocracy or semi-authoritarian regimes, whereas the European cases exemplify democratic success, even if they too exhibit fundamental democratic deficits (Ágh 2002; Lewis 2004). Thus, what we are in fact striving for in methodological terms is to compare the incomparable.

In our search for the keys to political development we asked six country specialists to paint a broad picture of what characterises the changes listed above. We asked them to follow the Tocquevillian tradition, a 'method' of indirect comparison where in-depth knowledge of a country based on linguistics and history is held up against existing concepts. In this sense, all case studies and empirical descriptions have a comparative core because comparable concepts are applied. Thus, we stress that the manner in which the four transitions are connected and shaped by their positions in the international context provides unique 'keys' to understanding the countries in question, and hence we called for contributions that place the choices made by the elites in a socio-economic and historical context.

The following six chapters, each dedicated to one country, constitute the main bulk of this book. The final task of comparing across the cases and discussing different pathways will be dealt with in our concluding chapter. This introductory chapter first gives an overview of the debate and describes the importance and impact of the different transition spheres. Second, we discuss the methodology applied in the final comparative chapter.

PERTINENT THEORY

Initially both optimism and scepticism thrived with respect to political developments in the aftermath of communist rule. In political science there was certainly room for optimism. Following the lead of Rustow (1970), a group of prominent researchers led by Schmitter and O'Donnell published a monumental four-volume study of the transitions to democracy in Southern Europe and Latin America, emphasising actors and stages in the process (O'Donnell, Schmitter & Whitehead (eds.) 1986a; 1986b; 1986c; O'Donnell & Schmitter 1986). The core of their argument rests on the intuitive fact that the initiation of democracy is an agreement made among concerned interests (Przeworski 1988; 1991; McFaul 2002) – a matter of 'craftsmanship' (di Palma 1990). Structural factors are consequently relegated to a status of being more or less benevolent factors for the survival of democracy rather than root causes for the development of democracy (Przeworski & Limongi 1997). The speed with which the Central and Eastern European countries embraced democratic procedures can be interpreted as the ultimate confirmation of their core argument.

The initial optimism was, however, soon laced with scepticism. The concerns about the viability of democracy were not unfounded. Stepan and Suleiman (1995), for example, warned about political instability in Poland, and the 'stolen revolution' in Romania (Tismaneanu 1997) was ample evidence of the difficulties associated with establishing democracy. Populism, not only as a general phenomenon (Carpenter 1997), endangered economic reform (Sachs 1992) and bore with it the seeds of authoritarianism (Eke & Kuzio 2000). Popular mistrust of new institutions and the political elite also became widespread (Misler & Rose 1997; 2001). However, perhaps because of the speed with which the Central and East European countries embraced free elections, the transition to and consolidation of democracy came to be used interchangeably, creating a conceptual fog between the end goal of political development and the process (Kopecky & Mudde 2000). In other words, the focus on getting the institutions right was confounded with internalisation and the acceptance of democratic norms and values.

The theories of transition from authoritarian regimes have focused on the development of democratic political institutions. In line with the scepticism noted above, it would seem odd to speak of a process of democratisation as there are few signs that this is occurring in Central Asia and the Caucasus. Instead a number of scholars have pointed to the rise of authoritarianism (Kubicek 1998; Treacher 1996), if not sultanism (Eke & Kuzio 2000; Blank 2004) or clan politics (Schatz 2004; Collins 2004; Matsuzato 2004). The last few years have seen a growing literature about these 'halfway houses' using vocabulary like 'competitive authoritarianism' (Levitsky & Way 2003) and 'Hybrid Regimes' (Diamond 2002) in their efforts to classify regimes and to understand the processes in countries that feature some elements of liberal democracy, but also major or minor democratic deficiencies. That is, while much of Eastern Europe is characterised by deficient democracy, democratic quality remains problematic even among more advanced countries (Lewis 2004, 162). So in terms of democratic choices, the outcomes of post-communist transitions range from defective democracies or de facto return to authoritarian regimes further to the East and in the Southern Balkans, to success stories of democratically consolidated systems that are now – or are about to become – members of the European Union. Even though there are undoubtedly some success stories, they are still marred by democratic deficits (Rupnik 2007; Mungio-Pippidi 2007). That is not to say that democracy is considered fragile in the new and coming EU member states. At a macro-level EU membership will safeguard democratic transition (Sadurski 2004). Still, 'there are democratic deficits, corresponding to the advanced democracies, acting as obstacles to further democratization' (Ágh 2002). So while the early process of building democratic institutions is finished and primarily interpreted as a top-down elite project, the development of efficient political decision-making systems capable of producing policies that maximise collective benefits to democratic majorities and the creation of state administrations to implement political decisions in transparent ways that include citizens' interests and concerns are much more difficult and time-consuming tasks.

In early transition studies much ground was gained with respect to the description and explanation of the sudden breakdown of the communist regimes, the subsequent negotiations (Elster 1993), and the study of the early choices in rebuilding institutions (Geddes 1996; Elster, Offe & Preuss (eds.) 1998; Nørgaard & Johannsen 1999). A large number of case studies discussed the political developments in individual countries in detail, but few scholars attempted comparative studies. Ágh's (1998) informative study of Central Europe and the Balkans and Geddes' (1999) seminal article, in which she uses game theory to lay the theoretical foundations for comparing military and party cadre preferences depending on their strength, are notable exceptions. Even though O'Donnell (2002, 7), one of the authors of the four-volume study mentioned earlier that paved the way for transitology, later emphasised that 'nothing [is] predestined about the transition', there has been a puzzling silence about the formation of actor preferences. This silence is justified in a rational choice model applying a short-term perspective that distinguishes between hard- and soft-liners (Karl 1986; Elster 1993); but Haggard and Kaufman (1997) have rightly challenged transition theory for using the short-term perspective because it fails to address the historical context and the political economy, without which it is not possible to understand the relative positions of the actors or their values.

The successes, deficiencies or democratic failures of various regimes within the region demonstrate that we will not be able to understand the trajectories or later developments unless the historical context and the values and strengths of the respective actors are factored into the equation. Although we emphasise the importance of the past, we do not necessarily see the past as a deadweight but, referring to Stark and Bruszt (1998), as the social logic that configured strategic choices and shaped future policy outcomes. However, following Kreuzer & Pettai (2004), merely referring to history is not sufficient. Instead, the impact of each historical phenomenon upon the present must be specified and, ideally, a weight must be assigned to the argument. Thus, rejecting the assumption of a *tabula rasa* situation after the breakdown of the Soviet communist regime, we contend that the political developments that formed the power structures of the elites were shaped by historical constraints as well as opportunities. Moreover, we not only focus on the political and economic transformation as being pertinent to the early transitology studies. Following Bunce as quoted above, our ambition is to analyse the way in which the present power structures and the opportunities and choices afforded to the elites were shaped by the past and intertwined in the four transition areas: political development, economic liberalisation, nation building, and state building. Furthermore, we seek to place the development of domestic power structures within the international context.

THE QUADRUPLE CHALLENGE

Our premise is that the roots of the current power structure that developed after communism should be sought in the way in which the elites have handled the four interconnected transformations. It is in this arena of connected processes that the battle between the incumbent and opposition elites was fought, and hence it is here that the roots of the new power structure are to be found. Originally, 'transition to democracy' simply denoted the process from the breakdown of an authoritarian regime to the agreement that establishes democracy (O'Donnell & Schmitter 1986). However, as noted above, establishing democratic procedures is not the same as democratic consolidation, and when we abandon the concepts of democratisation and democratic consolidation, the study of political development after communism becomes vastly more complex.

We now turn to a description of the four transformation areas and how they are interrelated. In doing so, we include illustrative examples from the region. Lastly, we consider how the international context constrains or furthers elite decisions.

Designing political institutions

Transitions from authoritarianism are frequently analysed with the aid of 'pacts' and 'imposition' (Karl & Schmitter 1991), highlighting exclusion and inclusion of the communist elite after regime breakdown. The communist elites in Georgia and the Czech Republic were effectively excluded, while Poland and Hungary are the standard examples of negotiated and inclusive East European pacts. An additional distinction, however, is how elites exploited the windows of opportunity that were open only in the early years of reform. Elster, Offe & Preuss (1998, 59-60) argue that such windows could either be 'invested' in the creation of new institutions or 'consumed' to accumulate power and deal with newly emerging problems on an ad hoc basis. Whereas Hungary, Poland and the Czech Republic illustrate how the windows of opportunity were invested in forming new democratic and economic institutions, the Georgian elite consolidated their power by using state institutions for private ends in a clientelistic network.

Inclusion or exclusion of the communist elite and the way elites operated are reflected in how the new political institutions evolved. At least three aspects are crucial. The first aspect concerns how political decision makers, presidents and parliaments, are chosen. On the one hand, election rules can be so constructed that the incumbent regime can ensure the election of its candidates through appointments to a quota of the Upper House and through stringent membership requirements for parties, which is the case in Kazakhstan. On the other hand, early decisions on election rules can be so liberal that representation becomes fragmented, and thus counterproductive to efficient and viable decision making. Conversely, the choice of an extremely high electoral threshold may effectively exclude significant parts of the population from parliamentary representation as seen in the Czech Republic.

The second aspect concerns how public demands and interests are channelled into political decisions: the development of political parties on the one hand, and that of civil society organisations on the other. Post-communist states are dominated for many reasons by weak and deformed civil societies (Bernhard 1996). Communism not only did its best, at least in theory, to stamp out socio-economic differences; it also attempted to destroy civil society in practice. At the dawn of democracy in 1989 Linz and Stepan (1996, 352) counted the number of independent movements in Poland, Hungary and Bulgaria to be a mere 60, 21 and 13, respectively. Although the number of associations has since increased massively (Ágh 2001; Mansfeldová et al. 2005), Howard (2000) argues that measured by membership, organisations in post-communist Europe remain weak.

The weakness of civil society is correlated with the persistent problems in forming party systems that reflect emerging socio-economic cleavages. The problem is related to a persistent political cleavage along the lines of a post-communist divide (Kitschelt 1995; Whitefield 2002) and the lack of coherent inter-party and coalition programmes, of which the Polish case is an all too good example. The main problem, not only in the Polish case, is to develop a stable party system to ensure that governments are accountable to the voters through the parties (Rose, Munro & White 2001). Toole (2003) demonstrates that the formation of a modern East-European party tends to be elite-driven and not so much rooted in society; but he also finds (2005) promising signs of decreasing electoral volatility, suggesting that the party systems are in the process of stabilising. Developments in the Czech Republic highlight another problem. Here The Communist Party of Bohemia and Moravia (KSČM) – the last unreformed communist party in Eastern Europe – wins between 11 and 18 per cent of the vote. But because of its extreme leftist position it is not considered a credible government partner. The danger is not so much that government must be formed among centrist forces; the risk is that the KSČM is forced to become, in Linz's (1978) terms, an anti-systemic and disloyal opposition, and secondly, that a forced coalition between centre and right-wing parties may eradicate political competition (Vachaudova 2005).

The third aspect focuses on the inclusion of civil society actors in decision-making processes. Inclusiveness is not merely a question of voice, however. There is empirical evidence that a responsive state, one characterised by dense cooperation between public authorities and a civil society based on values of participatory democracy, has a tendency to be kinder and gentler, promoting equality and reducing poverty (Johannsen & Pedersen 2008). In our country sample, the extended Slovenian corporatist system is a highly inclusive political system (Lukšič 2003), while in contrast, the Kazakhstani political system is based on central management with a largely demobilised civil society in which civil society organisations are mainly seen to monitor society and mobilise behind presidential policies. The remaining countries' attempts to activate tripartite institutions, partly in response to European Union requests, can be placed somewhere in-between.

Redistributing ownership

The economic structure under communism was based on state ownership and planning, according the communist elite nearly absolute power and control over economic decisions. Thus, the political system could not have been transformed without rearranging the economic institutions and redefining the relationship between political and economic power (Elster, Offe, & Preuss 1998). Rejection of the communist tradition of state-owned means of production and centralised economic planning obviously required a revision of property rights, implying privatisation and marketisation in the form of price liberalisation and exposure of domestic markets to global competition (Frydman et al. 1993). Choices in these areas determined who stood to gain and who to lose in the process.

Two approaches soon crystallised – radical 'big bang' versus gradual reform (Przeworski 1991; Williamson 1993), anticipating that economic hardship and unemployment would be inescapable consequences of reform. The two approaches primarily diverged in their estimation of how severe the crisis would be and how long it would take the economies to recover. Inspired by the neo-liberal so-called *Washington consensus,* the radical 'big bang' was thought to bring about a steep J-curve with initial contraction being followed by speedy recovery (Hellman 1998). Conversely, the gradual reform process was expected to produce a less steep J-curve and require a more prolonged period of economic recovery. Marketisation appears to have had its own set of political consequences for the functioning of democracy. Advocates of rapid economic reform claimed that, given the expected initial welfare loss (Fidrmuc 2003), the elite should utilise the 'extraordinary political capital' generated by the systemic change to implement policies and then see them through before electoral reaction set in (Balcerowicz 1994). However, such a top-down reform process constricts democracy and might well fuel anti-democratic and populist tendencies (Grabel 2000; Przeworski et al. 1995).

The initial choices of pace and sequencing of economic reform policies diverged radically among the countries. Estonia made the most radical and consistent choices in terms of price liberalisation, free trade policies, introduction of a flat tax rate system and large-scale privatisation (Nørgaard & Johannsen, 1999). The early stages of Poland's liberalisation in 1989-1991 were equally successful, utilising a strongly autocratic, autonomous 'change team' with a high degree of internal coherence that was relatively insulated from social actors and commanded extensive foreign expertise (Pedersen & Zubek, 2005). However, problems of how to privatise major state-owned enterprises are still pending, in part due to comparatively high levels of employee security and influence. Largely following neo-liberal recommendations, Prime Minister Vasclav Klaus introduced a voucher scheme for the Czech privatisation process, giving every adult Czech person a share of state property. With respect to economic liberalisation, Kazakhstan is in a completely different league as access to natural resources (oil) creates special conditions for the extraordinary extraction of windfall resources by the elites, which leads to discussions of 'rentier states' (e.g. Ross 2001). To some extent the same is true of Georgia, which controls Russian gas pipelines. However, ethnic conflict and chaos have derailed the successful strategic use of the resources.

The privatisation process has given the incumbent elites vast opportunities to strengthen their power bases in the economic sphere. Adjectives characterising the process more as *theft* than *fair trade* have been common. Moreover, in Poland unsettled issues of privatisation have enabled the elite to shift smoothly between political positions in parliament and private entrepreneurships, contributing to a general mistrust in elite behaviour and raising suspicions and accusations of corruption.

Dismantling or rebuilding the state

Although not in the frontline, transformation of the state – or state building – is closely related to political and economic transition. State building was somewhat overlooked in democratisation discussions (Linz & Stepan 1996), which initially confined themselves to the study of institutions and how post-communist countries revised and/or adopted new constitutions and electoral systems (Lijphart 1994; Geddes 1996; Pogany 1996; Frye 1997; Johannsen 2000). However, its connectedness to economic reform became evident only two years after the regimes broke down, when Offe (1991) posited that the Central and Eastern European countries faced a 'triple transition'. In addition to democratisation and marketisation, Offe argued that stateness, a conflation of state and nation building, was also an essential aspect of transition. But as made clear by Grzymala-Busse and Luong (2002), many scholars overlooked the need to reconstruct public authority in the post-communist countries, instead seeing the agenda as state dismantling in the face of the behemoth communist state.

Later contributions have emphasised other dimensions of state building, partly because the dust from the constitutional struggles has settled, partly because marketisation and privatisation created a demand-driven agenda (Fukuyama 2004). This agenda clearly goes beyond a concept of state building focusing on monopolising physical violence within a given recognised territory, even though this has indeed been particularly problematic in Georgia. Rather, the state-building agenda points to increasing governance capacity and ability to fulfil core obligations. Most importantly, the new economic order required as much attention as the rebuilding of the state's capacity to guarantee and protect the rights and liberties crucial to the enforcement of contracts and the protection of citizens' property. The rebuilding of the state's capacity to govern emphasises both elite decision-making and implementation capacity. On the one hand, decision-making capacity illuminates the importance of democratic bargaining and compromise within the elite and its responsiveness to public interests. This decision-making capacity emphasises the elite's ability to rebuild state functions, not only within the core obligations mentioned above, but increasingly in terms of securing the public infrastructure and service facilities necessary to ensure economic performance. On the other hand, insufficient state capacity impedes the implementation of decisions made by elected officials (see, for example, Pedersen & Johannsen 2004). Consequently, consolidated democracy becomes largely irrelevant if the laws passed by a democratically elected parliament are poorly implemented, and hence do not have the intended impact on citizens' lives. Thus, however important the establishment and acceptance of democratic procedures by state and non-state actors alike, the functionality of a democratic government is nullified if the state does not have the capacity needed to implement these decisions.

This debate emphasises that democracy requires not only Montesquieu's division of power, but also functioning and capable administrations guided by Weberian and democratic principles (Peters 1995; Linz & Stepan 1996; Bunce 2000). This emphasis comprises three aspects. First, the challenge of state building was coping with a public administration legacy from the communist regime based on 'command-and-control' principles and subordinated to the political interests of the regime (Verheijen, 1999; Obolonsky, 1999). Although this system did in many ways resemble a Weberian ideal type bureaucracy, it became the very antithesis of efficiency and transparency because of the highly politicised communist culture.

Second, the emphasis on state building has highlighted the issue of corruption. Corruption is not just a moral problem – it also circumvents democratic decision-making processes within the legislature and has an adverse impact on adoption and implementation (Pedersen & Johannsen 2006a; Johannsen & Pedersen 2007). While corruption may certainly be problematic in moral terms, some scholars argue that systematised corruption can result in a state administration that at least functions (Miller et al. 2001), which to some extent was the case in Georgia (Christophe 2004). Although the new EU-member states in particular have had increasing success in gaining control of corruption, it is still a considerable problem in these countries, and even more so in states that are not EU members (Johannsen & Pedersen, 2008). Third, the specific topic of lustration, elimination of people regarded as renegades during the communist regime by the new elite, elevated political criteria above experience and efficiency (Kaldor & Vejvoda 1997). On the other hand, while lustration policies were harsh in the Czech Republic, Poland only began to discuss the issue more than ten years after the Soviet regime broke down. Moreover, in the Czech Republic lustration is continuously criticised for being unjust, based on rumours and gossip, and for striking at random.

The issue of state building has thus become fused with an emerging literature on state capacity and administrative reform (Cummings & Nørgaard 2004; Goetz 2001). The central aspect of state building has been applied to administrative and judicial reform, civil service legislation, economically sustainable salaries and education, all focusing on a Weberian-inspired meritocracy in order to avoid arbitrary administrative decisions and informal empowerment of the elite (Nunberg 2000).

Who to include and who to exclude?

Nation building, as a process distinct from state building, is the building block that completes the quadruple transformation process (Lewis 2004), and when Schmitter and Karl (1994) ask 'how far east should [transitologists] attempt to go?', Kuzio (2001, 169) replies indirectly by arguing that transitologists did not 'go far enough' in their efforts to develop a framework capable of distinguishing between state building and the national question as two separate and conceptually different processes. In the post-communist patchwork of nationalities and minorities, anti-discriminatory policies had the potential to provoke dissatisfaction in the 'titular' population if they felt the 'new' state did not pay sufficient attention to their needs. So when the post-communist states had to change entire political and economic systems and rebuild their states, they were challenged by the fourth issue of nation building, compelling them to define who should be the 'people' constituting the political community (Kuzio, 2001).

The challenge of nation building emerges again because the states were founded in accordance with the Westphalian notion of *one nation* (Brubaker, 1996) through which it is decided who belongs to the state (inclusion) and who does not (exclusion). Defining *the nation* is far from an objective exercise, however. As argued by Benedict Anderson (1983), a nation reflects the way in which people within the borders of a given territory *imagine* belongingness to the political community. It is argued that imagined belongingness can be formed in either of two ways. First, belongingness can be established on the principle of citizenship, thus according every citizen within the territory equal rights and obligations. Second, belongingness can be built on a sense of shared cultural or ethnic characteristics, common language, tradition or history. In either case the image of a nation limits and thus stands in contrast to the images of *other nations*.

The distinction between a *civic* and an *ethnic* core of a nation was discussed at length after Brubaker's seminal book. According to Kuzio (2001), however, this implies that it should be possible to identify states empirically based on civic principles alone. But this is not the case. In contrast, he argues that *all* civic states have ethno-cultural cores, but they emphasise their ethno-cultural cores to varying degrees, and thus, with different implications for choices in the three other transformation areas.

Faced with the challenge of defining the nation, the elites often appealed to the nationalism of the 'titular' population as a strategy to consolidate their own power (Linz & Stepan, 1996). Besides, nationalism thrived well in these countries as it was commensurate with the Soviet legacy that based citizenship in the tradition of *Volk, blood, narod and race* (Crawford & Lijphart 1995; Bunce 1995b).

The issue of nation building may be played out in an exclusive and possibly hostile way, or it may be inclusive and pragmatic. Contrast, for example, the Kazakhstani rhetoric of inclusion and a 'Kazakhstani' state with the ethnic conflicts in Georgia. But even though the question of nation building was more apparent in countries further to the east, as the examples of Kazakhstan and Georgia show, it was not absent in Central and Eastern Europe. Looking beyond the countries considered in this book, Slovakia is a prime example of state formation being a nationalising project (Tesser 2003; Pridham 2002). Furthermore, Latvia and Estonia were criticised for building an 'ethnocracy' when they excluded Soviet-era immigrants from political participation in the early days of transition (Linz & Stepan 1996). Even Hungary had to face the question of nation building when the Antall government in the early 1990s had to deal with an irredentist claim that the borders with neighbouring

Slovakia and Romania should be reconsidered (see, for example, Vachaudova 2005).

The consequences of early decisions about nationhood are evident. The Estonian de facto exclusion of the Russian population from participating in early elections and in privatisation schemes created a momentum that enabled the titular Estonians to (re-)capture the economy and state apparatus. In contrast, the undetermined nation building in Georgia placed the country between ethnic and civil wars, delaying large-scale privatisation and administrative reconstruction. Defining the nation never really became an issue in Poland despite the existence of external territories with large groups of ethnic Poles in Lithuania and Ukraine. Nationality being a 'non-issue', the political struggle has concentrated on building and re-building institutions.

In more general terms, and following Rustow (1970), a nation is consolidated when the community is taken for granted and is above normal politics. Nation building is thus distinct from state building in the sense that it refers to a community based on shared or imagined values rather than on the state. However, nation building and state building are also matters of practice (Kopecky & Mudde 2000). Nationalist movements not only functioned as catalysts for bringing down the inner Soviet empire, as the popular movements in the Baltic states and elsewhere showed (Tuminez 2003; Bunce 2005). Part of the state-building process involves the creation of a positive identification, and an effective state requires the existence of an established and agreed political community (Rustow 1970; Kubicek 2000). The link between nation building and the other transformation areas thereby highlights the way in which decisions on inclusion/exclusion may impact the functioning of democracy, redistribution of wealth in the privatisation process, and rebuilding state administrative capacity.

The international context

Domestic transformation after communism did not take place in a vacuum. Globalisation and systemic pressures have increasingly called the distinction between politics within the state and politics among nations into question. The international context in many respects sets the stage for elite decisions. A central distinction argued by Levitsky and Way (2005) concerns the vulnerability of governments to external pressure and how committed they are to implementing internationally advocated reforms. For example, elite decisions regarding economic reforms were heavily influenced by the *Washington consensus*, even though its liberal recommendations were not followed by all transition countries.

The international context also shaped decisions on state building. This is most evident in Estonia, Poland, the Czech Republic and Slovenia, where the European Union set the stage in a process characterised as 'the most massive international rule transfer in recent history' (Schimmelfennig & Sedelmeier, 2005, 6). Outside the realm of direct EU conditionality, the international community, international donors and trade partners have put pressure on domestic elites. Eduard Shevardnadze's comeback and his long rule in Georgia can be seen as due to his close international connections – he was the 'pet of the West', which gave him the opportunity to divert Western financial assistance to serve his own interests and those of his proponents. In contrast, Kazakhstan reflects the importance of having natural resources, in this case oil. Oil income has given Kazakh leaders more freedom to make domestic policies without external powers having leverage on them. On the other hand, dependency on foreign investments to extract oil resources has made it necessary to enhance transparency and meritocracy in the financial sector as well as in pockets within the state administration.

In a similar vein the international context has been formative with respect to nation building. Related not only to the historical fact of Soviet occupation but also to fear of Russian irredentism, the Estonian elite was empowered to exclude a Russian minority from political influence with little criticism from the Western international community. In contrast, the number of Russians in Kazakhstan and its proximity to Russia made it difficult for the elite to construct the country on a concept of a *Kazakhi nation*.

Even though our understanding of domestic change is only complete when the international context is taken into consideration, we do contend that the choices made in regime transformation are solely contingent upon domestic forces and demands but are like intertwined strands in the quadruple transition process.

THE BEAUTY OF MAXIMISING VARIATION

The conceptual idea behind this book is that the way in which each aspect of the four transitions was handled by the elites constitutes the specificity of regime transition in each post-communist country. However, connecting the four transitions as well as the impact of the international context is a highly ambitious agenda. The challenge is to gain new theoretical and conceptual insights into factors that determined whether political development ran from authoritarian regime to consolidated democracy or not. In accordance with Karl and Schmitter's (1995) suggestions, we seek to combine the approaches used in area- and case-specific studies with those of cross-comparative studies. Our claim is that agency matters, but that it must be underpinned by the historical and socio-economic contexts within the interrelated transitions. In theoretical terms, this implies a sociological rather than a rational choice perspective on agency (March & Olson 1984; Hall & Taylor 1996), and in methodological terms it requires that we maximise variation.

The choice of Kazakhstan, Georgia, Estonia, Poland, the Czech Republic and Slovenia makes for a maximum of variation in background variables. In this sense there are resonances of the debate of the 1990s concerning transitology versus area studies, and thus more explicitly concerning the comparability of transitions in Latin America and Southern Europe with those that took place in the post-communist countries.

On the one hand, it was argued, the post-communist transitions should be utilised in systematic comparisons to reveal if there are differences between the regions, thus engaging in the process of theory building and operationalisation of concepts based on solid empirical research (Schmitter & Karl 1994; Karl & Schmitter 1995). On the other hand, it was argued, the differences between the regions were too extensive to permit fruitful comparisons, in part because the regime changes in the post-communist area involved more dimensions than those in Southern Europe and Latin America (Bunce 1995b). Instead it was emphasised that the post-communist experience constituted a 'comparative laboratory' (Bunce 2001, 793), not only because of the sheer number of cases but, more importantly, because they had all been exposed to similar 'homogenizing effects of the socialist experience' and shared defining characteristics with respect to dominant ideology and economic, social and political models (Bunce 1999). This is not to say that there are no differences. As Bunce (1999) herself makes clear, by 1995 Slovenia was about 25 times richer than Tajikistan.

The methodological implication of Bunce's argument of similarity in post-communist countries is that there is far less need to root studies in their historical context and the political economy. However, a simple comparative model will suffice only if we assume that all cases are alike. We argue instead that variation may be just as comprehensive within the post-communist countries, giving rise to an equally justified warning about comparing not just apples, but apples and kangaroos. Table 1, which compares the cases with respect to a number of variables, is ample evidence of the striking variance between the selected cases. Comparing their political and economic legacies, the Czech Republic and Poland belonged to the 'outer Soviet empire'. Estonia, Georgia and Kazakhstan were integral parts of the Soviet Union, whereas Slovenia was a constituent part of socialist Yugoslavia. With respect to traditions of statehood, Poland was ostensibly an independent state. The Czech Republic gained independence through the 'velvet divorce' from Slovakia. Estonia and Georgia could point to a few symbolically and politically important years of independence prior to their forced incorporation into the Soviet Union in 1940 and 1921, respectively. Kazakhstan was originally part of Tsarist Russia, and if Slovenia had ever experienced independence before achieving its current status, that legacy has faded even from public memory.

TABLE 1: SELECTED BACKGROUND VARIABLES IN SIX SELECTED POST-COMMUNIST COUNTRIES

	KAZAKHSTAN	GEORGIA	ESTONIA	POLAND	CZECH REPUBLIC	SLOVENIA
POLITICAL AND ECONOMIC INHERITANCE	1920: Soviet Republic	1921: Soviet occupation and annexation 1992: Civil war and de facto separatist regions of Abkhazia & South Ossetia	1940: Soviet occupation 1945: Forced collectivization, immigration and integration in Soviet planned economy.	1945: Soviet satellite 1952: People's Republic of Poland 1980: Solidarity 1981: Martial Law introduced	1948: Communist Coup d'etat. 1968: Prague Spring crushed.	-1918: Austro-Hungarian empire 1918: Kingdom of Yugoslavia 1945: Socialist Federal Republic of Yugoslavia
INDEPENDENCE	1991: Independence following the collapse of the Soviet Union	1991: Declaration of independence 1991: de facto independence following the collapse of the Soviet Union	1990: Declaration of independence 1991: de facto independence following the collapse of the Soviet Union	1918: Treaty of Versailles	1993: Velvet divorce.	1991: Declaration of independence and the 10-days war.
POPULATION	15.2 mill.	4.7 mill.	1.3 mill.	38.5 mill.	10.2 mill.	2.0 mill.
ETHNIC MINORITIES (PERCENT)	Russophone: 33.7 Uzbek: 2.5 German: 2.4 Tatar: 1.7 Uygur: 1.4 Other: 4.9	Azeri: 6.5 Armenian: 5.7 Russian: 1.5 Other: 2.5	Russophone: 29.0 Finns: 0.9 Other: 2.2	German: 0.4 Belarussian: 0.1 Ukrainian: 0.1 Other: 2.7	Moravian: 3.7 Slovak: 1.9 Other: 4	Serb: 2 Croat 1.8 Bosniak: 1.1 Other: 12
GDP/CAPITA, 2004 ($)	1,483	1,132	8,227	6,265	10,462	16,359
SYSTEM OF GOVERNMENT	De facto Presidential	Semi-presidential	Parliamentary	Semi-presidential	Parliamentary	Parliamentary
DEMOCRACY	No	No/Yes	Yes	Yes	Yes	Yes

Sources: Encyclopaedia Britannica; CIA – The World Fact book; UNCTD World Development Index, Freedom House Index

The countries also differ with respect to size, wealth and ethnic composition. Measured by population size, Poland is about 30 times bigger than Estonia. In ethnic terms Poland is the most homogenous country, minorities constituting approximately three per cent of the total population. At the other end of the spectrum, the titular inhabitants of Kazakhstan make up a bare majority, and in Estonia the minority comprises almost one-third of the population. In terms of wealth the four European countries are almost 15 times richer than Kazakhstan and Georgia (even though Kazakhstan has experienced almost double-digit growth in recent years).

If we look at the first institutional choices after the fall of communism, the differences between the cases become even more striking. Politically the six cases differ with respect to their form of government. Parliamentarianism prevails among the European countries (Johannsen 2000), even though Poland has chosen a more semi-presidential system. Likewise, the Slovenian system is fundamentally parliamentary despite its directly elected president. In contrast, the Georgian system is ostensibly semi-presidential, while the Kazakhi system can best be described as 'de facto' presidentialism.

By maximising variation in the background variables, we stress that the way in which elite preferences and choices are formed by the four transition areas and linked to the international environment provides unique 'keys' to understanding the political development in the countries in question. As a result, we called for contributions that root the elite choices in their socio-economic and historical context and asked each author to focus on the decisive feature for the outcome in his or her case. Put another way: 'what is the *key* to understanding the political development of the country in question?'

Identifying these keys was not the task of the contributing authors. But extracting the keys from their in-depth insights allows us to subsequently address the issue of comparability across the cases. Why is a feature decisive in one context but not in another? Why does an elite in one context obtain particular incentives and preferences not found in other contexts? In this comparison we offer, in methodological terms, a foundation for (re-)constructing an alternative view of transition trajectories in the post-communist space by deconstructing the 'keys' in the combinations of the four transitions. Rather than straying into a debate over democracy versus authoritarianism, we stress that the 'key' that results from a combination of circumstances can help us understand political development.

The structure of this book is based on country studies that take us from East to West. We start in Kazakhstan, go on to Georgia and then turn north to Estonia. After Estonia we jump south to Slovenia, before we end with the two 'traditional' core central European states, the Czech Republic and Poland. Although we are searching for connections between developments in five transition areas, the authors have been given a free hand to approach the issues in their own spirit and style of writing, focusing of course on the 'key' to understanding post-communist developments. In the concluding chapter our point of departure is 'keys to transition'. Applying our comparative strategy with the transition areas as the core unit, we look for possible pathways to political development, proposing that the 'keys' emerge from the combination of challenges and decisions against the backdrop of the historical context.

References

Balcerowicz, L. 1994. 'Understanding Postcommunist Transitions', *Journal of Democracy*, 5, 4, 75-89.

Bunce, V. 1995b. 'Comparing east and south'. *Journal of Democracy*, 6, 87-100.

Bunce, V. 1999. 'The Political Economy of Postsocialism', *Slavic Review*, 58, 4, 756-793.

Bunce, V. 2000. 'Comparative Democratization: Big and Bounded Generalizations', *Comparative Political Studies*, 33, 6-7, 703-734.

Bunce, V. 2001. 'The Postsocialist Experience and Comparative Politics', *PS: Political Science and Politics*, 34, 4, 793-795.

Bunce, V. 2005. 'The National Idea: Imperial Legacies and Post-Communist Pathways in Eastern Europe', *East European Politics and Societies*, 19, 3, 406-442.

Carpenter, M. 1997. 'Slovakia and the Triumph of Nationalist Populism', *Communist and Post-Communist Studies*, 30, 2, 205-219.

Christophe, B. (2004), 'Understanding Politics in Georgia,' *DEMSTAR Research Report* no. 22. Aarhus: Department of Political Science.

Collins, K. 2004. 'The Logic Of Clan Politics: Evidence from the Central Asian Trajectories', *World Politics*, 56, 224-61.

Cummings, S.N. & O. Nørgaard 2004. 'Conceptualising State Capacity: Comparing Kazakhstan and Kyrgyzstan', *Political Studies*, 52, 4, 685-708.

di Palma, G. 1990. *To Craft Democracies: An Essay on Democratic Transitions*. Berkeley: University of California Press.

Diamond, L. 2002. 'Elections Without Democracy: Thinking about Hybrid Regimes', *Journal of Democracy*, 13, 2, 21-35.

Eke, S.M. & T. Kuzio 2000. 'Sultanism in Eastern Europe: The Socio-Political Roots of Authoritarian Populism in Belarus', *Europe-Asia Studies*, 52, 3, 523-547.

Elster, J. 1993. 'Constitution-Making in Eastern Europe: Rebuilding the Boat in Open Sea'. In: Joachim Jens Hesse (ed.), *Administrative Transformation in Central and Eastern Europe: Towards Public Sector Reform in Post-Communist Societies*. Oxford: Blackwell, 169-218.

Elster, J., C. Offe & U.K. Preuss, a.o. 1998. *Institutional Design in Post-Communist Societies: Rebuilding the Ship at Sea.* Cambridge: Cambridge University Press.

Fidrmuc, J. 2003. 'Economic reform, democracy and growth during post-communist transition', *European Journal of Political Economy*, 19, 3, 583-604.

Frydman, R., A. Rapaczynski, J.S. Earle et al. 1993. *The Privatization Process in Central and Eastern Europe.* And *The Privatization Process in Russia, Ukraine and the Baltic States.* CEU Privatization Reports vols. 1 and 2. Budapest, London, New York: Central European University Press.

Frye, T. 1997. 'A Politics of Institutional Choice: Post-Communist Presidencies', *Comparative Political Studies*, 30, 5, 523-552.

Fukuyama, F. 2004. *State-building. Governance and World Order in the 21st Century.* Ithaca, NY: Cornell University Press.

Geddes, B. 1996. 'Initiation of New Democratic Institutions in Eastern Europe and Latin America'. In: Arend Lijphart & Carlos H. Waisman (eds.), *Institutional Design in New Democracies: Eastern Europe and Latin America.* Boulder: Westview Press, 15-42.

Geddes, B. 1999. 'What Do We Know About Democratization After Twenty Years?', *Annual Review of Political Science*, 2, 115-144.

Goetz, K.H. 2001. 'Making sense of post-communist central administration: modernization, Europeanization or Latinization?', *Journal of European Public Policy*, 8, 6, 1032-1051.

Grabel, I. 2000. 'The political economy of 'policy credibility': the new-classical macroeconomic and the remaking of emerging economies', *Cambridge Journal of Economics*, 24, 1, 1-19.

Hall, P.A. & R.C.R. Taylor 1996. 'Political Science and the Three New Institutionalisms', *Political Studies*, 936-957.

Johannsen, L. & K.H. Pedersen 2007. 'The Talk of the Town: Comparing Corruption in the Baltic States and Poland'. In: M.-B. Schartau, S. Berglund & B. Henningsen (eds.), *Political Culture: Values and Identities in the Baltic Sea Region.* Berlin: Berliner Wissenschafts-Verlag, 117-134.

Johannsen, L. & K.H. Pedersen 2008. 'Korruption – et permanent eller forbigående fænomen' (Corruption – a transitional or permanent phenomenon', *Nordisk Østforum*, 22, 3-4.

Johannsen, L. & K.H. Pedersen 2008. 'The Responsive State: Openness and Inclusion in the Policy Process'. In: A.A. Dani & A. de Haan (eds.), *Inclusive States: Social Policy and Structural Inequalities.* The World Bank, Washington D.C.: The International Bank for Reconstruction and Development.

Johannsen, L. 2000. *The Constitution and Democracy: The Choice and Consequence of the Constitution in Post-Communist Countries.* Aarhus: Politica.

Kaldor, M. & I. Vejvoda 1997. 'Democratization in central and east European countries', *International Affairs*, 73, 1, 59-82.

Karl, T.L. & P.C. Schmitter 1991. 'Modes of Transition in Latin America, Southern and Eastern Europe', *Journal of International Affairs*, 45, 269-284.

Karl, T.L. & P.C. Schmitter 1995. 'From an Iron Curtain to a Paper Curtain: Grounding Transitologists or Students of Postcommunism?', *Slavic Review*, Winter 1995.

Karl, T.L. 1986. 'Petroleum and Political Pacts: The Transition to Democracy in Venezuela'. In: O'Donnell, Schmitter & Whitehead (eds.), *Transitions from Authoritarian Rule: Latin America*, Baltimore: The Johns Hopkins University Press, 196-219.

Kitschelt, H. 1995. 'Formation of Party Cleavages in Post-Communist Societies: Theoretical propositions', *Party Politics*, 1, 4, 447-472.

Kreuzer, M. & V. Pettai 2004, 'Political Parties and the Study of Political Development: New Insights from the Postcommunist Democracies', *World Politics*, 56, 608-633.

Kubicek, P. 1998. 'Authoritarianism in Central Asia: Curse or Cure?', *Third World Quarterly*, 19, 1, 29-43.

Kubicek, P. 2000. 'Regional Polarisation in Ukraine: Public Opinion, Voting and Legislative Behaviour', *Europe-Asia Studies*, 52, 2, 272-293.

Kuzio, T. 2001. 'Transition in Post-Communist States: Triple or Quadruple?', *Politics*, 21, 3, 168-177.

Landman, T. 2000. *Issues and Methods in Comparative Politics. An Introduction.* London: Routledge.

Levitsky, S. & L.A. Way 2002. 'Elections Without Democracy: The Rise of Competitive Authoritarianism', *Journal of Democracy*, 13, 2, 51-65.

Levitsky, S. & L.A. Way 2005. 'International Linkage and Democratization', *Journal of Democracy*, 16, 3, 20-34.

Lewis, P. 2004. 'Democracy in Post-Communist Europe, Fifteen Years On: A Concluding Note', *Journal of Communist Studies and Transition Politics*, 20, 1, 162-165.

Lijphart, A. 1994. 'Democratization and Constitutional Choices in Czechoslovakia, Hungary and Poland, 1989-91'. In: Ian Budge & David MacKay (eds.), *Developing Democracy*. London: Sage.

Linz, J.J. & A. Stepan 1996. *Problems of Democratic Transition and Consolidation: Southern Europe, South America, and Post-Communist Europe.* Baltimore: The Johns Hopkins University Press.

Lukšič, I. 2003. 'Corporatism packaged in pluralist ideology: the case of Slovenia', *Communist and Post-Communist Studies*, 36, 509-525.

Matsuzato, K. 2004. 'A Populist Island in an Ocean of Clan Politics: The Lukashenka Regime as an Exception among CIS Countries', *Europe-Asia Studies*, 56, 2, 235-261.

Miller, W.L., Å.B. Grødelund & T.Y. Koshechkina 2001. *A Culture of Corruption? Coping with Government in Post-communist Europe.* Budapest: CEU Press.

Nørgaard, O. & L. Johannsen (1999). *The Baltic States After Independence*, with Mette Skak & Rene Hauge Sørensen, 2nd Ed., Studies of Communism in Transition. Cheltenham: Edward Elgar.

O'Donnell, G. 2002. 'In Partial Defence of an Evanescent "Paradigm"'. *Journal of Democracy*, 13, 3, 6-12.

Obolonsky, A.V. 1999. 'The Modern Russian Administration in the time of Transition: New Challenges versus Old Nomenclature Legacy', *International Review of Administrative Sciences*, 65, 4.

Pedersen, K.H. & L. Johannsen 2004. 'The Real Challenge for Change. Public Administration in New EU Member States'. *WeltTrends*, 43, 12, 93-105.

Pedersen, K.H. & L. Johannsen 2006a. 'Corruption: Commonality, Causes & Consequences: Comparing 15 Ex-Communist Countries'. In: Allan Rosenbaum & Juraj Nemec (eds.), *Democratic Governance in the Central and Eastern European Countries: Challenges and Responses for the XXI Century*. Bratislava: NISPAcee, 311-336.

Pedersen, K.H. & R. Zubek 2005. 'State of the State in Poland', *DEMSTAR Research Report*, no. 17, Aarhus: Department of Political Science.

Peters, G.B. 1995. 'The civil service in consolidation of democracy', *International Social Science Journal*, 127-140.

Pogany, I. 1996. 'Constitution Making or Constitutional Transformation in Post-Communist Societies?', *Political Studies*, 44, 3, 568-591.

Przeworski, A. & F. Limongi 1997. 'Modernization: Theories and Facts'. *World Politics*, 49, 155-83.

Przeworski, A. 1988. 'Democracy as a Contingent Outcome of Conflicts'. In: Jon Elster & Rune Slagstad (eds.), *Constitutionalism and Democracy*. Cambridge: Cambridge University Press, 59-80.

Przeworski, A. 1991. *Democracy and the Market: Political and Economic Reforms in Eastern Europe and Latin America*. Cambridge: Cambridge University Press.

Przeworski, A. et al. 1995. *Sustainable Democracy*, Cambridge: Cambridge University Press.

Rose, R., N. Munro & S. White 2001. 'Voting in a Floating Party System: the 1999 Duma Election', *Europe-Asia Studies*, 53, 3, 419-443.

Ross, M.L. 2001. 'Does oil hinder democracy?', *World Politics*, 53, 3, 325-3.

Rustow, D. 1970. 'Transitions to Democracy: Toward a Dynamic Model', *Comparative Politics*, 2, 3, 337-63.

Schatz, E. 2004. *Modern Clan Politics: The Power of "Blood" in Kazakhstan and Beyond*. University of Washington Press.

Schimmelfennig, F. & U. Sedelmeier (eds.) 2005. *The Europeanization of Central and Eastern Europe*. Ithaca: Cornell University Press.

Stepan, A. & E.N. Suleiman 1995. 'The French Fifth Republic: A Model for Import? Reflections on Poland and Brazil'. In: Chehabi & Stepan (eds.), *Politics, Society and Democracy: Comparative Studies (Essays in Honor of Juan J. Linz)*, Boulder: Westview Press, 393-414.

Tismaneanu, V. 1997. 'Romanian exceptionalism? Democracy, ethnocracy, and uncertain pluralism in post-Ceausescu Romania'. In Dawisha & Perrot (eds.), *Politics, Power, and the Struggle for Democracy in South-East Europe*. Cambridge: Cambridge University Press, 403-451.

Toole, J. 2003. 'Straddling the East-West Divide: Party Organisation and Communist Legacies in East Central Europe', *Europe-Asia Studies*, 55, 1, 101-118.

Treacher, A. 1996. 'Political Evolution in Central Asia', *Democratization*, 3, 3, 306-327.

Tuminez, A.S. 2003. 'Nationalism, Ethnic Pressures, and the Break-up of the Soviet Union', *Journal of Cold War Studies*, 5, 4, 81-136.

Vachaudova, M.A. 2005. *Europe Undivided. Democracy, Leverage & Integration After Communism*. Oxford: Oxford University Press.

Verheijen, T. 1999. 'Context and Structure' in Tony Verheijen (ed.) *Civil Service Systems in Central and Eastern Europe*, Cheltenham, UK: Edward Elgar.

Way, L.A. 2003. 'Weak States and Pluralism: The Case of Moldova', *East European Politics and Societies*, 17, 3, 454-482.

Whitefield, S. 2002. 'Political Cleavages and Post-Communist Politics', *Annual Review of Political Science*, 5, 181-200.

CHAPTER 2

Co-optation and control:

Managing heterogeneity in Kazakhstan

Sally N. Cummings*

Kazakhstan's politics is rooted in a heterogeneous regime. Its heterogeneity is the product of both history and choice. Various opposites, fragmentations or cleavages have both created and resulted from elite policies. The state is pulled in various directions, and causes and consequences in the regime's politics are thus often complex and contradictory. Bargaining by forces within and outside the state has demanded balance and negotiation in ideology, practice and policy.

In traditional Kazakh society central power was feeble and fragmented. Although they were a hereditary estate, members of the ruling elite had to earn their title through charisma or military skill, and rarely did a leader enjoy a monopoly of power. Moreover, rulers did not preside over a defined area: traditional Kazakh territory was occupied by three groupings, known as hordes, and a single horde did not necessarily concord with the territory over which the khan ruled. The inability of the khans to command specific tribes or slaves also made them weak and ineffective rulers. They often had to entertain lavishly to maintain the support of these tribes. When a formal state did develop it would not be a recognisably separate institution or 'set of institutions' with a bureaucracy, tax collection or standing army. Consequently, the traditional Kazakh steppe was devoid of a politico-administrative centre.

Imperial and Soviet rule profoundly transformed the nature of the Kazakh domain. Tsarist rule rested on the seizure of Kazakh land. Imperial policy introduced to the steppe a fundamentally different conceptualisation of power, one defined by territory, regulated by procedural elections and supported by a bureaucracy. Tsarist rule was, nevertheless, overwhelmingly pragmatic. Sovietisation was, by contrast, highly ideological, and again transformed the relationship between the political elite and society: a Europeanisation of the population and accompanying acculturation; a wholehearted transformation in the production basis of their society; a clear divide between urbanised, industry-employed Russians and rural Kazakhs; the achievement of mass literacy; a change in the

---

* This chapter draws on *Kazakhstan: Power and the Elite* (I.B. Tauris, 2005) and *The Dynamics of Centre-Periphery Relations* (London: Royal Institute of International Affairs, 2000).

character but an overall strengthening of kinship at the lower levels of society (for an excellent overview, see Rakowska-Harmstone 1994).[1]

The Soviet Republic of Kazakhstan was never intended to be an independent state; the Soviet system imploded and independence became a *de facto* reality for the republic. The post-independence Kazakhstani elite was not only initially reluctant to assume power but also constituted an ethnic minority. In 1991, Kazakhstan was the only Soviet republic in which the titular nationality was a minority population. According to the last Soviet census, taken in 1989, Kazakhs constituted 39.5 per cent of the population, while Russians made up 37.7 per cent. Combined with the Ukrainians (5.4 per cent) and the Belorussians (1.1 per cent), the Slavs constituted 44.2 per cent of the population. When considering the largely Russified Germans (5.8 per cent), non-Kazakhs formed a bare but absolute majority of the republic. Moreover, most of the non-Kazakhs were, and are, settled in communities in the northern part of the country on the border with Russia.

This chapter assesses the way in which history and choice have interwoven to create Kazakhstan's regime mix. It is organised around five challenges of transition: political development, state building, nation building, economic transformation and internationalisation.

POLITICAL DEVELOPMENT: SEMI-AUTHORITARIANISM AND ELITE FRAGMENTATION

Kazakhstan has passed through four main phases of political development since independence: liberalisation between 1992 and 1994, with the passing of Kazakhstan's first constitution in 1993; heightened institutional in-fighting in 1994-5; executive consolidation in 1995 and 1996, with the passing of Kazakhstan's second constitution in 1995; greater authoritarianism since 1997; and more open elite fragmentation within the context of continued authoritarianism between 2001 and 2007. In retrospect, the early independence years of greater liberalisation were a tactical concession rather than a long-term intention to liberalise. The Kazakhstani system continues to be an authoritarian rather than a democratic one. Government has not come to power by free and fair elections. In spite of the Constitution's references to checks and balances, no practical mechanisms are in place to control the executive. The executive continues to overwhelm all branches of government, and within the executive the president, his close entourage and the presidential administration continue to dominate. The state is a unitary state. While this regime is stable and effective it prevents the accession of new groups.

---

1 For an excellent overview of Soviet legacies, see Teresa Rakowska-Harmstone, 'Soviet Legacies', *Central Asia Monitor*, 1994, Vol. 3, pp. 1-23.

In December 1993, the President 'invited' parliament to dissolve itself. A decree granted the President plenipotentiary power until the new parliamentary elections of 17 March 1994. 42 of the 177 candidates for the parliamentary elections were picked from a 'state list' (*gosudarstvennyi spisok*) compiled by the President. In March 1995, the Constitutional Court, supposedly at the prompting of the President, dismissed this thirteenth parliament on the basis of an alleged complaint lodged one year previously by an Almaty candidate, Tatyana Kvyatkovskaya.[2] She complained that she had been disadvantaged by the large size of her own constituency, with smaller districts in Almaty enjoying disproportionately large voting powers. The Constitutional Court, on the basis of this single constituency, declared the entire elections of the previous year illegal. Nevertheless, the regional legislative bodies (maslikhats) that existed in 1994 were not dissolved. The dissolution of parliament (Majilis) reinstated the president's plenipotentiary powers until December 1995, when new parliamentary elections were held. The alleged almost unanimous support for the President in the 29 April 1995 referendum granted him the powers to push through the new Constitution of August 1995 with substantially increased powers. This April referendum also extended presidential rule to December 2000, permitting the president to avoid the competitive presidential elections scheduled for 1996, which would probably have been contested by two reportedly popular alternative candidates, Olzhas Suleimenov and Gaziz Aldamzharov.

The 1999-2004 Majilis was to house the smallest number of professionals and the largest number of pro-government or business representatives of all Kazakhstani parliaments sitting since 1991, and in the September 2004 parliamentary elections pro-government parties won 76 of the 77 seats. The 2000 and 2004 parliamentary elections distinguished themselves from the two preceeding ones above all by the harshness of regime repression and the multiplicity of laws passed to limit the activity of the opposition. Kazakhstan's September 2004 parliamentary elections were criticised by domestic and international observers for strong irregularities. While a delegation from the Commonwealth of Independent States announced that the elections were free and fair, the Organisation for Security and Cooperation in Europe (OSCE) concluded that the elections fell short of international standards. Several prominent Kazakhstani officials resigned in protest, including the late Minister of Information, Altynbek Sarsenbaev, who in early 2006 was found dead. Suspicion for causing his demise was laid on the National Security Committee.

After thus weakening parliament and keeping a tight rein on the execu-

---

2   This prompted Olzhas Suleimenov, poet, writer, politician and former leader of the anti-
     nuclear movement 'Nevada-Semipalatinsk' to state in March 1995: 'In Yeltsin's Russia, to
     dissolve parliament you need tanks; in Nazarbaev's Kazakhstan to dissolve parliament you
     only need one tank: Tatyana Kvyatkovskaya'.

tive, in 1998 Nazarbaev launched an informal election campaign for the 2000 presidential elections. Although Nazarbaev's televised national address on 30 September 1998 promised sweeping democratisation measures and ruled out early elections, he had meanwhile struck a deal with parliament to call early elections for January 1999 (*The Jamestown Monitor*, 1 October 1998). In return for their support, members of both houses of parliament would see their next term of office extended by one more year each (after the parliamentary elections of October 1999). New contenders would face greater impediments to elections, as parties and movements participating in parliamentary elections in October 1999 would need to pass only a 7 instead of a 10 per cent threshold of the popular vote to sit in parliament. But the most important of parliament's amendments was extension of the President's term of office from five to seven years (effectively, then, until 2006). The President's required minimum age was increased from 35 to 40, and the age limit of 65 lifted (Interfax Kazakhstan 7, 8 & 9 October 1998). All these amendments were incorporated in the October 1998 legislation.

Neither the presidential election of January 1999 nor its successor in December 2005 was democratic. In both cases the election was held prematurely, and placed the incumbent president at an unfair advantage financially and organisationally. In 1999 the election commission also barred the only serious contender to Nazarbaev, Akezhan Kazhegeldin (Prime Minister, 1994-7) because of accusations of money laundering in Belgium and of holding an unsanctioned meeting of his campaign movement. The commission claimed this was within constitutional practice since Clause 4.1 of the 8 May 1998 constitutional amendment to the electoral law stipulated that no-one with a criminal record, including minor offences, was allowed to stand for electoral office.[3] In both cases Nazarbaev won with an overwhelming majority, and in both cases serious irregularities were recorded, in particular with regard to excluding competition. The June 2000 Law on the First President of Kazakhstan confers on Nazarbaev, upon the expiration of his term, the lifetime 'rights' to: address the country at any time; issue 'policy initiatives' to state bodies and government officials; attend and address sessions of the parliament and the cabinet of ministers; hold a seat on the Security Council; and chair the Assembly of Peoples of Kazakhstan (an interethnic accord forum, made up of officially selected representatives of the country's ethnic communities). Under the same law, Nazarbaev gains lifetime immunity from legal liability for any of his actions as president, with the hypothetical exception of 'high treason'. The immunity extends to Nazarbaev's person, dwellings and offices, documents,

---

3 *Konstitutsionnyi zakon Respubliki Kazakhstan*, 8 May 1998, Astana, 'O vnesenii izmenenii I dopolnenii v ukaz prezidenta respubliki Kazakhstan, imeyoushchii silu konstitutsionnogo zakona, 'O vyborakh v Respublike Kazakhstan', published in *Kazakhstanskaya Pravda*, 9 May 1998.

means of communication and all personal possessions. Also, amendments to the Law on Elections passed in April 2005 prohibited voters and political parties from organising any public meetings from the end of the election campaign until the official publication of the results. Restrictions on campaigning were also enforced by the new Law on Extremism, amendments to the Law on Mass Media, and new legislation pertaining to national security.

Relative to other Central Asian states, with the exception of Kyrgyzstan, Kazakhstan boasted the most outspoken media in the initial post-independence period. The tabloid newspaper *Karavan* was Central Asia's only newspaper to have its own printing press. Even so, since 1993 Freedom House's annual *Freedom of the Press* survey has rated Kazakhstan's media 'Not Free'. 1997, in particular, witnessed increased tightening of control over the media, and this has continued. *Karavan* was bought by the establishment in 1997, and although it has changed ownership since the purchase, it remains in the hands of the incumbent elite. Independent regional radio and television stations were abolished and national television became increasingly monopolised by the state television company Khabar, run by the President's daughter, Dariga Nazarbaeva. Kazakhstan's private media outlets are predominantly associated with private elite groupings. Although competition over media control at the elite level has not abated, and even though in April 2004 a controversial new media law was withdrawn, presidential monopolisation of state media outlets has continued. A number of opposition newspapers were closed in 2005. For instance, *Respublika* was re-closed in May and *Zhuma Times – Data Nedeli* in December. In September 2005 control of the registration of Internet domains was also introduced. In June 2006, moreover, the Majilis (lower house of parliament) approved government-initiated amendments to the media law which promised further media crackdowns, and a protest rally organised by media interest groups, unprecedented in scale, followed (*Panorama* 23 June 2006).

As the political regime has become more authoritarian and foreign investment has increased, the political elite has become both more concentrated at the apex and apparently more fragmented within the top leadership. By 1997 the core elite had become considerably smaller than that of 1991, and was increasingly dominated by family and close allies. Nevertheless, maintaining a balance between such loyal Nazarbaev supporters and the technocratic elite, and between laissez-faire and repressive tactics, has been a key challenge in this period. Things came to a head in 2001. Since 1997 two of Nazarbaev's sons-in-law, Rakhat Aliev and Timur Kulibaev, had occupied top posts (Aliev as head of the Tax Inspectorate and later as Deputy Head of the National Security Committee, and Kulibaev as Deputy Head of what was then called Kazakhoil (the state national oil company)). In what was probably a reaction to this concentration of power, Aliyev was forced to resign in November 2001. But he was then publicly defended by Nazarbaev on television and reappointed, this time as Head of Halyk, the National Savings Bank. The apparent reconciliation between Nazarbaev and Aliyev prompted an alliance of technocrats, businessmen and parliamentarians to announce the formation of the Democratic Choice of Kazakhstan (DCK) that same month. The key founding members of this new movement were Deputy Prime Minister Uraz Djandosov, Labour and Social Protection Minister Alikhan Baimenov, Deputy Defence Minister Zhannat Ertlesova, and Pavlodar Governor Ghalymzhan Zhakiyanov, as well as Kazakhkommertsbank head Serjan Sukhanberdin (who also has interests in oil and metals) and Temirbank head Mukhtar Ablyazov, a former energy minister.

As a compromise candidate between Nazabarov and DCK, Imangaly Tasmagambetov was appointed prime minister in early 2002. Mishandling a land reform bill, he remained in this post barely over a year, becoming Kazakhstan's shortest-serving prime minister. In his successor, Daniyal Akhmetov, the president was again playing it safe by appointing a loyal protégé who had served reliably in the northern regions. Between March and May 2002 the government severely weakened the DCK, arresting its leaders and forcing it to split, creating a new group, Ak Zhol (White Path). In July 2002 Nazarbaev introduced a new law on political parties that would close down most opposition movements, and the DCK's two most prominent leaders were sentenced to prison on charges of corruption and abuse of office. In January 2003 opposition journalist Sergei Duvanov was imprisoned on trumped-up rape charges.

Credible opposition candidates have found registration difficult and access to the media restricted. These measures have been partly responsible for the weakness of the opposition, its lack of charismatic leaders and its beleaguered disunity. Uraz Dzhandosov was co-opted back into the elite and made a presidential aide in January 2003. In 2002 three main opposition movements – Kazhegeldin's RPPK, Azamat and the People's Congress of Kazakhstan – merged into the United Democratic Party (UDP), but have had to work hard to maintain a united position. Furthermore, in April 2005 Ak Zhol split. As mentioned briefly above, moreover, on 12 February 2006 Sarsenbaev and his bodyguard were found dead alongside a road near a farm located not far from Almaty (*Novoye pokolenie* 17 February 2006), and immediate accusations by the opposition of a governmental cover-up followed. Sarsenbaev had surprised many when he had joined the ranks of the opposition in 2004. In March 2006 Nazarbaev said the authorities would revise legislation, if necessary, to hold people accountable for libel or bribery (*Khabar TV* 1 March 2006).

In parallel with this weakening of oppositional movements, pro-presidential parties have gained increasing strength. In particular, the size of Kazakhstan's main ruling party, OTAN, formed in 1999, grew considerably when other pro-presidential parties decided to merge with it in December 2006. These pro-presidential parties are transmission belts rather than bottom-up movements, and severely diminish the prospects for a representative party system capable of shaping opinions and political will. The above political trends strengthen Nazarbaev's hand in steering the political succession.

Despite prime minister Akhmetov's difficulties in 2005, when he was strongly criticised for the scandalous takeover of PetroKazakhstan by the China National Petroleum Company (CNPC), the Russian-Ukrainian gas deal's detrimental consequences for the Kazakh economy, creeping inflation, the fuel crisis, and corruption in the top echelons of power, he survived the government reshuffle following Nazarbaev's re-election in December, which effectively only made one major change (the replacing of two deputy prime ministers with 40-year-old, Chinese-educated Karim Masimov). In January 2007, however, Akhmetov was replaced by this same Masimov. In what was a major reshuffle, Marat Tazhin was appointed as the new foreign minister and his predecessor Tokaev as the new head of the *Senat*, the position first in line to assume power in the event of the chief executive's death.

STATE BUILDING: COMPARTMENTALISATION AND CORRUPTION

The state has maintained its monopoly over the use of force. Kazakhstan is notable for its absence of insurgent or violent movements, and the Cossack and Slavic movements were squashed in the early 1990s. At the end of the 1990s there was some talk of extremist Islamic organisations operating in the south, but again, they appear to have gained little prominence. The late 1990s witnessed some popular protests over unpaid wages, pensions arrears and the role of foreign investors, but nothing large-scale. While drugs trafficking occurs through Central Asia, the influence of the drugs mafia, with input from regional elites, is only beginning. Kazakhstan's military spending is the biggest in the CIS, but because of economic growth it consumes only 1.2 per cent of GDP. This growing militarisation of the region may, however, pose an increased threat to regional stability.

The political elite's relationship to the state is thus ambiguous. It is both reforming and rent-seeking. Members of the political elite have attempted to reform the state, whose basic infrastructures are largely a Soviet legacy. They have introduced measures to rationalise decision making and streamline government. They have developed consultative mechanisms with groups outside the state. Under Kazhegeldin, the government introduced a comprehensive economic reform programme which locked the state into the global economy. It also undertook several reform rounds in an attempt to improve the quality of governance, particularly the March 1997 decree that reduced the number of ministries from 20 to 14 and state committees from twelve to two. There are pockets of reliable business infrastructure, notably the banking sector and foreign investment law.

By the close of the 1990s, however, state-building initiatives had stagnated, eclipsed by rent-seeking. Both mass privatisation and the flow of oil revenues have intensified corrupt practices. According to the Berlin-based *Transparency International Corruption Perceptions Index*, Kazakhstan rates among the top fifteen most corrupt states in the world. Although such accusations are not uncommon among emerging markets, the increasing controversy surrounding the Giffen affair has been distinctive. In the 1990s American-born businessman James Giffen served as advisor to the regime in negotiations over several large oil deals, and the US government alleges that in this period Giffen paid USD 78m in bribes to two high-ranking officials, who were named as Nazarbaev and Balgimbaev in 2004. Nazarbaev thus became the first sitting foreign head of state to be accused under the US Foreign Corrupt Practises Act since its inception in 1977. While 2005 also saw the introduction of supplementary legislation with respect to the professionalisation of the civil service, and the introduction of more competitive exams, recruitment continues to be dominated by personal loyalties and dismissals by political interference, and the January 2007 reshuffle reflected this.

A core feature of state building involves creating a workable relationship between the centre and the regions. During the Soviet period, much of northern and eastern Kazakhstan had been closely integrated with neighbouring areas in Russia. This integration involved economic production and distribution; energy systems; transport infrastructure; and elite recruitment networks. The Soviet state and Communist Party ensured the maintenance of these ties (Melvin 1999). With the collapse of these institutions, the regions bordering Russia became autonomous and no central institutions were readily available to replace those of the Soviet era. While during the Soviet era Moscow's relations with its republics had formed the essence of centre-periphery relations, these had now been supplanted by Almaty's relations with its own provinces. The construction of a unitary state became closely associated with increased authoritarianism. Partly as an attempt to secure greater control over these northern border provinces, the centre literally moved northwards; in 1998 Akmola (renamed Astana) in north-central Kazakhstan replaced south-eastern Almaty as the political capital of the republic.

The 1998 move of the capital was the fourth in seventy-five years. A Presidential Decree issued on 15 September 1995 confirmed the relocation. Official motives for this decision emphasise that Almaty is both situated in an earthquake zone and unable to expand physically because of adjacent mountains. Most unofficial explanations link the move to a desire to increase the government's hold on the northern regions and thereby the territorial integrity of the state, as well as to direct the process of internal migration, particularly the encouragement of ethnic Kazakhs to move to the northern regions. Again, then, politics is being dictated by this perceived need to adopt the centrist position and to overcome imbalance, in this case the ethnic-Russian numerical domination of the north. Responsible decentralisation has not occurred, although there were attempts in 2006 to make the centre-regional budgeting more transparent.

NATION BUILDING: MULTIETHNICITY AND SUB-ETHNICITY

Centre-region relations have also been complicated by Kazakhstan's multiethnic character, as ethnic Russians account for almost the same proportion of the population as Kazakhs in 1991. However, according to the 1999 census Kazakhs had attained an ethnic majority of the republic's total population. A key factor in the Kazakhs' newly won numerical majority was large-scale emigration of non-Kazakhs.

The creation of an independent state required its leadership to establish a new relationship with its territory. This relationship was on an emotional and practical level. The notion of a Kazakhstan as home to all ethnic groups is contested by many non-ethnic groups, and the sense of being a 'Kazakhstani', as opposed to, say, being a Kazakh or a Russian, is very weak. Important regional variations also exist in the degree to which populations regard the term 'Kazakhstani' as legitimate. People in the south are more comfortable about the co-existence of Kazakh and Kazakhstani, while those in the north see ethnic and state identities as competing. Accordingly, neither a state (Kazakhstani) nor a national (Kazakh) identity was readily available to the new nation and state builders. The central Kazakhstani elite feared the possible union of its Russian-populated northern provinces with Russia, and attempted to construct a civic identity which stressed affiliation to the state rather than to a nation. So it resisted dual citizenship, which it equated with dual loyalty and a possible north-south split. The choice of a unitary state further eliminated the granting of territorial mechanisms to maintain cultural differences, and the regime became significantly centralised.

Unitary systems in multiethnic states are often sustained by the persistent underdevelopment of one of the country's major ethnic groups. The ethnic Russian community, particularly prior to 1995, felt itself targeted as just one such group. It claims that Kazakhs have come to monopolise social, political and economic organisations; that the Kazakh language has been promoted at the expense of the Russian language; and that the territorial and cultural rights of non-Kazakhs have not been guaranteed in practice. Unitary systems are in this way particularly challenged in the context of multiethnic societies.

Up to 1995, provincial politics in the northern and eastern provinces was dominated by social movements advocating alternative political arrangements. The first substantial such organisation was the Russian Community (registered in 1992), soon to be surpassed in popularity by the broader Slavic Community, *Lad*, both of which demonstrated substantial provincial variations. In January 1994 a local community for Slavic culture organised a meeting in the city of Ust-Kamenogorsk. The participants demanded the creation of national autonomy for ethnic Russians in East-Kazakhstan, the elevation of Russian to the state language, and the introduction of republic-wide dual citizenship. Over 10,000 participated in the meeting. They even began to talk of creating a 'Republic of Southern Siberia' and supported Alexander Solzhenitsyn's controversial proposal to transfer this and other parts of northern Kazakhstan to Russia. In 2006 ethnic Russians continued to dominate numerically in the three regions of Kostanai, Pavlodar, and Northern-Kazakhstan.

The issue of multiethnicity dominated the agenda until around 1995. By then Russian emigration had peaked, the Kazakh birthrate was increasingly relatively faster than that of ethnic Russians, and issues of dual citizenship and the status of the Russian language no longer dominated the agenda. The new 1995 Constitution was in part a concession to the Russian population. It de-emphasised ethnic Kazakh historical rights over the new republic's territory, and raised the status of Russian from a language of interethnic communication to an official language.

Nation building has simultaneously been concerned with strengthening the Kazakh ethnos. While the 1995 Constitution grants equal civic rights to all ethnic groups, it also emphasises that the Kazakh ethnos is considered the titular nation and should thus be accorded special rights. Scholars differ in their assessment of the degree to which tribal affiliation matters in Kazakhstani identity politics. For historian Nurbulat Masanov, recruitment is shaped by this need for intra-Kazakh balance, primarily in terms of his or her horde or *zhuz* affiliation. The traditional Kazakh lands represented three distinct geographical units, and these units were given the political-territorial labels of horde (*zhuz*). They were known as the Senior, Middle and Junior Hordes. According to some historians, these groupings covered the three geographical steppe areas of South-East, Central/North and West Kazakhstan respectively.[4] Simplifying Masanov's argument, post-independence members of the Senior Zhuz have been accorded positions of low status but high influence; those of the Junior Zhuz, often in the past a broker between Senior and Middle Zhuz interests, have received positions of medium influence, high status and relatively high influence; and those of the Middle Zhuz have gained positions of high status but low influence.[5]

---

4   For this complex issue of horde formation and a map illustrating their borders in relation to those of contemporary provinces, see Akiner (1997).

5   See *Slovo Kyrgyzstana*, 3 April 1997 and The Economist, 4 June 1994 for variations on Masanov's theory. Writes The Economist: 'So, as ethnic Russians are disappearing from the corridors of Kazakh power, the Great Horde is asserting itself. Horde politics works

While Masanov's thesis is helpful because it emphasises the regional diversity of the Republic and the predominance of individuals from the south in positions of influence, the appointment process is more complex, and is based on both objective and subjective criteria (see Cummings 2005). Objectively, the Law on State Service, education and experience plays an important role in the appointment of some individuals. Subjectively, issues of loyalty to the president are of considerable importance, as are an individual's economic influence, and regional, economic or social networks of belonging may also matter. The importance of informal politics, however, is set to continue.

Defining citizenship is less an issue than an unspoken perception of rights that has real consequences for political and economic participation. Non-titular ethnic groups thus perceive discrimination whether or not it is actually present. Politically, all major posts have been Kazakhised and the Kazakh language is required by all major political office holders. Nevertheless, the Soviet legacy of internationalism is still an important factor in a general demobilisation of nations and nationalism in the post-Soviet era, and indigenous movements do not appear to be growing. There is no fundamental contestation that the state should exist, again probably because individuals are finding a niche and perhaps also because the most vociferous individuals left in the early 1990s. However, it may be that the Republic's economic success is slowly reinforcing the sense of Kazakhstani identity.

ECONOMIC TRANSFORMATION

The transformation of politics, state and nation has been strongly shaped by the country's economic development. Kazakhstan's macro-economic record, the market system's institutional framework, its reform of the financial sector and its foreign direct investment (FDI) legislation are the success stories of the post-Soviet space, where Kazakhstan has one of the best developed market-based systems of competition.

However, a strong informal sector exists in both politics and society, and the rules of the game are not equal for all participants. Since 2001 the government has aimed to increase the participation of small and medium-sized enterprises (SMES), but structural reforms still fall behind those enacted in the late 1990s. A law on private entrepreneurship was nevertheless adopted in November 2005 to simplify the bureaucracy faced by small businesses.

---

much like party politics. When a new speaker of parliament was chosen recently, members of the Middle and Little Hordes combined to vote against Mr Nazarbaev's Great Horde candidate'. One early discussion of the role of the zhuz factor in political appointments was published by the Institute of Development of Kazakhstan (IDK): Kazakh Tribalism today, its characteristics and possible solutions (Almaty: IDK, 1996).

Privatisation since 1991 has passed through three stages: small-scale privatisation, including housing (1991-2); mass privatisation and concurrent privatisation of agriculture (which involved the privatisation of livestock and equipment but not land) (1993-5); and case-by-case privatisation, which under the premiership of Akezhan Kazhegeldin (1994-1997) also involved the attraction of foreign management contracts. In the spring of 1991, still under communism when 'privatisation' was not a fully acceptable term, the Kazakh Supreme Soviet adopted a law on the more politically acceptable term de-statification (*razgosudarstvleniia*). The law was adopted, but was limited in this first phase to small and medium-sized enterprises. By March 1993 about 30 per cent of trading companies had been privatised, 40 per cent of construction companies, and 25 per cent of foodstuff companies (*Delovaia Nedelia*, 1998).

In March 1993 parliament passed a second law on destatification and privatisation. Covering a two-year period (1993-5), this second stage was largely based on the Czech voucher system, which was later also used in Russia. All Kazakhstani citizens received vouchers representing a set value which they were able to invest in various investment privatisation funds (IPFs). Fund managers would then use their vouchers to bid for up to 20 per cent of the shares in the medium-sized enterprises that were offered at privatisation auctions. 51 per cent of the shares were to be auctioned, 10 per cent to be given to workers and staff, and 39 per cent went to the government. Although the aim was to spread the number of funds, vouchers remained lodged predominantly in ten of the two hundred or so that were registered. But Nazarbaev faced broadbased opposition to market reform from the Twelfth Supreme Soviet, and this was part of the reason for its 'self-dissolution' in 1993.

In December 1994, dissatisfied with the course of privatisation and emboldened by their higher profile, leaders of these funds wrote an open letter to the President, urging him to include major rather than simply medium-sized industries in the privatisation process. Only light industry had been privatised, they argued, and giants that could generate profits for the IPFs, such as the giant steelmill Karmetkombinat, were excluded. When no response from the elite was forthcoming, the IPF leaders decided instead to form a movement, *Novoe Pokolenie* (New Generation). The key leaders included Kozykorpesh Esenberlin (Aziya-Leasing), Bulat Abilov (Butya), Nurlan Smagulov (Astana Motors), Nurlan Kapparov (Aktsept), Nurzhan Subkhanberdin (Kazkommertsbank), and Mukhtar Abliazov (Astana-Holding).

A third stage in privatisation was introduced at the end of 1993 with case-by-case privatisation. Initially this applied to companies with over 5,000 workers, and the first to be auctioned was the Almaty Tobacco Factory. The sale of this factory to Philip Morris was signed in November 1993, the same month that Kazakhstan's national currency, the *tenge*, was introduced. At the time this was the single largest foreign investment project signed, with Philip Morris earmarking USD 240 million over five years. However, relations with the company soured: the company accused the government of failing to provide fair operating conditions, such as the government's agreement in 1994 to allow RJR Reynolds to set up a competitive outlet at Shymkent's confectionery factory – on what Philip Morris argued were better production terms. The government had, it said, also refused to include tax norms in the contract (taxes were raised from 20 to 30 per cent already in spring 1994) (*Delovaia Nedelia*, 1998). The standoff between Philip Morris's local management and the government was only resolved when Nazarbaev firmly intervened. Unlike small and mass privatisation, these case-by-case tenders revolved around personal relations between the investor and state official involved, and needed a firm line from the latter. The incident was decisive for impressing on the President that Tereshchenko and his government were unable to deal effectively with foreign investors and had to be removed.

The appointment of the new Prime Minister, Akezhan Kazhegeldin, marked a new phase in this third case-by-case stage by introducing management contracts. While such management contracts have been practised elsewhere in the postcommunist world, Kazakhstan stands out in the number it signed. Whole sectors were given over to foreign management. Examples of key management contracts include the Joint Stock Company (JSC) of Pavlodar's Aluminium Factory (managed by Whiteswan Ltd.), the JSC of Zhezkazgan's copper concern, Zhezkazgantsvetmet (managed by Samsung Deutschland), JSC Dansk Mining Corporation (managed by Japan Chrome Corporation) and the Sokolovsk-Sarbai Mining Facility (managed by Ivedon International Ltd.). Most of these corporations were offshore investors.

Once entire economic sectors were under foreign management and, in some cases, eventually under foreign ownership, the process was stalled. Kazhegeldin's successor, Nurlan Balgimbaev, was appointed partly because he was a well-known opponent of privatisation policies. Under Balgimbaev, the stock-market flotation of Kazakhstan's blue-chip companies was temporarily halted. The centre tried to regain control over enterprises in the provinces, not least because it needed their export revenues to finance a gaping budget deficit. Attempts to re-nationalise provoked disputes with some foreign investors, even with well-known Western oil companies, who were charged with tax evasion. In contrast to Kazhegeldin's privatisation policy, Balgimbaev's industrial policy, sponsored and developed by his Trade and Industry Minister Mukhtar Abliazov, promised a statist approach to reform. Balgimbaev's successor and former Foreign Minister Kasymzhomart Tokaev replaced Abliazov with a former northern-based regional governor (*akim*) Danial Akhmetov. To some observers, this suggested a mere gesture towards including regional representatives in central policy.

Between 1998 and 2001, while politically we saw the onset of repression and the management of elites, privatisation began to stagnate. The period of political elite infighting described in the previous section came at a time of unprecedented economic growth for Kazakhstan. In 2000 Kazakhstan registered a budget surplus for the first time; part of the justification for the mass privatisation programme had been to close the budget deficit. It was now growing faster than any other post-Soviet state. Kazakhstan had successfully implemented a macroeconomic stabilisation programme, and continued to offer incentives to foreign investors.

Kazakhstan has the least extreme inequality of Central Asian states. Foreign trade has contributed significantly to economic development by improving the balance of payments, attracting FDI and promoting competition. Foreign trade is liberalised in principle, although significant exceptions remain, including differentiated tariffs and special rules for individual companies or sectors. Application to the World Trade Organisation, pursued since 1996, has stalled mainly because of tariffs. The country, however, trades very little with its Central Asian neighbours (only 3 per cent of its exports and 2 per cent of its imports). Export growth in 2006 was sustained by two main factors: maintenance of high world prices (coupled with expansion of oil production from new fields), and new export transport capacity (relieving existing constraints). The opening of a new route in late 2005 to the People's Republic of China and some shipment through Azerbaijan via the Baky-Ceyhan-Tbilisi (BCT) line were significant developments.

The president appears to have succeeded in isolating, or compartmentalising, a key section of the elite from political interference or populist pressures. The financial sector is one of the strongest elements in Kazakhstan's overall economic reform programme – if not the strongest element of all. The institutional foundations are laid for a solid banking system oriented towards international standards with functional banking supervision, minimum capital requirements and market discipline. In 2005 the first credit bureau was established during the year to help banks obtain information on the credit history of borrowers. A new budget code brought in significant changes to the budget system in 2005, streamlining centre-regional budget administration and simplifying major tax procedures. Difficulties in banking may arise if rapid credit expansion continues.

While the government succeeded in attracting major transnational companies and initially boasted a liberal foreign investment law (Dosmukhametov 2002), it was soon to have major disputes with each of the major transnational companies it attracted. The most notable were with the Belgian company Tractebel, the Canadian company Hurricane Hydrocarbons, and the American oil giant (then named) Chevron. The majority of these disputes were over levels of tax obligations and profit repatriation.

INTERNATIONALISATION: LIBERALISATION
AND MULTI-VECTOR FOREIGN POLICY

A key explanation behind Kazakhstan's successful integration into the international economy has been the country's liberalisation of foreign relations. Geopolitical constraints affect Kazakhstan's ability to benefit from its vast natural resources. According to the president, the republic holds 30 per cent of the world's proven reserves of chromium, 25 per cent of its manganese, 19 per cent of its lead, 13 per cent of its zinc, 10 per cent of its copper and 10 per cent of its iron. The President also claimed that Kazakhstan ranked first worldwide with respect to estimated reserves of uranium, and seventh worldwide for gold (*Panorama*, 1998; *Interfax-Kazakhstan*, 1998). Oil reserves estimated for the Caucasus and Central Asia as a whole vary greatly but range from 30bn to 200bn barrels. These estimates include proven and possible reserves (Forsythe, 1996). As recently as 1998 all existing oil and gas pipeline routes continued to run through Russia.

Attracting investors into the country has proven easier than getting resources out. The successful attraction of investors can be attributed partly to elite strategy. The republic was the first of the Soviet republics to introduce a privatisation programme in 1990. Under the premiership of Kazhegeldin (1994-1997) the government introduced foreign management contracts, whereby large domestic enterprises were handed over to foreign companies for management. By 1997 Kazakhstan had attracted the second largest amount of per capita foreign investment of all states (after Hungary). This foreign economic investment carries two major implications: the increased alliance between foreign and domestic actors (mentioned earlier in the context of centre-periphery bargaining), and the increasing emphasis since the late 1990s of an industrial policy that attempts to forge closer links between the state and domestic corporate actors.

As a landlocked state, it has been in Kazakhstan's interest to conduct friendly relations with its contiguous neighbours, two of which, Russia and China, are great powers. But rather than depending on one or the other or even on both, Kazakhstan has also sought new partners further afield, notably in the Middle East and the West. This 'multi-vector' foreign policy, as it came to be known, was primarily motivated by the republic's need to secure alternative oil pipeline routes. Kazakhstan remains unwilling to commit itself to any one power. As in domestic politics, Kazakhstan's foreign policy has been multifaceted, straddling various interests, its direction devoid of strong ideological content.

Foreign policy direction and content also compensate for internal cleavages. In particular, the regime's inability to legitimate itself strongly domestically vis-à-vis its ethnic Russian population encourages it to use foreign policy as a legitimation tool. Nazarbaev's major foreign policy initiatives may be understood in this context, particularly towards the Eurasian Union. Nazarbaev's strongly confederal orientation, with his emphasis on Kazakhstan being in a wider unit that includes Russia, has provided considerable psychological comfort to the Republic's large Russian community and is intended for their consumption.

While Kazakhstan has pursued its officially proclaimed multi-vector foreign policy since 1991, professing to seek allies in several different directions, including the West, Middle and Far East, Russia has repeatedly been declared its priority partner during the same period. A bilateral pact reached in May 2002 on the division of the Caspian Sea played a pivotal role in improving economic cooperation between Astana and Moscow. In January 2005 Russia and Kazakhstan signed a significant treaty delimiting the 7,500-kilometre-long frontier dividing the two states. More recent examples in 2006 alone included Nazarbaev's speech at his inaugural ceremony of January 2006 (Putin's attendance at the ceremony was seen as an unprecedented gesture, because it was the first time the Russian president opted to attend such an event on foreign soil); in his state-of-the-nation address of 1 March, in which he referred to his country's 'strategic partnership' with Russia;[6] and in May of that year, after talks with Russian President Vladimir Putin in Russia's southern Black Sea resort of Sochi, he said a strong Russia was important for its partners and allies. In addition, Nazarbaev was the only post-Soviet leader invited to attend the G-8 summit in St. Petersburg in July 2006.

Although Russia has continued to be emphasised in both rhetoric and practice, in practice the most significant development in foreign policy orientation has been Kazakhstan's increasingly close relationship with China. This continues to be portrayed as part of a multi-vector foreign policy, and such initiatives have often come either before or after overtures to other states, primarily Russia or the US. In an agreement with the Chinese National Petroleum Company (CNPC), in October 2004 Kazakhstan began construction of a 962 km oil pipeline from the Atasu settlement in the Karagandy region of Kazakhstan to Chinese Alashankou, which is expected to pump 10 million tonnes per annum and to make Russian oil shipments to China by rail economically non-viable. The deal was overwhelmingly in Kazakhstan's favour, with nearly 60 per cent of workers to be domestic, the projected cost (USD 700 million) to be covered equally, and the promise of thousands of jobs in the Karagandy, East Kazakhstan and Almaty regions (Yermukanov, 2004).

Meanwhile relations between Kazakhstan and the US have been mixed. Kazakh President Nursultan Nazarbaev's official visit to the United States in September 2006 was his sixth summit meeting with US President George W.

---

6   'Kazakhstan and Russia have similar or close positions on important international security issues,' Nazarbaev added (RIA-Novosti, March 1 2006).

Bush. Observers at the time commented that the US might be losing interest in Kazakhstan, but mutual interests continued to encourage a relationship. On the one hand, the Bush administration has expressed gratitude to the Kazakh peacekeeping battalion (Kazbat) that was deployed to Iraq in 2002; it remains the only Muslim country in Central Asia to have deployed a mission (albeit a non-combat one) to Iraq; it also appreciated assurances in 2006 by Deputy Kazakh Defence Minister Bolat Sembinov that Kazakhstan would not withdraw Kazbat from Iraq. Nazarbaev can use this deployment as a bargaining chip for increased financial and technical aid, and in his country's drive for membership of WTO in 2007 and chairmanship of the OSCE in 2009.

To date, Kazakhstan has succeeded in conducting a safe multi-vector policy that has managed to avoid intensifying geopolitical collisions between the United States, China, Russia and their allies, but regional challenges have grown in importance. These have been exacerbated by an increasingly unilateralist government of Uzbekistan, and in 2006 the government's statements reflected an increased urgency over securing a leadership role in the closer region of Central Asia. Tashkent's inclination towards unilateralism is an attempt to reassert its regional hegemony. Uzbekistan is the most populous Central Asian state and has pretensions to regional dominance. In 2000, Tashkent unilaterally demarcated its border with Kazakhstan in the Saryagach region of South Kazakhstan province, despite the absence of any border agreement between the two countries. Given the presence of strategic Uzbek communities in regions of neighbouring states – such as South Kazakhstan – there are fears that Tashkent may feel justified in expanding its borders. The presidents reportedly share a personal rivalry which reflects their states' competition for regional leadership in Central Asia. These differences will probably be accentuated by divergent domestic and foreign policy priorities.

Economically, while Kazakhstan has opted for the most ambitious economic liberalisation programme in Central Asia, Uzbekistan has preferred state-led, gradual reform. With only 11 per cent of Central Asia's total territory, Uzbekistan has 46 per cent of the region's population. Thus, compared to Kazakhstan's population density of six people per square kilometre, Uzbekistan's 46 people per square kilometre exert greater pressure on land and water resources. Even though the Uzbek diaspora is primarily situated in Kazakhstan's southern regions, this has previously not stopped Uzbekistan from cutting off gas supplies to southern Kazakhstan to gain economic leverage. In April 2006 Bauyr-zhan Akhmetov, a 24-year-old resident of Saryagash district, South Kazakhstan, was beaten unconscious by Uzbek border guards and abducted to Uzbekistan, where he was later hospitalised with life-threatening head injuries. The Kazakh Foreign Ministry issued a note of protest that described the behaviour of the Uzbek border guards as 'unacceptable [and] unlawful in legal and political terms.' The border incident, which took place one month after the Tashkent meeting between Nazarbaev and Uzbek President Islam Karimov, points to the lack of bilateral trust endemic to the region (Fuad, 2006). Nor do Kazakhstan's ties with other Central Asian countries inspire much confidence in a Central Asian Union. Thus while in his February 2005 state-of-the-nation address Nazarbaev emphasised the possibility of a union on the basis of agreements for eternal friendship between Kazakhstan, Uzbekistan and Kyrgyzstan, one year later in the same address it was given no mention (ibid).

International problems become domestic ones and, by the same token, with its limited defence possibilities, Kazakhstan will be forced to internationalise a looming domestic issue. In the immediate term, the reaction of Kazakhstan to security threats, as with other states, has been to close borders and tighten security. Despite short-term temptations to become self-reliant and self-protective, Kazakhstan has nevertheless continued to cooperate with outside powers. In particular, it has participated in the cooperation between China and Russia. The Shanghai Five, comprising the five states on the former Soviet-Chinese border (Kazakhstan, Kyrgyzstan, Tajikistan, China and Russia), was enlarged in June 2001 to include Uzbekistan and its functions expanded to include cooperation on regional security threats. Without such interlocking agreements, Kazakhstan's external sovereignty is likely to be severely diminished.

CONCLUSIONS

How these cleavages and different driving forces are balanced will depend on how oil income (and expectations thereof), industrial policy, elite groups and new external challenges are managed. Significant oil income revenue is projected for Kazakhstan. The political elite has established a fund to channel these revenues, but given Kazakhstan's corruption and distribution record, the oil revenues are likely to be poorly managed, with rent-seeking and Dutch disease a likely by-product. Overall, oil revenues will increase the political stakes for all the actors outlined in this chapter, domestic and foreign alike.

By the end of the 1990s elite fragmentation had emerged more clearly. While by no means as fully developed as the financial-industrial groups in Russia, these groups have their own media outlets and their representatives in the government and presidential administration. Although they are highly fluid entities, they include state agencies and regional networks, financial institutions and economic groupings. One major task has been to balance these disparate interests within the incumbent elite. In certain cases, oligarchic and regional interests have reinforced each other. This occurs when Soviet-era recruitment networks have not been disrupted by the influx of foreign investment and where Soviet-era groupings continue to exist. This is particularly the case in the south, where Soviet-era networks were not directly controlled by Moscow. A coincidence of regional and oligarchic interests can also be observed when new foreign investment has forged new alliances between foreign capital, the regional governor and the regional governor's relations with the centre. Oil is the principal example of this phenomenon, and it increases these groups' bargaining power in relation to the centre.

An industrial policy has already been started to counter the effects of income revenue flows and underlying economic, social and political trends. The precise nature of this policy is unclear, in particular the degree to which it may become a cover for mercantilism and protectionism. Again, given the substantial pressures on the government and on the presidency, some protectionism is likely. At one level the reaction is part of the general resentment that arises from the ambitious expectations of locals with regard to foreign investors. Quite apart from whether foreign companies are fulfilling their contractual obligations, there is the need to change perceptions that foreign investors aim to exploit. The discontent suggests that perceptions are not changing, and that workers feel they are not being treated fairly or equally (compared to foreign workers), and that promised social amenities have not been delivered. The Kazakhstani regime is likely to criticise: 1) the behaviour of foreign companies that do not actively promote or are inconsistent with the economic and social goals of the host country (in the name of national interest); 2) the potential lack of control over foreign corporations' policies in the republic (in the name of national sovereignty); and 3) foreign companies' lack of understanding of and concern for policies and practices compatible with local conditions, ways and aspirations (in the name of national identity).

The September 11 terrorist attacks and their consequences for Central Asia provided the background for the open expression of divisions. In November 2001 elite fragmentation appeared to become an open struggle. The government crisis made explicit a number of trends that have been developing since the late 1990s: the fragmentation of the elite, particularly in anticipation of oil revenues; competing oligarchic media ownership, and a renascent, albeit weak, opposition. These trends are likely to intensify once expected oil revenues begin to flow, and the political stakes get higher.

Russia's pledges and its foreign policy in the short term promise a pro-active policy. Russia's involvement in the Shanghai Forum, along with China, is also salutary for the republic in the medium term, even if only symbolically. Both trends strengthen Kazakhstani sovereignty and the security of foreign investments. The influence of the US in Central Asia as a whole has increased post-September 11, but Kazakhstan's domestic and foreign policies will probably continue to emphasise Russian interests. The failed US strategic partnership with Uzbekistan demonstrated how Central Asian strategic partnerships with the US may not be durable, and Kazakhstan is most likely to rely on longer-term relationships with its immediate neighbours Russia and China, with China likely to continue to grow in importance.

The balancing evident in Nazarbaev's domestic politics has thus been reflected in his foreign policy. Unlike other Central Asian republics, Kazakhstan initially took only observer status in the Muslim-dominated Economic Cooperation Council, largely to avoid appearing too 'Muslim'; simultaneously, Nazarbaev has drawn on overtures made by Iranians to help develop transportation links, by Omanis to build oil pipelines, by Egyptians to build mosques, and by Saudi Arabians to help develop trade links. In his rhetoric, Nazarbaev has capitalised on his country's ethnic heterogeneity by portraying his Republic as a bridge between Europe and Asia. This has also facilitiated his ability to pursue a multi-vector foreign policy.

The re-election of President Nazarbaev in December 2005 marks the beginning of what will probably prove a protracted period of preparation for his political succession. He and his regime aim to ensure that when the presidential succession does occur, it takes place in an orderly manner and follows the course he desires. We can expect the jockeying by key elite groupings to continue as they compete to ensure their place in the post-Nazarbaev era. Within this context, the repression of civil society activity and the independent media is likely to continue, and any fundamental change in the direction of political reform will need to come from within the government itself. Overall, economic change will receive priority attention over political change. Addressing parliament on 10 January 2007, Nazarbaev outlined his priorities for the new government: to pursue his pet project of making Kazakhstan one of the world's 50 most competitive countries, continue administrative reform, improve state and budget planning, develop the regions, boost the pension system, continue the focus on macroeconomic policy, train a competitive work force, improve infrastructure, bring the best of corporate management into the running of the state, and diversify the economy. The key economic challenge for the regime will continue to be the management of substantial oil revenues (a source of rampant corruption), and of potential overheating of the economy.

Kazakhstani politics is imbued with a strong sense of pragmatism which has managed to avoid ideological confrontation. The future of the Kazakhstani state will depend on the maintenance of this balance. Olcott warns of the consequences if this balance is ignored:

> Whatever the desires of its leadership or of any single constituency within the state, Kazakhstan will remain a heterogeneous society for some time to come, with enormous regional as well as ethnic diversity. It is impossible that the interests of all these many groups should coincide, and the pressures inherent in the country's makeup will need venting (Brill Olcott 2002, 125).

Kazakhstan's political developmental path is not predetermined. Certain cleavages outlined above are the product of history and shape the environment within which elites operate, ethnicity and geopolitics being the most important. But to suggest that the development is culturally predetermined or historically instilled is erroneous. Kazakhstan's already varied regimes within these early independence years demonstrate that choice and strategy matter. While certain historical legacies may have contoured the decisions within which institutions and the state have been built, they have not determined them. They have resulted in unclear outcomes, partly because this state is still in flux and because balance has often encouraged pragmatism over ideology. The regime's short history suggests a polity open to innovation and change, where decisions by a small number of individuals can have important consequences for political development. For the moment, Kazakhstan remains a complex political system where numerous cross-cutting tensions are balanced by centrifugal forces.

References

Akiner, S. 1997. *The Formation of Kazakh Identity*. London: Royal Institute of International Affairs.

Brill Olcott, M. 1992. 'Central Asia's Catapult to Independence', *Foreign Affairs* 71(3), 118-28.

Brill Olcott, M. 1995. *The Kazakhs*. 2nd Edition. Stanford: Hoover University Press.

Brill Olcott, M. 2002. *Kazakhstan: Unfulfilled Promise*. Washington, D.C.: Carnegie Endowment for International Peace.

Brown, B. 2000. 'New Political Parties in Kazakhstan', *Radio Liberty*, 23 August 1990.

Cummings, S.N. 2000. *The Dynamics of Centre-Periphery Relations*. London: Royal Institute of International Affairs.

Cummings, S.N. (ed.) 2002. *Power and Change in Central Asia*. London: Routledge.

Cummings, S.N. (ed.) 2003. *Oil, Transition and Security in Central Asia*. London: Routledge.

Cummings, S.N. 2005. *Kazakhstan: Power and the Elite*. London: I.B. Tauris.

Delovaia nedelia No. 1, 1998.

Dosmukhametov, E.K. 2002. *Foreign Direct Investment in Kazakhstan: Politico-Legal Aspects of Post-Communist Transition*. St. Anthony's Series. London: Palgrave Macmillan.

Economist Intelligence Unit (EIU) *Country Reports*, Kazakhstan (1994-2001).

Eurasia Daily Monitor. The Jamestown Foundation.

Fierman, W. 1998. 'Language and Identity in Kazakhstan: Formulations in Policy Documents 1987-1997', *Communist and Post-Communist Studies*, 31, 2, 171-86.

Forsythe, R. 1996. *The Politics of Oil and The Caucasus and Central Asia*. London: International Institute for Strategic Studies, Adelphi Paper 300.

Fuad, H. 2006. 'Astana's Integration Dreams Suffer Setbacks', 19 May 2006, http://www.jamestown.org/edm/article.php?article_id=2371152

Interfax Kazakhstan 7, 8 and 9 October 1998.

Interfax Kazakhstan 4 June 1998.

Kazakhstanskaya Pravda 9 May 1998.

Khabar TV, 1 March 2006 cited at http://www.jamestown.org/edm/article.php?article_id=2371237

Luong, P.J. & E. Weinthal 1999. 'The NGO Paradox: Democratic Goals and Non-Democratic Outcomes in Kazakhstan', *Europe-Asia Studies*, 51, 7, 1267-84.

Masanov, N. & I. Savin 1997. *Kazakhstan: Model Etnopolitichesgo monitoringa*. Moscow: Institut etnologii i antropologii RAN.

Melvin, N.J. 1999. 'Russian Kazakhstani Cross-Border Relations'. For the conference *Central Asia in a New Security Context*, The Swedish Institution of International Affairs, Stockholm, 2-3 September 1999.

Nazarbaev, N. 1991. *Bez pravykh I levykh*. Moscow: Molodaia Gvardiia.

Novoye pokolenie 17 February 2006.

Panorama 23 June 2006.

Peck, A.E. 1999. 'Foreign Investment in Kazakhstan's Mineral Industries', *Post-Soviet Geography and Economics*, 40, 7, 471-518.

Rakowska-Harmstone, T. 1994. 'Soviet Legacies.' *Central Asian Monitor* 3, 1-23.

RIA-Novosti 1 March 2006.

Schatz, E. 2004. *Modern Clan Politics: The Power of 'Blood' in Kazakhstan and Beyond*. Seattle, WA: University of Washington Press.

The Jamestown Monitor 1 October 1998.

Yermukanov, M. (2004). 'Chinese Pipe Dreams Come True in Kazakhstan', 5 October 2004, located at: http://www.jamestown.org/programs/edm/article.php?article_id=2371237

CHAPTER 3

Shevardnadze's political strategies:

The rise and fall of the incumbent

Nina Dadalauri and Lars Johannsen

Consider a small mountainous state marred by civil and secessionist wars, a depressing record of de-industrialisation and social impoverishment, almost total failure by the state to provide public goods, pervasive corruption and serious shortcomings in developing liberal democracy.

Most people would probably conclude that such headlines describe state failure and a lack of nation building and call into question the survival of the state, and rightly so. This description fits Georgia in its post-Soviet independence period, but it was happily supplanted by hopes for a new beginning after the Rose Revolution in 2003, when people took the issue of electoral fraud to the streets and ousted incumbent president Eduard Shevardnadze. The new president and leader of the Rose Revolution, Mikheil Saakashvili, promised to 'unify the nation' and professed a strong belief in the principles of free and fair elections and support for a market economy.

Brought in by the instigators of the 1992 coup, Eduard Shevardnadze had managed to stabilise the country and build a personal powerbase that served him well for eleven years. The Georgian state had survived against all odds and proved capable of being a front runner in the so-called colour revolutions. The task at hand is to explain the whys of the Rose Revolution, and to find out why Eduard Shevardnadze was able to stay in power for so long.

The debate over the 'Colour Revolutions' focused on the issues of electoral fraud and the organisation of the opposition, including the youth movement Kmara ('Enough'), which was instrumental in organising rallies and demonstrations (Fairbanks 2004; Karumidze & Wertsch 2005; Wheatley 2005; Jones 2006). Thus, the structure of the Rose Revolution corresponds to what we saw in the Serbian 'Bulldozer' Revolution and the Ukrainian 'Orange' Revolution (Herd 2005).

However, this does not explain why the revolution did not happen earlier. How did the Shevardnadze regime manage to survive for eleven years when every election was openly flawed? In these modern times even autocrats are expected to pay at least token respect to electoral institutions (Levitsky & Way 2002; Bunce 2003). Moreover, Gandhi and Przeworski (2007) argue that authoritarian leaders can consolidate their rule and prolong their tenure by incorporating the potential and actual opposition into the political institutions through semi-free elections.

All these explanations are relevant to the case at hand, but it will be demonstrated that the nexus of the survival of Shevardnadze's regime was the political strategies he used to stabilise the country and to build his political power base. However, the strategies he used to remain in office also proved to be the bane of his rule and eventually led to his downfall in the Rose Revolution. It is argued that Shevardnadze's three-tiered strategy of cooptation, soft coercion and clientelism made for what we have decided to call 'Absurdity Fair', that is, utter legal chaos with rampant corruption, where people are compelled to break the rules and participate in bribery simply to survive.

In order to track the development of Shevardnadze's strategies, we first outline the massive difficulties surrounding Georgian independence. Against this backdrop we trace Shevardnadze's initial stabilisation efforts and the strategies he developed to retain power. We end with a discussion of why these strategies failed in the long term and paved the way for a new beginning.

SETTING THE SCENE

Modern Georgia was born in the midst of the Soviet collapse. As was the case elsewhere in the Soviet empire, memories of previous statehood infused dissidents and popular movements with nationalistic credos and ambitions to restore self-determination and independence. Seasoned dissidents like Zviad Gamsakhurdia and Merab Kostava were quick to grasp the opportunities afforded by glasnost and anti-Soviet sentiments to establish the movement 'Round Table – Free Georgia' (Mrgvali Magida – Tavisupali Sakartvelo) (Slider 1997, 161).

In October 1990 'Round Table – Free Georgia' competed in the first multiparty elections for the Supreme Soviet of the Soviet Republic of Georgia and won a majority of the seats. Independence from Moscow became the policy of the day. In January 1991 Gamsakhurdia initiated the establishment of a national guard (Erovnuli Gvardia). A referendum was held and independence was declared on 9 April 1991 (Aves 1996, 5).

After the final dissolution of the Soviet Union in December 1991, very few people were prepared for the chaos that accompanied independence. The self-imposed economic blockade of Russia by Georgia had caused severe shortages (Gurgenidze et al. 1994, 261; Jones 1997). In addition, the Georgian government prioritised nation-building policy over economic restoration (Nodia 1998). Clothed in populist garb as the 'national awakening' and the 'spiritual mission of Georgia', these nationalistic policies soon polarised rather than unified the country (Jones 1994, 133).

In the multi-ethnic state of Georgia, where about 30 per cent of the population belong to different ethnic groups (Jones 2000, 63), tensions and ultimately armed clashes soon followed. In 1991 fighting erupted in South Ossetia, and there was armed conflict between Georgian troops and Abkhazian separatists in 1992-1993. The conflicts left Georgia with around 300,000 internally displaced persons (IDMC 2007), and in both cases the disaffected regions achieved de facto independence from Georgia (Demetrious 2002).

Reflecting the hardships found elsewhere in the Soviet Union and the priority given to nation building, the economy was in free fall. The economy began to contract in 1989, and when growth finally resumed in 1994 GDP per capita was only 23 per cent of the level in 1988. In 1992 alone the loss was about 44.1 per cent compared to the previous year (see table 1). Inflation ran rampant with a record-breaking high of more than 15,000 per cent in 1993. The pace of economic reform was slow and consisted initially of only price liberalisation, followed by small-scale privatisation. Other deep structural reforms such as banking, trade and exchange reforms and enterprise restructuring did not begin in earnest until 1995. In addition to economic despair, Georgia also became a vastly more unequal society, as reflected by the GINI index (table 1). Thus, by 2003 Georgia was more unequal than, for example, Estonia, Moldova and Armenia, but on a par with Russia.

The poor economic policies and ethnic tensions led to increased political tension among Georgians. Criticised by nationalists for the military failures, by reformers for the lack of reform, and by the cultural elite for his ultra-nationalist policies, Gamsakhurdia's political base, 'Round Table – Free Georgia', began to crumble (Jones 1997). With easy access to weapons and the growth of paramilitary groups, the stage was set for a violent coup d'état and civil war.

In December 1991 a Military Council (*samxedro sabcho*) headed by Tangiz Sigua (a former Minister of the Economy), Tengiz Kitovani (Head of the National Guard) and Jaba Ioseliani (Commander of the paramilitary group Brotherhood (*Mkhedrioni*)) commandeered a coup d'état. The besieged Gamsakhurdia managed to escape Tbilisi and flee the country (Slider 1997, 166). With the insurgencies in Abkhazia and South Ossetia continuing, the infant Georgian state was bleeding. Chaos, collapse and state failure seem fitting terms here.

The Military Council, now renamed the State Council (*saxelmzipo sabcho*), decided in March 1992 to invite Eduard Shevardnadze to return home, ostensibly to create a new 'Foundation for Georgian Revival and Democracy' (Slider 1997, 187). A couple of days later he became Chair of the State Council and Parliament. The coup makers saw Shevardnadze as the ideal person to help put the country back together again. As former First Secretary of the Georgian Communist Party in the 1970s, Shevardnadze had a reputation for being tough on corruption (Simis 1982; Fuller 1985). Furthermore, in his

TABLE 1: ECONOMIC DEVELOPMENT AND ECONOMIC REFORM. 1988-2006. SELECTED INDICATORS

	GDP PER CAPITA PPP (CONSTANT INTERNATIONAL US $, YEAR 2000)	GDP GROWTH PER CAPITA (ANNUAL %)	GINI INDEX	INFLATION GDP DEFLATOR (ANNUAL %)	ECONOMIC REFORM (EBRD)
1988	5840	4.6	..	-2.3	..
1989	5396	-7.6	..	5.4	1.00
1990	4606	-14.6	..	22.4	1.00
1991	3666	-20.4	..	62.1	1.00
1992	2050	-44.1	..	1314.2	1.29
1993	1478	-27.9	..	15442.3	1.49
1994	1351	-8.6	..	6041.6	1.46
1995	1412	4.5	..	162.7	2.08
1996	1595	13.0	37.1	43.0	2.63
1997	1787	12.0	..	6.5	2.83
1998	1865	4.3	..	6.9	2.87
1999	1940	4.0	38.0	9.7	2.87
2000	1998	3.0	..	4.7	3.00
2001	2118	6.0	36.9	5.4	3.00
2002	2260	6.7	..	5.9	3.00
2003	2538	12.3	40.4	3.4	3.00
2004	2714	6.9	..	8.4	3.04
2005	2994	10.3	..	8.3	3.13
2006	3304	10.3	..	5.7	..

Source: World Development Indicators (online, 2008); Economic Reform: Calculations based on EBRD (http://www.ebrd.com/pubs/econo/6520.htm). The figure shows an unweighted average of the scores for 1) large-scale privatisation, 2) small-scale privatisation, 3) enterprise restructuring, 4) price liberalisation, 5) trade and foreign exchange system, 6) competition policy, 7) banking reform and interest rate liberalisation, and 8) securities markets & non-bank financial institutions. The scale is 1.0 (planned economy) to 4+ (fully functional market economy).

capacity as Foreign Secretary of the Soviet Union he played a key role in the détente with the West, which gave him access to a huge international network (Cohen 2004).

War and economic decline changed the political agenda of the Georgian state. Building peace through political and economic stabilisation supplanted national state building. The difficult start to Shevardnadze's rule in Georgia is described very well by Nodia (2002, 426), who argues that the anarchistic militias left little room for state institutions to function, and that whatever hopes had been tied to democracy had been discredited by war, economic collapse and the ousting of Gamsakhurdia. Apathy became the order of the day, and the country was deeply divided.

STABILISATION: THE FIRST THREE STEPS

As the Chair of the State Council and Parliament Shevardnadze was endowed with very broad powers, but his political base was quite weak. He did not command a parliamentary majority (Aves 1996, 9), and parliament itself was more a platform for emotional statements than a lawmaking institution (Jones 1997, 523). What is more, Shevardnadze was entirely dependent on the goodwill of the coup-makers, especially Kitovani and Ioseliani, who each controlled their own 'armed forces'. The state as such had no army of its own, only militia groupings (Nodia 2002). And by then Gamsakhurdia was plotting and planning to return.

Shevardnadze employed three strategies. First, Russia was approached in order to secure her help, initially against the separatists and then against Gamsakhurdia. Second, the coup-makers were outmanoeuvered one by one, either by coopting them or by pitting one against the other. Finally, Shevardnadze sought western assistance to reform and rebuild the Georgian economy.

Russia to the rescue

Shevardnadze's relations with Russia have been characterised as inconsistent and incoherent (Nodia 2000, 198). Russia was seen as a strategic partner, but was at the same time blamed for aiding the Abkhaz separatists (Darchiashvili 2000, 73). Never as radical as Gamsakhurdia in 'blaming Russia', he managed to obtain Russian support at two crucial junctures, albeit at a heavy price.

By the autumn of 1993 a ceasefire had been achieved in Abkhazia with Russian troops acting as peacekeepers. Meanwhile, unrest was growing in Western Georgia. Into this cauldron Gamsakhurdia returned from Chechnya, where he had been granted asylum, advocating rebellion against the central government. Shevardnadze had to find a way of dealing with the 'Zviadist' challenge. Once again Russia came to the rescue. On the pretext of securing essential railroads, Russian troops entered Georgia to help suppress the riots

(Rotar 1998). Massive arrests and the disarmament of 'Zviadists' followed, but it was not until Gamsakhurdia died (he allegedly committed suicide) in December 1993 that the main challenge had been met (Rotar 1998). A second round of arrests followed the failed attempt on Shevardnadze's life in 1998 (Nodia 2000, 189).

With the ceasefires in Abkhazia and South Ossetia and the 'Zviadists' locked up, Shevardnadze was again in control, but Russian troops guarded the border with Turkey and acted as peacekeepers, and a Russian protégé was appointed as head of the Ministry of Defence (Nodia 2002, 418). In addition, Shevardnadze joined the Commonwealth of Independent States (CIS) – an organisation founded on the remains of the Soviet Union and often seen as serving Russian economic, security and political interests in the former Soviet republics.

The price was too steep for nationalistically inclined Georgian politicians, and to them CIS membership amounted to betrayal. But Shevardnadze stood firm and sought to balance his foreign policy by involving western organisations in restructuring the economy. Overall, Shevardnadze tried to manage his relations with the West while not upsetting the 'partnership relations' with Georgia's northern neighbour.

Outmanoeuvring the paramilitary groups

Nominally in control of the territory, the main challenge to Shevardnadze's rule came from his allies Kitovani and Ioseliani and their respective paramilitary groups. Both resisted having their influence curtailed by Shevardnadze's efforts to institute law and order. Without an army loyal to the state, Shevardnadze would definitely lose an open conflict (Wheatley 2005). Instead he developed a strategy that served him well for the coming decade.

Rather than risking open conflict with his adversaries, Shevardnadze tried to co-opt Ioseliani in a bid to marginalise Kitovani. It began as an attempt by the Georgian parliament to reduce the power of Ioseliani's 'Mkhedrioni'. As chairman of the parliament Shevardnadze formed a committee charged with this task. The fiendishly clever ploy on Shevardnadze's part was to include Ioseliani in the committee and accept his proposals. With a pacified Ioseliani on his side Shevardnadze could now turn to Kitovani. The National Security and Defence Council was dissolved and the National Guard abolished (Wheatley 2005).

With Kitovani out of the game, Ioseliani's time was up after an attempt on Shevardnadze's life in August 1995. Blaming the 'Mkhedrioni' for the plot, massive rounds of arrests started. Ioseliani was also imprisoned. Shevardnadze had at last managed to put down the armed challenges to his rule. On 17 October the new Constitution of Georgia was adopted. This served to institutionalise and consolidate Shevardnadze's political hegemony even further, and in November 1995 Shevardnadze could let himself be elected President of Georgia (Aves 1996; Demetriou 2002, 878).

Rebuilding the economy

When Shevardnadze returned in March 1992 the Georgian economy was in free fall, a situation that was to deteriorate further in the first two years of his rule as the wars took their toll. Only by 1995, the year that Shevardnadze achieved political supremacy, did the economy get back on track (table 1).

Economic restructuring was not only a question of introducing market reforms, however. The capacity and the instruments available to the state also had to be considered. Tax collection did not work, resulting in a spiralling budget deficit (Papava 1995). What is more, the government had little control over monetary policy. Initially the printing press was in Moscow and the interim currency, the coupon that was introduced in April 1993, had little credibility. With the assistance of the IMF, reforms were set in motion and a strict fiscal policy adopted for the 1995 budget. Inflation had been tamed already by the spring of 1995, and backed by a new IMF loan a new Georgian currency, the Lari (GEL), was introduced in September 1995.

As in the political sphere, Shevardnadze tried in the economic sphere to balance between various interests. There were western commitments to the economic reforms, and American security interests were taken care of through an agreement to convey some of Azerbaijan's oil exports through Georgia (Nodia 2000). Meanwhile, three Russian military bases were granted permission to stay on Georgian soil, and new economic ties were established with Turkey and Iran.

Credited with ensuring order, rebuilding state capacity and restoring economic growth, by the end of 1995 Shevardnadze had plenty of political capital. Most importantly, however, he had found the tools required to maintain and expand his powerbase.

IN THE GREY ZONE: POWER STRATEGIES

The first years of stabilisation moved Georgia from the category of 'failed state' to that of merely 'weak state'. Apart from Abkhazia and South Ossetia, the government controlled the territory and the political situation appeared stable (Aves 1996). Some elements of a democratic state were present, at least in the form of state institutions with legislative, executive and judicial powers (Aves 1996; Nodia 2002). Because of the election Shevardnaze had achieved nationwide legitimacy, and the once-thriving crime and racketeering circles had been reduced to a point where they no longer threatened the political order (Nodia 2002).

Georgia was nevertheless still a weak state, and therefore remained for years to come in what has been termed the 'grey zone' (Carothers 2002), 'competitive authoritarianism' (Levitsky & Way 2002) or 'hybrid regimes' (Diamond 2002), regimes that feature some elements of liberal democracy but also have serious democratic deficiencies. However, the strategies Shevardnadze used to maintain political power did not suffice to improve state capacity beyond the initial gains. They also bore within them the seeds of destruction of his power.

Shevardnadze's political strategies have been characterised as a series of Machiavellian political manoeuvres (Demetriou 2002, 877). To secure his position he had to make sure others were dependent upon him for resources through appointments, tolerance of rampant corruption and an elaborate patron-client system. Whenever possible Shevardnadze co-opted and balanced different groups against each other. Nor did he shy away from creating an atmosphere of distrust and uncertainty among his clientele in order to control them.

Building the machine: co-opting and balancing

Shevardnadze's political machine rested on three pillars. First, Shevardnadze created the 'Citizens Union of Georgia' (*saqartvelos mokalaketa kavshiri*) as his political organisation, elite hub and campaign vehicle. Second, he used the appointive power vested in the presidency, and finally, he negotiated an unofficial modus vivendi with regional leaders and powerbrokers.

The 'Citizens Union of Georgia' (CUG) was created in November 1993. It was Shevardnadze's formal political base in elections (Aves 1996, 15), and it won comfortable majorities in both the 1995 and the 1999 parliamentary elections. It was also the 'party of the establishment', and it infiltrated state institutions through appointments based on membership of and loyalty to the establishment rather than merit (Jones 2000, 52). So, just like in the old times of the Soviet Union, membership of 'the party' became a requirement for career advancement and the members controlled most of the political, social and economic life in the country (Demetriou 2002).

The secessionist wars and the nationalistic rhetoric of Gamsakhurdia made the CUG an important organisation that cast itself in civic terms and supported the development of minority policies. This is not to argue that Georgia should pride itself on having developed minority policies (Demetriou 2002); but the nationalistic rhetoric was replaced by reference to the concept of citizenship, and the CUG also sponsored a number of cultural festivals for minorities (Aves 1996).

The CUG became an elite hub encompassing diverse groupings. It included regional *apparatchiks*, managers of state enterprises, former communist party members and intellectuals, and also a group that would later become known as *the young reformers* (Jones 2000, 52; Demetriou 2002, 878). As a party of power rather than one of conviction, the CUG had outlasted itself by the beginning of the new millennium. The split between reformers and non-reformers became evident in 2001, when the later leaders of the Rose Revolution left the CUG. The CUG was now seriously fragmented. Thus, for the fraudulent 2003 parliamentary elections Shevardnadze backed the pro-governmental alliance 'For a New Georgia' (*akhali sakartvelostvis*).

Shevardnadze also used his presidential power to appoint high-ranking officials and build a political system designed to reward supporters and punish defectors. Shevardnadze's power ranged from the prefects or governors (*rts-munebuli*) of the provinces (*mkhare*) to the selection of local executive officials (*gamgebeli*) among those elected to the local councils (*sakrebul*). Furthermore, in his efforts to balance different interest groups and make sure no group grew strong enough to challenge him, Shevardnadze mirrored the very same mix as that in the CUG by appointing reformers and non-reformers where appropriate. Finally, since local tax collection was limited the local councils were heavily dependent on transfers from the central budget. Fiscal decentralisation developed, albeit slowly, and through amendments to the local governance law in 2001 major cities (like Tbilisi and Poti) could now elect their own mayors by popular vote. The president now held the vertical lines of control throughout Georgia. As noted by one observer, this chain of control expanded the patron-client system even further (Jones 2000, 67).

The strategy of balancing also involved a modus vivendi with Aslan Abashidze, leader of the autonomous region of Adjara. Adjara enjoyed a special status, allowing Abashidze to build his own patron-client network. This could be maintained through toll collections at the border with Turkey or oil transit revenues from the port of Batumi, tolls and revenues that were never sent on to Tbilisi (Christophe 2004, 15) but remained in Adjara as a part of a 'silent pact' between Abashidze and Shevardnadze, with each refraining from challenging the other (Chiaberashvili & Tevzadze 2005, 194, 196). Aslan Abashidze was too powerful to threaten, and Shevardnadze dared not risk another civil war. Others, however, could be kept in line using *kompromats*.

Staying tuned: the policy of kompromat

In Soviet times collecting *kompromats*, that is, compromising material on an individual, was a tool frequently used by party officials to keep citizens under control. For example, a party official kept compromising records for later use against bosses and industrial managers, who often broke the rules in order to reach production quotas (Wheatley 2005, 21). The secret services also kept files on members of the ruling elite. Corrupt practices could thus be tolerated and then exposed at the right time (Simis 1982, 34). Knowing that *kompromats* were collected and filed rendered the 'sinners' vulnerable and subject to the power of the collector. The *kompromat* became a means of controlling the clients of the political power brokers.

The old Soviet rules of the game were transmitted to Georgia (Jones, 2000;

Chiaberashvili & Tevzadze 2005), and the use of *kompromats* was evident when the Minister of Internal Affairs of Georgia, Kakha Targamadze, announced in 2000 that his ministry possessed quite a lot of *kompromats* on the 'reformers' among CUG members (Wheatley 2005, 105). The reformers were thus warned to keep in line with those in power.

Feeding the machine: corruption and patron-client relations

The strategies and tools were expensive. In a country where the average monthly salary of a minister was GEL 165 (approximately USD 85) and civil servants got GEL 65 per month in 2000 (Nations in Transition 2001, 195), salaries alone would not be enough. Shevardnadze turned a blind eye to rampant corruption, extortion and the embezzlement of state funds. Corruption greased the wheels, supplemented salaries, and created a channel of communication between citizens and the state.

The study of corruption is still in its infancy, but indicators developed in recent years provide an overview of how widespread bribery actually was during this period. Since 1999 Transparency International has consistently ranked Georgia among the countries where corruption is most massive (CPI report 2003). Despite the Law on Corruption and the Incompatibility of Interests in Public Service (1997) and the creation of an anti-corruption commission in parliament in the 1996-1999 sessions, corruption survived in various forms in the everyday life of Georgians (Nations in Transition 2001, 1992). Attempts to control corruption were largely a failure – the World Bank found that between 1996 and 2002 Georgia was ranked among the 20 per cent of countries that had the least control over corruption (The World Bank 2007).

As it encouraged *'major players [to remain] interested in the preservation of the status quo'* (Nodia 2002, 430), some observers considered corruption to be a means of maintaining stability during Shevardnadze's reign. Corruption fed into the patron-client network. The extended family of Shevardnadze dominated various economic spheres (Chiaberashvili & Tevzadze 2005), and in 2000 a working group on corruption found that 184 of 384 high-ranking public officials had amassed properties estimated to be worth more than GEL 1 million (approximately USD 500,000). In view of the general tolerance of widespread corruption, the arrest of civil servants for corrupt practices was perceived to be politically motivated (Wheatley 2005, 106). The strategies and the way in which the machine was fed not only created a special kind of political, economic and social system, but also proved dysfunctional in the long term.

'Absurdity Fair', where rules are made to be broken

Shevardnadze's strategies created an environment we have called 'Absurdity Fair'. The most pertinent description of the state and the economy is the 'grabbing hand' (Frye & Shleifer 1997), and relations between citizens and between citizens and the state were characterised by a complete absence of social capital. Inspired by the description in William M. Thackeray's (1847-48) novel *Vanity Fair* of a place where all is frivolity and empty show, 'Absurdity Fair' is in fact a broader and more complete description of an environment marked by legal chaos, a place where rules are made to be broken and people feel compelled to use underhand methods in order to get around them. In the environment of 'Absurdity Fair', mistrust has replaced trust and institutions become vehicles for personal gain.

Distrust and confusion were achieved in part through *kompromats*, but mainly by deliberately created legal chaos. The legal chaos was the end result not only of a lack of will to implement the laws passed by parliament, but also of the vagueness of the rules, leaving citizens at the whim of bureaucrats. The development of the tax code is an instructive example of legal chaos during Shevardnadze's tenure. It was adopted in 1997 and then amended no less than 58 times. New rules often conflicted with previous ones, or were left on the books because there were no implementation mechanisms, technological equipment or the professional skills one would normally require of tax inspectors. So the Tax Code became notorious (Wheatley 2005, 106; Chelidze 2003, 9-13).

Bureaucrats were given extensive discretion, and in conjunction with poorly developed systems of accountability there was fertile ground for corruption. Bus drivers were compelled to take alcohol or blood pressure tests. Small kiosk holders had to comply with certain architectural designs (Christophe 2004, 21). All rules were subject to arbitrary decisions by public officials. Insecurity became the order of the day.

Because of the extent of the corruption the majority of people, bribe takers and givers alike, had engaged in moral wrongdoing which they wanted to keep secret. In 'Absurdity Fair' all are sinners and the likelihood of a challenge to the ruling system by 'clean hands' was minimised.

A great deal of scholarly work has been done on corruption and its relations with economic development and political consequences (Vishney 1993). Some argue that corruption may in some cases enhance state capacity (Darden 2002). Others find that corruption is detrimental to democracy and governance (Hellman et al. 2000; Rose-Ackerman 1999). However, when it comes to the incumbents and their opportunity to lengthen their tenure regardless of their performance record, corruption is considered to be one of the key factors in building a loyal power base for incumbents (Manzetti & Wilson 2007; Keeper 2005). According to this argument, Shevardnadze's decision to tolerate corruption was an intuitively 'appropriate' tool to enhance and sustain his power. However, as the following discussions illustrate, corruption as a source of 'feeding the patron-client' machine was a poor long-term strategy.

THE WELL DRIES UP

By the turn of the millennium political and economic development had reached a dead end. The Russian financial crisis in 1998 led to a devaluation of the GEL by 50 per cent (Nodia 2002, 432). Foreign direct investment slowed down. The country and the state were dependent on foreign aid. Foreign aid covered between 45 and 86 per cent of government expenditure, or USD 50-64 per capita in the years between 1997 and 2001 (World Development Indicators, 2008). In comparative terms Kenyans received USD 17 and 24 per cent of expenditures in 2001, and while the Kenyan figures had fallen compared with previous years, the Georgian figures had risen (World Development Indicators, 2008).

'Absurdity Fair' meant that while other developing countries struggled with adjustment programmes, state capacity remained low in Georgia. Debt continued to spiral. Between 1997 and 1999 central government debt rose from 43 to 72 per cent of GDP (World Development Indicators, 2008). Against this backdrop the IMF threatened to call in its credits in 1998 (Nodia 2002, 432), and when another negative assessment was published in 2003, other international organisations concerned with the magnitude of Georgian corruption and crime followed suit (Nations in Transition, 2003). The flow of aid that had greased the wheels threatened to slow to a trickle. The government came under severe financial strain and had to renege on a promised salary increase of GEL 35 (USD 16).

Georgia was not a closed authoritarian regime with strict censorship, and critical TV shows such as the cartoon '*Dardubala*' and the persistence of the investigative journalists in the local version of '60 Minutes' helped to expose high-level corruption to the broad public. In addition, the frozen conflicts and the inability of the government to improve the life of average Georgians from 1998 onwards led to a decline in Shevardnadze's popularity. Public opinion was slowly being turned against the regime, the incumbent and his clients. Mounting dissatisfaction with the regime and the emergence of an alternative elite meant that Georgia was ripe for change. Something was in the air.

The emergence of alternative elites

Although not a democracy under Shevardnadze, Georgia was neither a closed nor an authoritarian system. It was, as discussed above, something in between, and there were elements of liberal democracy. It is true that the regime was corrupt and that meaningful political competition was a farce, but at the same time there were extensive freedoms.

Parallel to the state, a non-governmental sector gradually emerged. According to Stephen Jones (2000, 68), there were no NGOs in 1992, but by 1997 almost 3,000 had been registered. Because of poor state performance and low capacity, many of the NGOs played important roles in education, training and information. As the NGOs grew stronger they also became a driving force behind policy initiatives.

Many of the NGOs were either run by or allied with the ever-increasing cadres of western-trained youngsters and reformers. Intensive exchange programmes in education led by the US government had given a large number of young people experience and knowledge of democracy and of how well-functioning states actually work. Shevardnadze was initially able to use the returnees in his mix of different interests, making sure that the balance was maintained. However, once the young reform elite reached the highest political positions people such as Mikheil Saakashvili, a lawyer trained in the US who had been named Minister of Justice, grew in numbers, general despair over 'Absurdity Fair' set in. The balance was lost and the reform elite started to defect.

The turning point came in 2001. In September Minister of Justice Saakashvili protested against the ever-increasing corruption and what he saw as Shevardnadze's failure to do anything about it. A month later Zurab Zhvania, the speaker of parliament, resigned. Zhvania had previously served as General Secretary of the CUG, and had been instrumental in recruiting young reformers such as Saakashvili to the party. Zhvania's resignation, which came in reaction to a raid by the Ministry of Security on the Rustavi 2 TV channel, split the CUG into several factions and the reformers began to set up their own parties. Preparations for the parliamentary elections in November 2003 were now underway.

THE COLLAPSE AND THE ROSE REVOLUTION

The election was scheduled for 2 November 2003. For the first time, Shevardnadze now faced a coherent and organised opposition. His political alliance For a New Georgia (*axali sakartvelostvis*) competed alongside Abashidze's 'Union of Democratic Revival' (*demokratiuli agordzinebis kavshiri*) – against Saakashvili's 'United National Movement' (*gaertianebuli erovnuli modzraoba*) and Zhavnia and Nino Burjanadze's (by then speaker of parliament) Burjanadze Democats (*burjanadze demokratebi*).

The election was flawed. The OSCE found that the election did not live up to international standards, and exit polls indicated that the opposition had won. Saakashvili urged the voters to protest, and at the opening of parliament a huge number of demonstrators stormed the session, forcing Shevardnadze to flee. A state of emergency was declared and the country once again found itself on the brink of bloodshed. This time around, however, violence was avoided when Shevardnadze resigned as President the following day after a meeting with Saakashvili and Zhavnia. On 25 November the Supreme Court (*uzenaesi sasamartlo*), somewhat belatedly, annulled the parliamentary elections. New elections for both the presidency and parliament could therefore be called for 2004. The Rose Revolution was over.

Could Shevardnadze have remained in power? Was it necessary to step down? It is certainly obvious that the strategies he had used to maintain power were bankrupt. So the only option left to him would have been to crush the opposition with military force when the state of emergency was declared. There is no indication that Shevardnadze contemplated this option, even though leaders of the NPD called on him to do so. Moreover, as sections of the police and military began to defect already on 22 November to join the demonstrations, such a course of action would undoubtedly have thrown the country into another civil war.

It is not the structural context that gave rise to the decision. The fall of Shevardnadze's regime and the transition to a new beginning – to many a democratic breakthrough (Beissinger 2007; Bunce & Wolchik 2006; McFaul 2005) – were accomplished by the three men who met on 23 November against the backdrop of the structural context and the thousands of demonstrators outside.

The structural analysis can, however, provide us with an understanding of what shaped events. True, many strong analytical points can be made about insiders who defect and leave their clients in limbo (Hale 2006). Our concern here is how the strategies of power shaped the structural context in the long term. Shevardnadze was propelled to power in a country that was chaotic, deeply divided and in dire economic straits. During the first years of his rule he managed to calm the situation and restore a degree of order. The strategies he used to secure order and later maintain power proved dysfunctional in the long term, however.

Shevardnadze's leadership style was in many ways typical of Soviet-era leaders in that he evinced a strong preference for constructing *ad hoc* coalitions consisting of different ideological and interest groups, and had a dislike for arrangements that restricted his room for manoeuvre (Aves 1996, 14). Shevardnadze's strategies should therefore not be seen as instrumentally designed to fit Georgia. That argument is certainly a rational afterthought. The strategies should instead be seen in the following light: Shevardnadze did what he was trained to do, and his actions were in line with the political system he was brought up in. As a highly skilled Soviet politician he used the 'tools of control' he had grown up with, and students of the Soviet Union will immediately recognise the *kompromat*. As a Georgian he had extensive experience of the 'tribal fragmentation' that was rampant even in the communist period, where 'favourites' received tributes from protégés (Simis 1982, 36-7).

We have called the outcome of the strategies 'Absurdity Fair'. 'Absurdity Fair' implies that the state could not modernise and develop beyond a few rudimentary functions. NGOs gradually came to provide what was seen as core state functions, thus commanding loyalty and legitimacy. To this should be added the diffusion of ideas from the outside. The young reformers who had studied and worked abroad were able to draw a picture of a credible alternative. In 'Absurdity Fair' everyone is a sinner, which implies that no opposition should be expected; but with the returnees came the message that the original sin was committed by the regime – not by the people.

In this message lies optimism for Georgia's future, the new beginning and the democratic breakthrough. On the other hand, generally speaking Shevardnadze only managed to stabilise a divided country. Nation building is still unsolved. The conflicts are still frozen and there are increasing calls for recognition of Abkhazia, for example. Furthermore, if the sins – corruption and clientelism – were not washed away by the Rose Revolution but are in fact ingrained in everyday life, the question remains if the reformers will be compelled to revisit history.

References

Aves, J. 1996. 'GEORGIA: From Chaos to Stability?' London: The Royal Institute of International Affairs, Russia and Eurasia Programme.

Beissinger, M. 2007. 'Structure and Example in Modular Political Phenomena: The Diffusion of Bulldozer/Rose/Orange/Tulip Revolutions', *Perspectives on Politics*, 5, 2, 259-276.

Bunce, V. 2003. 'Rethinking Recent Democratization. Lessons from the Postcommunist Experience', *World Politics* 55, 2, 167-192.

Bunce, V. & S. Wolchik 2006. 'Favorable Conditions and Electoral Revolutions', *Journal of Democracy*, 17, 4, 5-18.

Carothers, T. 2002. 'The End of Transition Paradigm', *Journal of Democracy*, 13, 1, 5-21.

Chelidze, D. 2003. 'Tax evasion schemes and their analysis'. Research Report published on the TRACCC-GO website www.traccc.cdn.ge (last accessed on March 27, 2008).

Chiaberashvili, Z. & G. Tevzadze 2005. 'Power Elites in Georgia: Old and New'. In: P.H. Fluri & E. Cole (eds.), *From Revolution to Reform: Georgia's Struggle with Democratic Institution Building and Security Sector Reform*, Bureau for Security Policy at the Austrian Ministry of Defence; National Defence Academy, Vienna; and Geneva Centre for the Democratic Control of Armed Forces in co-operation with PfP-Consortium of Defence Academies and Security Studies Institutes, Vienna and Geneva, pp. 187-207.

Cohen, A. 2004. 'Shevardnadze's Jouney, The Silver Fox bows out gracefully.' Hoover Institution website: http://www.hoover.org/publications/policyreview/3439296.html

Darchiashvili, D. 2000. 'Trends of Strategic Thinking in Georgia. Achievements, Problems, and Prospects'. In: Gary Bertsch, Cassady Craft, Scott A. Jones & Michael Beck (eds.), *Crossroads and Conflict. Security and Foreign Policy in The Caucasus and Central Asia,* Routledge, New York and London, 66-74.

Demetriou, S. 2002. 'Rising From the Ashes? The Difficult (Re)Birth of the Georgian States', *Development and Change,* 33, 5, 859-883.

Diamond, L. 2002. 'Elections Without Democracy. Thinking About Hybrid Regimes', *Journal of Democracy,* 13, 2, 21-35.

Fairbanks, C.H. Jr. 2004. 'Georgia's Rose Revolution', *Journal of Democracy,* 15, 2, 42-57.

Frye, Timothy & Andrei Shleifer 1997. 'The Invisible Hand and the Grabbing Hand', *The American Economic Review,* 87, 2, 354-358.

Fuller, E. 1985. 'A Portrait of Eduard Shevardnadze', July 3, Radio Liberty Research, RL 219/85.

Gandhi, J. & A. Przeworski 2007. 'Authoritarian Institutions and the Survival of Autocrats', *Comparative Political Studies,* 40, 11, 1279-1301.

Gurgenidze, L., M. Lobzhanidze & D. Onoprishvili 1994. 'Georgia: From Planning to Hyperinflation', *Communist Economies & Economic Transformation,* 6, 3, 259-289.

Hale, H.E. 2006. 'Democracy or Autocracy on the march? The colored revolutions as normal dynamics of patronal presidentialism', *Communist and Post-Communist Studies* 39, 305-329.

Hellman, J.S., G. Jones & D. Kaufmann 2000. 'Seize the State, Seize the Day: State Capture, Corruption and Influence in Transition', World Bank Paper published online: http://wbln0018.worldbank.org/Research/workpapers.nsf/0/9a0cdcfc7388d0ab8525699a0062f9d3/$FILE/wps2444.pdf (accessed on March 27, 2008).

Herd, G.P. 2005. 'Colorful revolutions and the CIS: "Manufactured" Versus "Managed" Democracy?', *Problems of Post-Communism,* 52, 2, 3-18.

Jones, S. 1994. 'Populism in Georgia: The Gamsaxurdia Phenomenon'. In: D.V. Schwartz & R. Panossian, *Nationalism and History. The Politics of Nation Building in Post-Soviet Armenia, Azerbaijan and Georgia.* Toronto: University of Toronto, Centre for Russian and East European Studies, 127-149.

Jones, S.F. 1997. 'Georgia: the Trauma of Statehood'. In: I. Bremmer & R. Taras (eds.), *New State, New Politics: Building the Post-Soviet Nations.* Cambridge: Cambridge University Press, 505-543.

Jones, S.F. 2000. 'Democracy from Below? Interest Groups in Georgian Society', *Slavic Review,* 59, 1, 42-73.

Jones, S.F. 2006. 'The Rose Revolution: A Revolution without Revolutionaries?', *Cambridge Review of International Affairs,* 19, 1, 33-48.

Karumidze, Z. & J.V. Wertsch 2005. *"Enough!" The Rose Revolution in the Republic of Georgia 2003.* Hauppauge, NY: Nova Science Publishers, Inc.

Keeper, P. 2005. 'Democratization and clientelism: Why are young democracies badly governed?', *Development Research Group.* Washington, D.C.: The World Bank.

Levitsky, S. & L.A. Way 2002. 'Elections without Democracy: The Rise of Competitive Authoritarianism', *Journal of Democracy,* 13, 2.

Manzetti, L. & C.J. Wilson 2007. 'Why Do Corrupt Governments Maintain Public Support?', *Comparative Political Studies,* 40, 8, 947-970.

McFaul, M. 2005. 'Transitions from Postcommunism', *Journal of Democracy,* 16, 3, 5-19.

Nations in Transition 2001. *Country Report on Georgia.*

Nations in Transition 2003. *Country Report on Georgia.*

Nodia, G. 1998. 'Dymanics of State-Building in Georgia', *Demokratyzatsya,* 6, 1.

Nodia, G. 2000. 'A New Cycle of Instability in Georgia: New Troubles and Old Problems'. In: G. Bertsch, C. Craft, S.A. Jones & M. Beck (eds.), *Crossroads and Conflict. Security and Foreign Policy in The Caucasus and Central Asia.* London: Routledge.

Nodia, G. 2002. 'Putting the State Back Together in Post-Soviet Georgia'. In: M.R. Beissinger & C. Young (eds.), *Beyond State Crisis: Postcolonial Africa and Post-Soviet Eurasia in Comparative Perspective.* Washington DC: Woodrow Wilson Center Press.

Papava, V. 1995. 'The Georgian Economy: Problems of Reform', *Eurasian Studies,* 2, 2.

Rose-Ackerman, S. 1999. *Corruption and Government: Causes, Consequences and Reforms.* Cambridge: Cambridge University Press.

Rotar, I. 1998. 'Mingrelia: Georgia's New "Hot Spot"?', *The Jamestown Foundation,* 4, 8. Online: http://www.jamestown.org/authors_details.php?author_id=80

Simis, K. 1982. *USSR: Secrets of a corrupt society.* London: J.M. Dent & Sons Ltd.

Slider, D. 1997. 'Democratizaton in Georgia'. In: K. Dawisha & B. Parrot (eds.), *Conflict, Cleavage, and Change in Central Asia and the Caucasus.* Cambridge: Cambridge University Press, 156-198.

Wheatley, J. 2005. *Georgia from National Awakening to Rose Revolution: Delayed Transition in the Former Soviet Union.* London: Ashgate Publications.

World Bank 2007. 'Georgia Governance Indicators, Country Data Report for Georgia 1996-2006', online: http://info.worldbank.org/governance/wgi2007/pdf/c81.pdf (accessed March 27, 2008).

CHAPTER 4

Understanding politics in Estonia:
The limits of tutelary transition

Vello Pettai*

Estonia has long been hailed as one of the most successful transition countries in Eastern Europe. From being a little-known Soviet republic in the late 1980s, it wrestled its way to the forefront of the group of countries that entered the European Union in 2004. It has sustained some of the strongest economic growth and development of any emerging market. It has maintained overall political stability, despite having adopted an entirely new constitution in 1992. It has even made notable progress in addressing what some believed would be its biggest challenge: relations with its sizeable Russian-speaking minority.

This chapter will seek to make sense of this success by analysing Estonia in terms of the four central transformation areas outlined in this book – political development, economic liberalisation, nation building and state building. In the Estonian case, I will argue that the key notion that accompanies all of these fields is "tutelary transition". In other words, I will examine both the origins and the consequences of a post-communist transition, which has been characterised by the dominance of political elites in making decisions and steering society in a direction that the elites see as necessary for the development of society and the good of the people.[1] Although this transition has still been subject to electoral corrections and it has certainly not been immune to public criticism, it has – for reasons that will be discussed in this chapter – remained surprisingly unchanged with respect to its original course in favour of liberal

---

1   In this respect, my approach offers a corollary to that presented by Ted Hopf (2002), who examines perceptions of transition from the bottom up, using focus groups among average people in Estonia, Ukraine and Uzbekistan. Hopf's key concepts centre on the 'legitimation' of reform strategies among the populace as well as their 'naturalisation' (or internalisation) over time. Hopf shows how Estonians have tolerated much of the transition because they see it as legitimate and 'natural'.

*   The author is deeply grateful to Lars Johannsen and Ole Nørgaard for their help and forbearance in commissioning this article. Support for this research came from a Targeted Financing Grant (no. 0180128) of the Estonian Ministry of Education and Research.

market economic policies, Western foreign policy orientations, and a steady preference for new and young political leaders. In comparison to most other Eastern European countries,[2] Estonia's tutelary transition has lasted far longer and been more durable.

After explaining what is meant by the concept of tutelary transition, I will turn to some indicators of this phenomenon in the Estonian case across such issues as economic reform, political institutionalisation, Russian minority integration and European Union accession. I will then analyse the 'limits' of this kind of integration, which Estonia has begun to reach some fifteen years after it began. These limits include growing social stratification and record-low levels of popular confidence in political institutions. More specifically, these strains have been evident in societal debates on the emergence of a 'second Estonia', meaning those in Estonia who have not benefited from the economic progress of the last decade. The fact that such a metaphor has gained credence in popular discussions reveals precisely the growing perception of a gap which now exists between different social strata, and which has therefore begun to undermine the previously unquestioned choices of post-communist development in Estonia.

Thus, in the course of the chapter I will look at some of the more profound reasons for this lengthy stretch of elite rule, and also at how some of these reasons are coming to an end. One of the more interesting explanations that I will examine derives from the patterns of party-political coalition building during the years of transition. The thesis will be that it was a special combination of nationalist as well as centrist-liberal political forces which made it possible to install a formidable ideology of reform and elite-led change. The more such coalitions are formed during the transition period, the easier it is to sustain a consistent transformation policy over time. Or put in another way, the more such forces (nationalist and centrist-liberal) are detached from each other or insufficiently inter-linked, the more fragmented the political spectrum will be and the less likely it is that such forces will predominate in society for long.

In the Estonian case, I will examine how the emergence of a relatively strong centre-right political bloc in 1992 helped to anchor the political system much more than it did in Latvia or Lithuania, for instance, and claim that as a result the hegemony of liberal market policies, a Western foreign policy as well as steady political institutionalisation has been much more durable, and even 'tutelary'. Of course, to some extent this sounds tautological: a centre-right political coalition causes centre-right policy domination. Thus, one should really ask where such orientations come from within society. While some scholars are tempted to proffer cultural or even civilisational explanations for

---

2   There may be a possible exception of Slovenia, where Prime Minister Janez Drnovsek was also in power for over seven years from 1993 to 2000.

such trends, in this paper I will be more cautious. The emergence of a strong and balanced centre-right pole in the Estonian political system could well be seen as serendipitous, since it was the result of choices made in the context of the particular division of votes and seats after Estonia's first post-independence elections in 1992. Because this division was such that a three-party centre-right coalition could emerge, Estonia was off to a good start. Going any farther back in the causal chain would require an examination of how voter preferences divided so fortuitously between the different parties, which would be a far more difficult task.[3] Suffice it therefore to say that well-balanced nationalist and centrist-liberal political coalitions augur well for developing transition paradigms, which remain dominant over extended periods of time.

TUTELARY TRANSITION

The central phenomenon behind the concept of tutelary transition is elite leadership. It is well known that political elites in society make decisions and *lead* their people in directions generally thought to be in the latter's best interest. Under modern democracy, of course, this autonomy of elites is somewhat (and in some cases even greatly) tempered by parallel mechanisms of popular input or reaction. On the most direct level, this happens through elections, where voters can replace the governing elites with competing ones. More indirectly, however, elite dominance is also circumscribed by watchdog institutions such as a free press, civil liberties that are guaranteed by the courts, and administrative rules that derive from the rule of law. Indeed, it is a fundamental principle of democracy that leaders must be *responsive* to the electorate: they must lead as people instruct them to lead, not as they may necessarily want to lead. This makes it all the more interesting to study cases in which demo-

---

3   One thesis I have examined elsewhere concerns the degree to which among the three Baltic states Lithuania was ahead of Estonia and Latvia in terms of electoral cycles. Namely, Lithuania's first free election in 1990 was much more party-political (nationalists vs. reform communists) than those of Estonia and Latvia, where competition remained on the level of loose coalitions and movements. As a result, the nationalist Sajudis movement came to power in Lithuania as a true party government, whereas the Popular Front governments in Estonia were still seen as transitional authorities. This, in turn, meant that the nationalists in Lithuania were judged in the 1992 elections as an incumbent power and were defeated by the reform communists, while in Estonia and Latvia the first post-independence elections were much more a free-for-all. See Pettai (2004a).

cratically accountable elites succeed in sustaining a certain agenda of societal transformation over a relatively lengthy period of time.[4]

The 'tutelary' aspect of elite rule in a transition society arises to the extent that elites are able to maintain a stance in which their policy choices regarding change in society are continually explained or justified in terms of imperatives other than direct popular preferences or input. This is the essence of the word 'tutelage', that is, the actions and responsibilities of a person viewed as the caretaker for someone else and therefore entitled to make decisions on behalf of that person, which do not necessarily derive from the immediate wishes of that person.[5]

To be sure, this relationship exists to some degree in all leadership situations. Leaders are rarely chosen (nor do they tend to act) merely as administrators of decisions reached directly through popular will. Leaders are always allowed a measure of strategic vision as well as tactical choice in carrying out their duties. 'Tutelary transition' is therefore a concept of *degree*, not of absolute content. Yet despite this caveat, I would argue that the notion has merit in attempting to *compare patterns of societal transformation in the post-communist world*.

A final point about tutelary transition relates to the second half of this term, namely, transition. Naturally, the fact that a society is in a self-acknowledged period of transition from some previous, failed era to a new future widens the parameters of leadership and therefore the opportunities of elites to make and sustain sweeping decisions. Such leadership has much greater leeway than in more stable societies, and therefore this too should be taken into account when critically examining the usefulness of 'tutelary transition' as a concept. If 'transition' already implies extraordinary prerogatives or processes, then how could it somehow be even more extraordinary or 'tutelary'? The answer to this question lies again in comparative degree, and in particular against the empirical backdrop of how most Central and Eastern European post-communist states have fared with sustaining transition policies across the last fifteen years. Each of them probably wanted to maintain control over economic policy and political consolidation for as long as possible in order to be able to implement the agenda they aspired to. However, in most cases after only 3-5 years either electoral reversal or more open social protest prompted a change in course.

---

4   In the literature, Pempel (1990) comes close to this same theme, where he studies how certain political parties (e.g. the Liberal Democrats in Japan or the Christian Democrats in Italy) are able to remain in power for long periods of time and across numerous democratic elections. His concept of 'one-party dominant regimes' captures this first dimension of tutelary transition, which is rule by a single political orientation across several elections.

5   Cf. the definition given by the Oxford English Dictionary: "1. The office or function of a guardian; protection, care, guardianship, patronage; governorship of a ward." OED Online (1989).

In Estonia, this paper will argue that a liberal pro-market economic agenda as well as an increasingly cartelised political class have endured together through a decade of post-communist transition. The question thus arises, how could this be?

IMPERATIVES FOR TUTELARY TRANSITION

Across all of the major dimensions of Estonia's post-communist transition, one can see how elite decisions and choices have been made which have largely emanated from a desire to push society forward for its own good, and which have not always been linked to immediate popular preferences. In the next section I will outline some of these decisions in more detail. For the moment, however, it is worth examining some of the country-specific aspects of Estonian tutelary elite behaviour. What are some of the particular dimensions of the tutelary imperative among Estonian elites?[6]

It is readily obvious in the Estonian case that country size has a lot to do with generating a feeling that each elite decision can have extremely important (if not existential) consequences for the country and the nation. In order to survive as an independent state and viable society in the modern word, leaders must be ready to have a long-term perspective. Moreover, the people themselves are likely to have a keen sense of their vulnerability, and so this too will generate acceptance of hard choices.

Nevertheless, it is essential to note the factors which still further accentuate this feeling of vulnerability in Estonia, given (a) the country's geopolitical location alongside Russia and (b) the very severe nature of Estonian-Russian relations during the 20th century. Put very simply, Estonian elites during the current era of independence have had a very clear sense that their mission is to secure Estonia's independence and future as a sovereign state within as little time as possible, since past experience has taught them that history comes as 'windows of opportunity' and that such windows must be consolidated as quickly as possible before they invariably close. The historical lessons begin with Estonia's first period of independence, which started in 1920 after the collapse of the Czarist empire. This event also marked the collapse of Russia as a regional power, and thus for Estonia it was a first window of opportunity to

---

6   In discussing these particularities, I should note that I am not trying to add an explanatory variable to the thesis about how such tutelary transition emerges. That is to say, describing why certain elites might want to sustain tutelary power over the transition is never sufficient for explaining how and why they were actually able to do this. Such an analysis would confuse motive with explanation. Notwithstanding adages like 'where there's a will, there's a way', in social science one must attempt to move beyond such circular (or unfalsifiable) explanations, since we often don't get what we want, no matter how much we want it.

secure statehood after nearly seven centuries of foreign domination.[7] Moreover, the continued weakness of Soviet Russia during the following decade meant that Estonia could attempt to build its own relations to the West and thereby hope to free itself once and for all from the orbit of its Eastern neighbour.

This effort failed of course – and for a number of reasons.[8] For the Estonian elites of the 1990s, the moral was clear: the country cannot rely on Russia remaining weak or suddenly becoming a permanently benevolent neighbour. Estonia and its elites must do all they can not only to insulate the country from Russian influence, but also to push cooperation and integration with Western partners in order to keep the inter-war scenario of merely temporary independence from repeating itself. Put in the starkest of terms, Estonia could be said to have again received perhaps at best a 20-year window of opportunity to secure its sovereignty and freedom, and if its elites were unable to realise this opportunity the country would probably face even greater doom than in 1940. As a result, the imperative to push Estonian society and its people in this direction (even if the people themselves did not always remain conscious of this need) was predominant in the minds of Estonian elites during much of the 1990s.[9]

Naturally, it would be wrong to paint a picture of Estonian leaders as obsessed with some kind of geopolitical fear or as suffering from psychological complexes. The drive for a Western-oriented and developed Estonia had a lot to do with a very basic desire to improve the living standards and well-being of Estonian society. But the tempo or zeal with which this effort was undertaken belies a likelihood that more profound stimuli were under the surface. Fortunately for Estonia, during the 1990s Russia remained relatively weak, not only because of the collapse of the Soviet Union, but also because of the chaotic leadership of Boris Yeltsin. It was only with the advent of Vladimir Putin that Russia could hope to develop a long-term recovery. However, Estonian leaders (along with those of Latvia and Lithuania) could by no means take this eventual course of events for granted. Thus, from the very beginning it was

---

7   Estonia's domination by foreign rulers began in the beginning of the 13th century, when German crusaders conquered Estonian lands and eventually settled down as landed nobility. During the 16th century, Sweden came to dominate over the Baltic lands, until in 1721 present-day Estonia and Latvia were taken over by Peter the Great and imperial Russia. For historical background, see Raun (1991), Taagepera (1993).

8   The rise of Stalinist Russia, the signing of the Molotov-Ribbentrop Pact between the USSR and Nazi Germany, and the occupation and annexation of the Baltic states by the Soviet Union in 1940.

9   For more analysis of security discourses among Estonian elites, see the extensive work by Merje Kuus (2002), (2003), (2004).

clear that strong (tutelary) measures would be needed for Estonia to do all it could to guarantee a better prospect of long-term independence.

ECONOMIC REFORM AND SHOCK THERAPY

By far the most prevalent dimension of tutelary rule by political elites concerns the implementation of difficult economic reforms, when such steps are seen as necessary for immediate economic recovery or longer-term prosperity. Examples abound from history and from around the world, where severe economic recession or breakdown has induced elites to drastically cut state spending, restructure inefficient economic sectors, or take other harsh measures to improve the national economic situation, while simultaneously suffering the wrath of the populace, which disapproves of or must endure these moves (Weyland 1998). Following the collapse of communism in 1989, the countries of Central and Eastern Europe were all the more prompted to adopt sweeping economic reform since their planned economies had all failed and the market system seemed the only alternative. To get from A to B, however, would not be easy.

The specific challenges of post-communist economic reconstruction reached far beyond the 'standard' type of macro-economic stabilisation seen often in Latin America, Africa or Asia, i.e. balancing budgets, taming inflation, liberalising trade and restoring economic confidence. Rather, it entailed a wholesale restructuring or redistribution of property in society away from the state and into private hands. Moreover, this was not the kind of piecemeal sale of a few state companies known in the West during the 1980s. Rather, it concerned all forms of industry, agriculture and services from heavy steel plants down to single-kiosk shoe repair shops. In the planned economy, all of these had belonged to the state.

A second dimension of property reform involved real estate owned by single individuals, and here again on two levels. The first was the privatisation of socialist-era housing stock, meaning the ubiquitous, dull, pre-fabricated apartment buildings erected across Central and Eastern Europe as part of socialist progress. Under this reform, tenants were generally allowed to 'purchase' their apartments from the state using vouchers distributed to them according to the number of years worked by them in the national economy. The second dimension of private property reform involved property 'restitution' or the return of houses, land or other property nationalised by the communist authorities up to 50 years ago, but now seen as having been seized unjustly and in need of amends. This was a gargantuan task in itself, since it would require incalculable numbers of man-hours to investigate, process and in many cases arbitrate the millions of restitution claims that would result. In addition, such restitution often meant that people currently living in these old houses would have to either move or find some *modus vivendi* with the new/old owner.

Lastly, in the former republics of the Soviet Union there was an additional need to create an entirely new and independent monetary system in the wake of the failed Soviet rouble. This task required setting up a competent central bank, developing procedures for the flow of accounts and cash, and establishing interest and exchange rates.

With so many challenges ahead, it was no wonder that the most popular policy prescription was 'shock therapy', which would involve carrying out as many reforms as possible and as quickly as possible in order to gain some headway before further economic anarchy, popular discontent or some other complication set in. The degree to which elites adhered to this shock therapy recipe could be taken as a measure of their tutelary behaviour.

In Estonia, there was a belief in far-reaching economic reform stretching all the way back to 1987. In September of that year, four well-known social scientists (Siim Kallas, Tiit Made, Edgar Savisaar and Mikk Titma) published a newspaper article essentially calling for economic autonomy in Estonia and for disengaging the republic from central Soviet rule. But even the best laid reform plans were of little help in a situation where the Soviet economy as a whole was rapidly grinding to a halt, and the Kremlin was becoming more and more an obstacle, rather than an impetus for change. In March 1990, Estonia held its first free elections since the Soviet occupation, and the opposition Popular Front came to power with its leader, Edgar Savisaar, as prime minister. Seizing the opportunity to begin a transformation, Savisaar initiated a triple policy of price liberalisation, small enterprise privatisation, and initial steps towards an independent monetary system. These efforts, however, were undermined by the even more drastic breakdown of the Soviet system; thus it is difficult to assess how much Savisaar was able to stem the tide of decline or simply hold off the worst.

In the event, the advent of independence following the failed Soviet coup in August 1991 kicked the reform process into new gear. Indeed, one of the central ideas to come from the 1987 four-man reform programme – the creation of a separate, convertible currency in Estonia – suddenly became an immediate imperative. This became a new landmark of reform ideology among Estonian elites, as in early 1992 the decision was taken by the prime minister at the time, Tiit Vähi, to rebuff contrary advice from the International Monetary Fund and introduce a new Estonian currency, the *kroon*, as early as June of that year.

To a large extent, Tiit Vähi had an easy time adopting this and other reform measures, since he had taken office in January 1992 with the express task of carrying the country to new elections in September. He did not intend to run for re-election and so did not have to worry about experiencing the political consequences of his decisions. This fate would fall to his successor and winner of the September elections, Mart Laar, leader of the nationalist Pro Patria party, which won 29 seats in the 101-seat parliament. Indeed, it would be Laar who would not only confront these consequences, but also instil much of the tutelary ethos that would follow throughout the rest of the 1990s.[10] He would also lay the foundations for a very youthful streak in Estonian politics, being just 32 years of age when he took office. His partners in the new coalition would be the equally nationalist Estonian National Independence Party (with 10 seats) and the more centrist Moderates (with 12 seats).

Two major crossroads of reform faced Laar in the fall of 1992. The first was the task of drawing up the first state budget in Estonian kroons since 1940. In technical terms, the introduction of the new currency had been remarkably successful: no serious problems were encountered. Monetarily and fiscally, however, the difficulties – true market competition, reduced economic growth, diminishing tax revenue – were only emerging. Laar's fiscal strategy was therefore radical not only in that he insisted on avoiding any deficit spending, but also in that he succeeded in pushing through a wholesale restructuring of the tax system, introducing a flat rate of just 26 per cent on all personal and corporate income. Laar gambled by cutting both spending and taxes at once. Second, Laar stood steadfast in the face of another consequence of the new kroon: a drastic wave of bankruptcies and business failures, especially among banks. The young historian-turned-politician's stance was that only strict discipline would provide any hope for the future.

These early moves were followed by further reforms, including the initiation of a large-scale privatisation programme (July 1993), the opening-up of Estonian trade through a drastic reduction in import and export tariffs (September 1993), and the attraction of extensive foreign investment to the detriment of building up local industry (beginning especially in 1994). Housing privatisation was kicked off in earnest during 1993. Property restitution (already approved in 1991) proceeded more slowly because of the sheer number of restitution claims as well as frequent controversies over true ownership or inheritance rights. However, its principle remained unquestioned (see Staehr, 2004).

In a word, the Laar government founded an entirely new economy for Estonia, all the while knowing that this would be neither simple nor popular. On the one hand, the complexity of these reforms was daunting. But in a strikingly self-assured manner, Laar would later argue that the youth and simple pro-market zeal he and his comrades had at the time was actually the key to their success. Speaking about how in 1992 the Pro Patria party had practically no experts on economics or finance amongst its top leaders, but still had to

---

10 Laar very much exudes this self-confidence and conviction in his memoirs from 1992-2002 originally published in German (2002b) and later in Estonian (2002a). In English, see Laar (1996).

write an economic policy platform for the September elections, Laar would comment:

> In retrospect this [deficiency] wasn't perhaps the worst aspect of things, since it allowed us to approach issues without any complexes. This is also what foreign experts who advised Pro Patria said about us, since according to them the advantage of people like us was that we knew nothing about economic theory – neither socialist nor capitalist. (Laar 2002a, 50)

POLITICAL DEVELOPMENT

In comparison to economic reform, Estonia's political transformation can be dated much more precisely to the period stretching from August 20, 1991 to June 28, 1992. These two dates mark the beginning and the end of Estonia's process of writing a new constitution and of thereby founding an entirely new political system. Moreover, the relative smoothness of this transformation stands in contrast to the experiences of Latvia and Lithuania. In the former country, the Latvian Supreme Soviet decided simply to reinstate the country's constitution from 1922 and therefore shied away from a wholesale renewal of the political system. In Lithuania, crude attempts were first made to reconfigure leftover Soviet institutions into a presidential system, but only when these failed in May 1992 was a hasty decision made to write a new constitution, which was ratified in October 1992.

In Estonia, one could say that the choice in favour of creating a new constitution was also serendipitous in that the decision came amid tense negotiations among rival Estonian politicians on August 19th and 20th 1991 about how to respond to the attempted coup against Mikhail Gorbachev in Moscow.[11] Both moderates from the ruling Estonian Popular Front and radicals from a movement known as the Congress of Estonia were wary of the other side gaining the upper hand just as the ultimate opportunity for restoring independence had arrived. Thus, they compromised on the creation of a special 60-member Constitutional Assembly, which would be appointed jointly by the existing Estonian Supreme Soviet and by the Congress of Estonia. During the next nine months, the new constitution would be drafted, discussed among the broad public and finally ratified with a 91 per cent popular approval rating on June 28, 1992.

In this respect, Estonia's new political system does not fit the model of a tutelary transition in its entirety. Although Estonia's elites were able to agree

---

11 For accounts of the August 1991 attempted coup in Estonia, see Must (2000) and *20. augusti klubi ja Riigikogu kantselei* (1996). For broader background see Taagepera (1993), Laar, Ott and Endre (1996).

quickly on the need to overhaul their political institutions, the institutions they chose were on the whole consensual or meant to spread out power, rather than to concentrate it in any one person's hands. It was tutelary, however, in the sense that public opinion polls from the time showed that Estonians would have preferred a more presidential regime, which was consciously forestalled by elites in the Constitutional Assembly. Eventually Estonia opted for a strongly parliamentary system, where executive authority is vested in a prime minister, who is appointed by the legislature and dependent on a majority coalition. Although Estonia does have a president, this post is largely ceremonial and is elected by the parliament or by a special electoral college, not by popular vote.

A second political dimension of Estonia's tutelary transition concerns the steady cartelisation of Estonian party politics. Cartelisation, as defined by Katz and Mair (1995), involves a narrowing of competition among political parties in contemporary democracies because of special institutional rules, which favour larger, long-standing parties over newer, smaller ones. Increasingly the system is configured to obstruct the entry of new political parties into the electoral marketplace. In addition, existing political parties also become less responsive to popular pressures, as they are less and less tied to large-scale collective organisations (such as trade unions) or dependent on mass membership; instead, they rely on single financial contributors or special interests. Lastly, the political message these parties propagate becomes more and more simplistic, relying on 'feel good' slogans and hype, rather than on a presentation of ideological principles or a discussion of political issues at hand.

Of course, judging by a number of standard indicators of political fragmentation Estonia would not seem to have a very consolidated or cartelised party system. The number of parliamentary parties has averaged 5.7 through the four compositions of the *Riigikogu* (or parliament) from 1992 to 2007.[12] The 'effective number of electoral parties' has also averaged 6.4.[13] Lastly, with each election there have always been new parties aiming for seats and actually getting into parliament. Thus, on the face of it, there would seem to be plenty of room for party competition.

Nevertheless, during the 1990s a number of institutional changes occurred which narrowed the field of political competition in Estonia and therefore concentrated political opportunities and resources in the hands of a few dominant

---

12 Included here are the main parliamentary party groups as they formed immediately after an election, for they represent the real political actors as far as parties are concerned. Electoral alliances (such as the Coalition Party-Country People's Union in 1995) are thus more validly broken up into the separate groups they themselves formed following the election.

13 This indicator, devised by Laakso and Taagepera (1979), weights the parties in a parliament (or an election) according to their proportional size (or vote share). Here electoral alliances are counted as one party; the vote shares of independent candidates have been excluded.

parties (See also Sikk 2003). The first decision was taken in 1994 with the adoption of a new Party Act, which mandated that all political parties must have at least 1,000 members. In comparison to Latvia and Lithuania, where the figure was just 200 and 400 respectively and where the populations were also many times larger, this minimum number was considerable. Second, the new party law instituted a system of state subsidies for all parties that succeeded in getting into parliament in proportion to their electoral strength. As a result, not only did this system favour existing parties over newcomers, it also favoured the strongest political parties in parliament. Thirdly, during the second half of the 1990s, these subsidies grew steadily to a total of roughly 1.25 million euros per year. With this kind of money it is true that parties as a whole were able to reduce their dependence on private contributions. Indeed, in 2003 an amendment to the Party Act was passed which banned contributions to political parties from commercial organisations (companies and firms). Likewise, it can be said that democracy was enhanced by state financing to the extent that parties were able to use this money to set up real party headquarters and institutionalise their relations with their members and voters. At the same time, the money also meant that newcomers would not have these kinds of advantages.

Finally, a certain degree of party cartelisation derived from Estonian electoral law (Sikk 2004; Mikkel & Pettai 2004). For example, since 1992 the electoral threshold has been 5 per cent. This has meant that during 1990s an average of nearly 10 per cent of the vote during each election was lost to parties that did not cross this threshold. After 2000, this number was down to less than 5 per cent; but this trend indicated the same phenomenon: voters had simply given up supporting smaller parties. In addition, in 1998 the electoral law was changed so that so-called electoral coalitions were henceforth banned and only single political parties could now field candidates for parliament. Lastly, in 2002 an attempt was made to extend the ban on coalitions to municipal elections. Although this was eventually overturned by Estonia's Supreme Court, it did force a number of local politicians to join one or another political party, whereas previously they had remained independents.[14]

Thirdly, Estonia's civil service became increasingly politicised during the 1990s, as cabinet ministers attempted to fill key ministerial posts with politically reliable party colleagues rather than professional civil servants. If there was a belief during the early 1990s that the director general in each ministry should be a professional civil servant who would maintain continuity between different cabinet shake-ups, then by the end of the decade it was more the practice that each minister had the prerogative to shake up his or her ministry,

---

14 For further examination of citizen electoral alliances in Estonia, see Pettai, Toomla Joakit (2007).

including the director general. In addition, ministers increasingly began hiring special advisors and aides who served as a link to the political party – enabling the minister to perform political functions and the party to maintain control over the minister. More and more politicians took a very cynical, zero-sum attitude to politics, saying that if they did not take such 'safety measures' first, their competitors would do so for them. (See also Sikk 2006.)

ELECTORAL COMPETITION

One famous tenet of democracy is that political outcomes are always uncertain (Przeworski 1991). Democracy is the kind of political system in which no-one is meant to have a built-in edge. The loser in one election is supposed to have a reasonable chance of becoming the victor in the next. This is even more the case in a parliamentary democracy, where victories are rarely absolute; instead, politics and governments are built on coalitions and coalitions can always include different players. As a result, the variety of different governing coalitions should be an indicator of representative vs. tutelary democracy.

In Estonia, the post-independence history of electoral outcomes and parliamentary coalitions has been very lop-sided. Between the first *Riigikogu* election in September 1992 and March 2007, a total of ten cabinets have been in office. (See table 1.) Of these, seven were either centre-right or centrist, totalling in terms of days 74 per cent of the time period in question.

In addition to this political dominance, the sense of tutelary transition also comes from the degree to which one party in particular – the Centre Party – has consistently been shunted into the opposition, although over time it has become the strongest and most popular party in the country. The Centre Party was founded in 1992 as the successor to the Estonian Popular Front, which led the country to independence in 1991. Although after independence many sections of this original umbrella movement peeled off to form their own political parties, a solid core remained around the Front's vigorous leader, Edgar Savisaar. It was this core that Savisaar aimed to mould into a centre-left political force.[15]

By the same token, many of the groups which had left the Popular Front did so precisely because of dissatisfaction with Savisaar's authoritative leader-

---

15 Admittedly, experts in Estonia often differ as to whether the Centre Party is truly a left-wing party. Based on its official programme, it would seem to be a rather liberal, market-oriented party. Indeed, in 2002 it was admitted into the Liberal International. However, on the domestic political scene and during elections, the party has consistently courted the votes of those who have been less advantaged by the economic transition, to wit, pensioners, low-wage workers and the Russian-speaking population. In this sense, the party anchors very much the 'left' of Estonian politics.

TABLE 1: GOVERNMENTS IN ESTONIA, 1992–2007

RIIGIKOGU	PRIME MINISTER	DATE OF INVESTITURE	DATE OF RELEASE	DAYS IN OFFICE	PARTY SUPPORT	POLITICAL PROFILE
VII	Mart Laar	21.10.1992	08.11.1994	748	Pro Patria, Estonian National Independence Party, Moderates	centre-right
	Andres Tarand	08.11.1994	17.04.1995	160	Pro Patria, Estonian National Independence Party, Moderates	centre-right
VIII	Tiit Vähi	17.04.1995	06.11.1995	203	Coalition Party/Country People's Party, Centre Party	centre-left
	Tiit Vähi	06.11.1995	05.12.1996	391	Coalition Party/Country People's Party, Reform Party	centre-right
	Tiit Vähi*	01.12.1996	17.03.1997	106	Coalition Party/Country People's Party [minority cabinet]	centre
	Mart Siimann	17.03.1997	25.03.1999	738	Coalition Party/Country People's Party, Development Party [minority cabinet]	centre
IX	Mart Laar	25.03.1999	28.01.2002	1040	Pro Patria Union, Reform Party, Moderates	centre-right
	Siim Kallas	28.01.2002	10.04.2003	423	Reform Party, Centre Party	right-left
X	Juhan Parts	10.04.2003	13.04.2005	734	Res Publica, Reform Party, People's Union	centre-right
	Andrus Ansip	13.04.2005	2.04.2007	719	Reform Party, Centre Party, People's Union	right-left

*Technically only a cabinet reshuffle following the departure of the Reform Party. No formal re-investiture by the parliament, although the government henceforth became a minority and its base of party support changed.

ship style. Savisaar was widely recognised as a superb tactician and organiser. Analysts and observers named him 'the best politician in Estonia' on numerous occasions. However, precisely for these same qualities, a number of other politicians became increasingly wary of his power and turned against him.

The key characteristic of tutelary transition to appear in this connection is that over time a major cleavage has developed between the Centre Party and Estonia's remaining political parties – not so much over policy differences, but over the singular persona of Edgar Savisaar. Throughout the second half of the 1990s Estonia's centrist and right-wing parties attempted to isolate the Centre Party primarily because they believed that cooperation with Savisaar – regardless of his party's support among the electorate – would be dangerous for the stability of Estonian democracy. At different points in time, leaders of these parties said that while they could imagine working together with the Centre Party on certain policy issues and getting along with 'reasonable' elements of the party, cooperation on a formal level was excluded because they did not trust Savisaar as a leader.

To be sure, this image of the Centre Party as a pariah in the Estonian party system was partly Savisaar's own doing. The history of wariness towards Savisaar began in January 1992, when as prime minister under the Popular Front he attempted to assume emergency powers amidst the severe economic crisis immediately following independence. This move was seen as excessive by a number of deputies in the Estonian parliament at the time, and it soon led to his being forced out of office. Following the parliamentary elections in September 1992, Savisaar and his party still did well, drawing 12 per cent of the vote and 15 seats in the Riigikogu. As such, the Centre Party became the third largest faction, but was clearly relegated to the opposition, since it was Pro Patria that dominated the parliament with 29 mandates.

In advance of the March 1995 elections, the Centre Party had a good chance of gaining electoral support. However, the actual mantle of an opposition set to take power was seized by the centrist Coalition Party, which formed a bloc with a number of agrarian parties and thus came out as the big victor in the elections with over 32 per cent of the vote. The Centre Party did increase its vote share to 14 per cent, but it remained in a tenuous position. During negotiations to form a new government, the leader of the Coalition Party, Tiit Vähi, eventually turn to Savisaar, and a cabinet was agreed soon thereafter with Savisaar as Minister of the Interior. However, once again the tensions around Savisaar began to mount, and in October 1995 a scandal broke in which it was revealed that during the recent coalition talks Savisaar had secretly taped a number of his conversations with various politicians. This example of mischief soon became a new cross on which to try to crucify the Centre Party leader. After he refused to resign as minister, he was formally dismissed by President Lennart Meri and the Coalition-Centre government collapsed. Moreover, the reverberations eventually reached inside the Centre Party, and Savisaar was forced out as chairman some weeks later.

Still, Savisaar was able to use his skills as a politician to manoeuvre himself back in as party chairman by the spring of 1996. This comeback amazed most political observers, while confirming for others the extent of Savisaar's real grip on the party. At the same time, the increasing polarisation around Savisaar soon became an electoral trump card for the party, since the early years of economic reform were now beginning to bite, and more and more voters began to view the Centre Party as the one remaining party that could provide an alternative. For those who had been hit worst by the economic transition, the ostracising of Savisaar made him look more and more like a martyr worthy of support. The party itself played this very skilfully, criticising the rising levels of economic inequality and promising to devote more resources to the disadvantaged if elected. As a key dividing line between it and other parties, it promised to roll back Estonia's flat-rate tax system and install instead a progressive income tax. By the next elections in March 1999, Savisaar expected to triumph as far-and-away the strongest party.

Indeed, Savisaar and the Centre Party did emerge victorious with 23.4 per cent of the vote and 28 seats in parliament. This amounted to a 7 per cent victory over the party's closest rival, the Pro Patria Union, which garnered only 16 per cent and 18 seats. However, the ganging-up on Savisaar continued, since the electoral arithmetic also revealed that the Pro Patria Union could equally form a governing majority together with the Reform Party and the Moderates. Indeed, this had been the aim of the three parties when three months before the elections they announced the formation of a 'Triple Alliance' or pledge to create a centre-right government and thwart Savisaar if they secured a majority of seats. When the electoral results showed this was possible, they pressed President Lennart Meri to entrust the formation of a new government to the leader of the Pro Patria Union, Mart Laar, despite the fact that democratic tradition should have given this right to Savisaar. Ultimately, Meri, as a former member of the PPU, happily obliged, and Savisaar was outmanoeuvred again.

The Triple Alliance government of Mart Laar was, in the event, the longest serving cabinet to date. However, on many occasions it held together more in defence against Savisaar than in the name of any specific policies. Likewise in the Tallinn City Council, where the Triple Alliance tried to hold power, the anti-Savisaar posture was particularly trying since it required special support from a number of Russian parties (thus making it into a quadruple alliance). By mid-2001, the strain of all this personality-cleaved politics began to show. The pro-market Reform Party became fed-up with cobbling together majorities, and in the Tallinn City Council it finally crossed the dividing line in December 2001, offering to form a new, stable municipal government with Savisaar and the Centre Party. Savisaar readily accepted the invitation, and within a week a new majority was formed. The move, however, could not help but rock the Triple Alliance at national level, and in early January Prime Minister Mart Laar announced that he would resign over what many in the Pro Patria Union as well as the Moderates saw as treason by the Reform Party.

In this respect, the decision by the Reform Party was a daring one. Politically it was shrewd because the leader of the party, Siim Kallas, himself became prime minister even though the reformists had ten seats fewer in parliament than the Centre Party. (Savisaar contented himself with becoming mayor of Tallinn.) Likewise, the move mixed up the party-political deck of cards, since if there was one party that was diametrically opposed to the policies of the Centre Party, it was the pro-market Reform Party. Indeed, for the year-long period during which the two would govern, they agreed to freeze their main policy difference over tax policy – namely the Centre Party's call for a progressive income tax and the Reform Party's desire not only to preserve the flat tax, but also to scale it back to just 20 per cent. It seemed, therefore, that the ice had been broken.

However, a coalition so anomalous as that existing between the Reform and Centre parties surely made no sense as the March 2003 parliamentary elections approached. The two were natural competitors, and this competition did heat up as the campaign progressed. However, for these elections there was a new player on the political scene – one who was determined to resume the anti-Centre Party crusade. The Union for the Republic – Res Publica (or simply known as Res Publica) was based on a long-standing political club comprised of assorted (usually young) supporters of either the Reform Party or the Pro Patria Union. For years they had simply been a social organisation; however during 2001 the leaders of the club became increasingly restless (i.e. ambitious), and eventually they announced an intention to form their own political party.

The party initially trod cautiously as it lacked a convincing leader. Eventually, however, they secured the support of the state auditor, Juhan Parts, who resigned his position in the summer of 2002 in order to jump into the party melee. After spearheading the party to a respectable showing in the municipal elections of October 2002, Parts and Res Publica came to epitomise the new alternative for those voters who were disgruntled with the Triple Alliance, but were also anti-Savisaar. The strategy of clearly opposing the Centre Party worked perfectly, and on election night Res Publica staged an upset by winning exactly the same amount of seats as the Centre Party, 28, albeit trailing in the vote count by some 3,900 (out of nearly 500,000 votes cast).

Following the elections, therefore, Estonia returned to its lop-sided politics: although Savisaar and the Centre Party had technically won the election with the most votes, Juhan Parts and Res Publica lost no time in seizing the momentum to sideline the Centre Party once again. Res Publica immediately turned to the Reform Party and the agrarian People's Union to begin talks on forming a stable 60-seat coalition. Savisaar protested loudly and accused the media of having demonised him, causing him to lose. But once again, Savisaar had to reconcile himself with the opposition. Moreover, the polarised split over him and his party was now more serious than ever. In an exit poll conducted by the Department of Political Science at the University of Tartu, fully 54 per cent of voters said that the Centre Party was the one party for whom they knew they would absolutely not vote.

But in April 2005 the Centre Party would get another opportunistic chance to enter government, when the Parts government collapsed and the Reform Party (led now by Andrus Ansip) turned to Edgar Savisaar to form a new coalition (still including the People's Union). This 'right-left' government even made Savisaar Minister of Economics and Communications, a position which he used to carry out high-profile projects such as buying back Estonia's privatised railway network in order to rebuild a state role in the economy. However, by the time the 2007 Riigikogu elections arrived, the anti-Savisaar rhetoric again began to mount amidst a fear that this time the Centre Party was sure to triumph. However, again it was not to be. The Reform Party pulled off a surprise upset and topped the Centre Party, 31 seats to 29. Andrus Ansip continued as prime minister and explicitly avoided negotiating a coalition with Savisaar, even though this would have been the easiest arithmetical option. Instead, he opted (almost astonishingly) for an oversize coalition on the centre-right with the (now merged) Pro Patria and Res Publica Union, the Social Democrats (former Moderates) and the newly-created Green Party.

In sum, such stark cleavage over one man and his party epitomised the idea that for those opposing Savisaar there was only one acceptable path for development, and that anything else was not only objectionable, but dangerous. To be sure, much of this was simple political rivalry. But behind the rhetoric was a party system in which the centre-right retained power from year to year not simply through a positive programme of success, but equally through demonisation of the one party able to form a possible alternative. In turn, this prompted the Centre Party to become equally vindictive, as some of its own political tactics showed. While the Estonian party system was far better balanced in terms of stable ideological orientations amongst its parties (in comparison to its Baltic neighbours), this occasional personification of politics was a definite weakness.

STATE BUILDING AND EUROPEAN UNION ACCESSION

From an empirical-analytical standpoint, it is difficult to distinguish in many of the post-communist countries of Central and Eastern Europe the processes of state building and European Union accession. To be sure, the issues of establishing an efficient bureaucracy, rule of law, effective policy implementation and civil society feedback were all inherently necessary goals to be achieved as part of democratic transition and consolidation. However, in most instances the perspective from which most of these challenges would be tackled involved the almost concomitant goal of joining the European Union. Thus, almost inevitably the way in which the details of state building would be approached would be that of first analysing the way in which such processes were conducted within the European Union's member states. And where such rules and regulations were actually a part of the *acquis communautaire*, the state-building process was even more guided by the EU model.

It is important to note that while the EU has always been seen as a kind of elite project and therefore equally characteristic of 'tutelary' tendencies, this applied in particular in the Estonian case, since popular misgivings about the accession process mounted quite ominously in the run-up to the country's final referendum on the issue. But Estonia's elite remained determined to see the development go through. In this sense, state building, too, took place in an intensified atmosphere, since the backdrop of the EU was always there.

Estonia's formal road to EU membership began in November 1995, when the country deposited its official application to join. Since the Baltic states' independence in 1991, Brussels had treated the three countries equally, first signing free-trade deals with each state, then concluding association agreements and other accords (Pettai 2003a). In 1997, however, the EU shifted tack by proposing a two-stage process of enlargement and by including Estonia in the first wave, with Latvia and Lithuania in the second. This idea was eventually abandoned in 1999, when Riga and Vilnius also began official accession negotiations. However, it was an indication of just how eager Estonian political leaders were to be considered for membership that they lobbied hard in 1997 to be included in this 'first wave'. While most average Estonians still had very little sense of what the EU implied, some of the country's leaders were already hopeful that membership could be secured by the turn of the century.

The actual accession process therefore proceeded apace; but curiously enough, public support among Estonians and non-Estonians began to decline noticeably. The EU's regular 'barometers' of public opinion in the accession states from 1998 to 2003 showed rising levels of opposition to membership especially in 2000 and 2001. When asked whether they thought membership 'would be a good thing', only a third responded 'yes'. Moreover, quite indicative of the extent to which accession was being perceived by the people as a tutelary process, nearly 40 per cent of respondents in 2001 said that the pace of negotiations should be slowed down; only 25 per cent wanted them to go as 'fast as possible' (European Commission 2002). This was the highest rate of scepticism among any of the Central and Eastern European candidate states (see also Ehin 2001, 2002/2003; Vetik 2003, Pettai 2005).

These sentiments placed Estonian elites once again in a position of having to coax the public to accept a project which they earnestly believed in, but whose value (and possible pain) was still questioned by average Estonians. This challenge reached its crescendo in advance of the final, September 14 2003 referendum on EU accession. Estonia's main political leaders – President Arnold Rüütel, Prime Minister Juhan Parts, parliamentary speaker Ene Ergma – issued joint statements calling on Estonians to vote with their conscience, but also declaring their own personal support for membership. President Rüütel was seen as particularly instrumental in convincing more sceptical rural voters to vote in favour because of his great popularity in the countryside. Meanwhile, Juhan Parts's Res Publica party staged its own pro-EU campaign, appealing to younger voters with amusing ads that predicted 'more sexy men' for Estonia if the country joined. The youth movement of the Reform Party also chimed in by distributing condoms with the slogan 'Better to be inside' (Past 2005).

However, the campaign also evoked graver themes. For example, a poster sponsored by the Estonian Chamber of Commerce and Industry posited the referendum as a choice between having either a lush, full-meat sandwich in the West (EU) or a dried-out, scraggly piece of bread in the East (Russia). What's more, these dietary choices were laid out against a map of Europe painted confidently blue in the West, and ominously red in the East. The poster admittedly caused a slight furore, since its implicitly anti-Russia message was seen as potentially scaring away as many Russian voters as it was meant to attract among Estonians. Thus, it was soon withdrawn. But it did show that for many opinion-makers the meaning of EU membership was linked just as much to Estonia's very survival as an independent nation-state in Europe as it was to economic benefits. So if nothing else could convince voters, the existential dimension was always there.

Estonia's EU accession process thus contained numerous moments at which elite choices were increasingly being questioned by average Estonians. After all, Estonia was now a good decade into its post-communist transition, and the readiness of the public to follow every proposition put forward by political leaders was beginning to wane. However, Estonian elites did squeeze out a respectable 67 per cent approval rating from the voters on September 14 2003. This was all they needed. Moreover, for the next EU hurdle – approval of the EU Constitution – Estonian leaders had already agreed that this would take place in parliament (Pettai & Veebel 2005). Thus, on the EU front elite decision making would continue.

MINORITY INTEGRATION AND NATION BUILDING

Estonia's ethnic relations come under the category of tutelary transition most clearly in terms of how the country determined its citizenship policy in 1991 and how the issue of minority integration subsequently evolved. In November 1991, the Estonian parliament passed a resolution stating that all Soviet-era immigrants and their descendants (roughly 30 per cent of the population in 1991) would not be accorded automatic citizenship in the restored Republic of Estonia, since in the eyes of most Estonians the Soviet era had been an illegal occupation and therefore all those who had settled in Estonia during that time could not be viewed as rightful citizens. This was part of a broader Estonian political doctrine of 'legal restorationism', which viewed Estonia's re-independence in 1991 as a direct restoration of its pre-1940 statehood and of all that this entailed. (Citizenship was only one part of this; the principle of property restitution discussed above was another.) As a result, Soviet-era settlers were now considered 'persons of undetermined citizenship' who could become either naturalised Estonian citizens (if they passed certain language and civics tests), or Russian Federation citizens (which was relatively easy during the 1990s). Alternatively, they could also remain as stateless, permanent residents in Estonia.

This decision was quite stark in the sense that it removed from national politics a sizeable part of the population, as non-citizens could no longer vote in parliamentary elections. (They were, however, given the right to vote in municipal elections as well as being guaranteed all social rights and benefits.) Moreover, because the overwhelming majority of non-citizens (being Soviet-era immigrants) were Russian, politics itself became heavily skewed in favour of the ethnic Estonian population. For example, the first *Riigikogu* to be elected in 1992 was 100 per cent ethnic Estonian, even though the population at large was only some 62 per cent Estonian. Russian parties were represented in the Estonian parliament in 1995-2003, but since then they have failed to overcome the 5 per cent electoral threshold. Special language laws were adopted instituting Estonian as the sole official language in the country; and the civil service (as in most countries) was made eligible for citizens only.

For the Estonians, this was all a question of historical and legal justice, since the very influx of Russians into Estonia since 1945 had been the product of a conscious Soviet policy to dilute the native population, and in this sense the Estonians insisted on a right to restore their nation state. Notably, in 1945, Estonia's Russian minority had numbered a mere 2-3 per cent. For Estonia's political leaders, meanwhile, the Russian minority was also a matter of security, since in their minds Russia could not be trusted not to use the minority as means of keeping control over Estonia despite the latter's independence. Moscow's frequent assertions during the 1990s that it retained a right and a responsibility to look after all Russian minority populations living in the former Soviet republics evoked ominous reminders of Hitler's defence of the Sudeten Germans before World War II. Thus, once again broader geopolitical issues weighed heavily on Estonian thinking.

For the Russian minority itself, there was little left but to accommodate to the Estonian rules. While considerable international attention was paid to Estonia's citizenship policy, there was never any direct pressure applied to reverse any of its main principles. Individual procedures for naturalisation were eased from time to time, but not even the European Union made an obstacle of the fact that Estonia would eventually join the community with some 150,000 stateless persons.[16] Instead, efforts were made to encourage the development of a meaningful integration policy for ethnic minorities – one that would contain Estonian language training for minorities, educational reform, and support for minority cultural groups as well as public information campaigns to improve Estonian attitudes towards minorities. In 1997, the first minister without portfolio specifically tasked with integration policy was appointed. By March 2000, a full-scale, 100-page policy document was adopted, setting out concrete measures to be taken across a range of administrative areas. At the same time, from among the international community the European Union, the United Nations Development Programme, the Soros foundation, Canada, and the Nordic countries all contributed tens of millions of Estonian kroons to supporting different integration programmes, many of which yielded significant results. This proved perhaps the most substantive dimension of international influence on Estonian minority policy.

All told, Estonia and its political elite decided to exercise a rather legalistic interpretation of the Soviet era and its aftermath in order to steer the country once again in a certain desired direction. Indeed, it could well be said that Estonia would never have been able to adopt such decisive political and economic reform in the early 1990s if power had not been so disproportionately in ethnic Estonian hands. Had Russian minority presence in Estonian politics been greater, there would have inevitably been more pressure to retain economic and political links with Russia, or at the very least economic reform (e.g. privatisation, industrial restructuring, attracting foreign investment) would have been much slower. The aim to remove Estonia once and for all from Moscow's shadow would have been a dream. Rather, Estonia might well have ended up more like Moldova, struggling with inter-ethnic tension and caught in an ambiguous geopolitical grey zone (Pettai & Hallik 2002).

Such speculation is naturally fraught with serious normative contradic-

---

16 Figure reported by Estonia's Minister for Population Affairs, Paul-Eerik Rummo, Postimees (2004). On international reaction to Estonia's citizenship policy, see Pettai (2001), Kelley (2003), Galbreath (2003).

tions: how could the political exclusion of minorities be justified in terms of some other collective good? This would seem to go beyond the latitude of even tutelary transition. But it was nevertheless a paradox of Estonia's ethnic relations that minority Russians enjoyed better living conditions in Estonia than in Russia, and that this relative prosperity was the result of a rapid market transformation. Indeed, one of the arguments (both in the media and in scholarly publications) as to why Russians in Estonia never protested more loudly against their denial of automatic citizenship involved precisely 'a rational calculation' that economically they would be better off if they refrained from doing so (Laitin 2003; Lauristin & Heidmets 2003). In this sense, the Russian minority could be said to have acquiesced even more than the Estonians to tutelary transition.

WILLING SUBJECTS?

While arguing that Estonia's four major transformations can fruitfully be understood via the concept of tutelary transition, it would be foolhardy not to consider the role of those who are ostensibly the objects or beneficiaries of this stewardship – the people of Estonia at large. To some extent the predominance of elite decision making in Estonian society can be explained by many of the rewards that such transition has objectively brought. Economic growth in Estonia has been stronger for a longer period of time than in most other Central and Eastern European countries (and certainly in comparison to the rest of the former Soviet Union, including the other two Baltic states). Estonia has received countless reform accolades from a variety of outside experts, including international financial institutions (World Bank), innovation researchers (Economist Intelligence Unit), corruption analysts (Transparency International), and competitiveness studies (Bertelsmann Foundation). Much of this positive news has also been reported in the Estonian press. Thus, a certain amount of optimism has continually existed in Estonian society. Even surveys conducted during the hardest period of transition (1992-93) showed that both Estonians and non-Estonians had more optimism than pessimism towards the future, both with regard to the country as a whole and in terms of their own household's well-being (EMOR 1993). As a result, it is not perhaps such a surprise to see that centre-right political forces and liberal ideologies have endured in Estonia, since people see them as producing results and thus regard them as the right way to go (Lauristin & Vihalemm 1997, 116-26).

FIGURE 1: ELECTORAL TURNOUT IN ESTONIA, 1990-2007

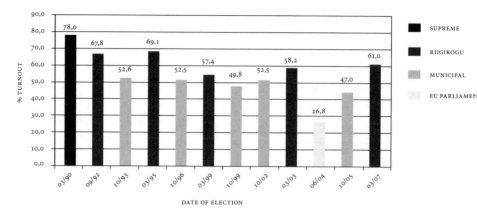

DATE OF ELECTION

FIGURE 2: TRUST IN GOVERNMENT INSTITUTIONS IN ESTONIA, 1995-2004

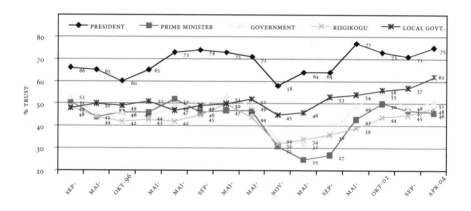

However, dissatisfaction with Estonia's elite-driven transition has manifested itself in different modes, starting with continually declining levels of electoral turnout and modest levels of trust in political institutions. (See Figures 1 and 2.) While electoral participation has dropped across Central and Eastern Europe since the heyday of the early 1990s, it is perhaps more striking to see this occurring in Estonia, where the example of high electoral participation in the Nordic countries[17] is closer at hand. Meanwhile, satisfaction with the performance of Estonia's political institutions dipped sharply in 2001, when the second government of Mart Laar was racked with controversy over the privatisation of Estonia's railways and the attempted sale of the country's main electricity plants. In this sense, such polls often reflected merely temporary

---

17 An average of 80.8 per cent for 16 elections between 1990 and 2001. See Siaroff & Merer (2002).

FIGURE 3: SOCIO-ECONOMIC VALUE CHANGE IN ESTONIA 1990-1999

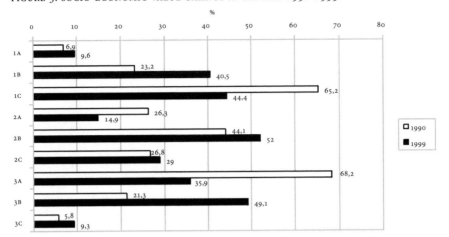

Source: Saar (2001).

Values juxtapositions:
1a Incomes should be made more equal.
1b Incomes could be more equal, but individual effort also matters.
1c There should be greater incentives for individual effort.
2a Individuals should take more responsibility for providing for themselves.
2b Both the individual and the state should take responsibility.
2c The state should take more responsibility to ensure that everyone is provided for.
3a Competition is good. It stimulates people to work hard and develop new ideas.
3b Competition is both good and bad.
3c Competition is harmful, it brings out the worst in people.

attitudes connected with specific individuals, rather than inherent trust in the institutions as such. The recovery in trust levels following the change of prime minister in January 2002 illustrates this effect. Nonetheless, other institutions such as the president or the courts retained much higher ratings during this period. Even the police and the tax authorities outstripped the government and the parliament, ranking respectively 60 and 69 per cent in April 2004.

Likewise, by the year 2000 it was becoming increasingly clear that Estonians' belief in hard-line market economics was waning and that a greater awareness of social issues was developing. Comparing data from the European Values Survey from 1990 and 1999, Andrus Saar (a leading Estonian pollster) revealed that Estonian attitudes towards competition, income inequality and individual self-responsibility had all declined (Saar 2001). Although in most cases these levels continued to be higher than in Latvia or Lithuania, the change over this 10-year period of liberal reform had been stark (see Figure 3). Even though in 1990 68.2

per cent of Estonians (both ethnic Estonians and Russians) believed that 'competition is good', by 1999 this figure was down by almost half, to just 35.9 per cent. Likewise, whereas in the beginning of the decade 65.2 per cent of respondents agreed that a person's income should be linked most of all to his/her own individual effort, some 10 years later only 44.4 per cent concurred with this opinion. The people of Estonia were genuinely becoming more left-wing in their attitudes.

CONCLUSION

The concept of 'tutelary transition' put forth here in order to understand politics in Estonia is admittedly highly contingent. For example, on a methodological level we must be careful not to create new terms at whim or without sufficient analytical reward. As Collier and Levitsky warn,

> In a literature in which conceptual confusion is a recurring problem, the analytic gains from precising [a] definition must be weighted against the cost of unsettling the semantic field. Hence, it is important that scholars avoid "definitional gerrymandering" [...], in the sense of introducing a new definition every time they encounter a somewhat anomalous field. (Collier & Levitsky 1997, 445)

Secondly, in an empirical sense the idea of tutelary transition does not encompass every single aspect of Estonian political development since 1992. Nor is it entirely consistent across even those phenomena to which it seems to apply. In this respect, therefore, 'tutelary transition' is a *heuristic concept* or an aid to 'understanding' transformation rather than necessarily explaining it. It seeks to 'explain' only to the extent that Estonia's staunch Western orientation, centre-right political profile and pro-market transition have all lasted longer than in most other post-communist Eastern European countries.

Thirdly, the model will certainly not last forever. Estonian elite perspectives on the perceived threat from Russia, the possibility for greater welfare spending, the prospects for minority integration, or a more balanced role for the Centre Party can all change. Factors such as European integration will diminish the feeling that Estonia is alone against Moscow. Economic development via the EU will also help balance out social inequalities. Lastly, a more even keel will be reached in party politics as older generations pass on.

However, the example of Estonia shows what kind of a delicate leadership balance democratic transition can entail. On the one hand, national politicians along with foreign observers will often want stable and commanding leadership in order to get a country 'on the right track'. But the point at which this hard line becomes 'tutelary' and counter-productive is less clear. Even now Estonia is not out of the woods, although it has certainly gained much from its strident development path.

References

20. augusti klubi ja Riigikogu kantselei 1996. *Kaks otsustavat päeva Toompeal, 19.-20. august 1991*, Tallinn: Eesti Entsüklopeedia Kirjastus.

Collier, D. & S. Levitsky 1997. 'Democracy with Adjectives: Conceptual Innovation in Comparative Research', *World Politics*, 49, 3, 430-51.

Ehin, P. 2001. 'Determinants of public support for EU membership: Data from the Baltic countries', *European Journal of Political Research*, 40, 1, 31-56.

Ehin, P. 2002/2003. 'Estonian Euroskepticism: A reflection of domestic politics?', *East European Constitutional Review*, 11/12, 4/1, 96-100.

EMOR 1993. 'Majandus: Hetkehinnangud, optimism-pessimism', *Infoleht*, November 13, 14-18.

ES Turu-uuringute AS 2001. 'Kümme aastat taasiseseisvumisest'. Tallinn: Riigikantselei.

European Commission 2002. 'Candidate Countries Eurobarometer'. Brussels: European Commission.

Galbreath, D. 2003. 'The Politics of European Integration and Minority Rights in Estonia and Latvia', *Perspectives on European Politics and Society*, 4, 1, 35-53.

Hopf, T. 2002. 'Making the Future Inevitable: Legitimizing, Naturalizing and Stabilizing. The Transition in Estonia, Ukraine and Uzbekistan', *European Journal of International Relations*, 8, 3, 403-36.

Katz, R.S. & P. Mair 1995. 'Changing Models of Party Organization and Party Democracy: The Emergence of the Cartel Party', *Party Politics*, 1, 1, 5-28.

Kelley, J. 2003. 'Does Domestic Politics Limit the Influence of External Actors on Ethnic Politics?', *Human Rights Review*, 4, 3, 35-54.

Kuus, M. 2002. 'European integration in identity narratives in Estonia: A quest for security', *Journal of Peace Research*, 39, 1, 91-108.

Kuus, M. 2003. 'Security in Flux: International Integration and the Transformations of Threat in Estonia', *Demokratizatsiya*, 11, 4, 573-86.

Kuus, M. 2004. '"Those Goody-Goody Estonians": Toward Rethinking Security in the European Union Applicant States', *Environment and Planning D: Society and Space*, 22, 2, 191-207.

Laakso, M. & R. Taagepera 1979. '"Effective" Number of Parties: A Measure with Application to West Europe', *Comparative Political Studies*, 12, 1, 3-27.

Laar, M. 1996. 'Estonia's success story', *Journal of Democracy*, 7, 1, 96-102.

Laar, M. 2002a. *Eesti uus algus*. Tallinn: Konrad Adenaueri Fond.

Laar, M. 2002b. *Das estnische Wirtschaftswunder*. St. Augustin: Konrad Adenaueri Fond.

Laar, M., U. Ott & S. Endre 1996. *Teine Eesti: Eesti iseseisvuse taassünd, 1986-1991*. Tallinn: SE & JS.

Laitin, D.D. 2003. 'Three models of integration and the Estonian/Russian reality', *Journal of Baltic Studies*, 34, 2, 197-222.

Lauristin, M. & M. Heidmets (eds.) 2003. *The Challenge of the Russian Minority: Emerging Multiculturalism in Estonia.* Tartu: Tartu University Press.

Lauristin, M. & P. Vihalemm 1997. 'Recent Historical Developments in Estonia: Three Stages of Transition (1987-1997)'. In: L. Weibull (ed.), *Return to the Western World: Cultural and Political Perspectives on the Estonian Post-Communist Transition.* Tartu: Tartu University Press, 73-126.

Mikkel, E. & V. Pettai 2004. 'The Baltics: Independence with Divergent Electoral Systems'. In: J. M. Colomer (ed.), *The Handbook of Electoral System Design.* New York: Palgrave Macmillan, 332-46.

Must, K. 2000. *Iseseisvuspäeva sünd.* Tartu: Ajalookirjanduse sihtasutus Kleio.

OED Online 1989. 'tutelage', Internet source: http://www.oed.com/, accessed on 5 February 2005.

Past, L. & P. Palk 2005. 'The Pre-Referendum Campaign'. In: V. Pettai & P. Ehin (eds.), *Deciding on Europe: The EU Referendum in Estonia.* Tartu: Tartu University Press, 63-88.

Pempel, T.J. (ed.) 1990. *Uncommon democracies: the one-party dominant regimes.* Ithaca: Cornell University Press.

Pettai, V. 2001. 'Estonia and Latvia: International influences on citizenship and minority integration'. In: A. Pravda & J. Zielonka (eds.), *International Influences on Democratic Transition in Central and Eastern Europe.* Oxford: Oxford University Press.

Pettai, V. 2003a. 'Introduction: Historic and historical aspects of Baltic accession to the European Union'. In: V. Pettai & J. Zielonka (eds.), *EU Enlargement, Volume 2. The Road to the European Union: Estonia, Latvia, and Lithuania.* Manchester: Manchester University Press, 1-13.

Pettai, V. 2004a. 'Narratives and Political Development in the Baltic States: History Revised and Improvised', *Ab Imperio*, 1, 405-33.

Pettai, V. 2005. 'Unfounded worries? Euroscepticism prior to the referendum'. In: V. Pettai & P. Ehin (eds.), *Deciding on Europe: The EU Referendum in Estonia.* Tartu: Tartu University Press, 41-61.

Pettai, V. & K. Hallik 2002. 'Understanding processes of ethnic control: Segmentation, dependency and cooptation in post-communist Estonia', *Nations and Nationalism*, 8, 4, 505-529.

Pettai, V. & V. Veebel 2005. 'Navigating between Policy and Populace: Estonia, its Accession Referendum and the EU Convention', *Politique européenne*, 1, 113-35.

Pettai, V., R. Toomla & E. Joakit 2007. 'Citizen Electoral Alliances In Estonia: Citizen Democracy Vs Cartel Parties'. Paper presented at the conference 'Independent Local Lists: A Comparative Perspective'. Martin-Luther-University, Halle-Wittenberg, 13-14 April.

Postimees 2004. 'Rekordarv uusi kodanikke', 29 December.

Przeworski, A. 1991. *Democracy and the market: political and economic reforms in Eastern Europe and Latin America.* Cambridge: Cambridge University Press.

Raun, T. 1991. *Estonia and the Estonians.* Stanford: Hoover Institution Press.

Saar, A. 2001. 'Muutused väärtushinnangutes aastail 1990-1999: uuringu aruanne'. Tallinn: Saar Poll.

Siaroff, A. & J.W.A. Merer 2002. 'Parliamentary Election Turnout in Europe since 1990', *Political Studies*, 50, 5, 916-27.

Sikk, A. 2003. 'A Cartel Party System in a Post-Communist Country? The Case of Estonia'. Paper presented at the ECPR General Conference, Marburg, September 18-21.

Sikk, A. 2004. 'Estonia'. In: D. Nohlen (ed.), *Elections in Europe.* Oxford: Oxford University Press.

Sikk, A. 2006. 'From Private Organizations to Democratic Infrastructure: Political Parties and the State in Estonia', *Journal of Communist and Transition Politics*, 22, 3, 341-61.

Staehr, K. 2004. 'Economic Transition in Estonia: Background, reforms and results'. In: E. Rindzeviciute (ed.), *Contemporary Change in Estonia.* Huddinge: Baltic & East European Graduate School, 37-68.

Taagepera, R. 1993. *Estonia: Return to Independence.* Boulder: Westview Press.

Vetik, R. 2003. 'Élite vs. People? Eurosceptic Public Opinion in Estonia', *Cambridge Review of International Affairs*, 16, 2, 257-71.

Weyland, K. 1998. 'The Political Fate of Market Reform in Latin America, Africa, and Eastern Europe', *International Studies Quarterly*, 42, 4, 645-74.

CHAPTER 5

Understanding politics in Slovenia:

Constitutional corporatism and politico-administrative relations

Miro Haček

Slovenia's political history is above all the struggle of a small nation resisting foreign domination and assimilation over many centuries as a constituent part of various monarchies, kingdoms, a fascist state and, finally, a socialist federation. The impact of the pre-World War I period is still evident today in the traditional attachment to the German and Austrian models of the political system, parliamentary traditions and certain features of the political culture. However, the most important historical periods for understanding contemporary Slovenia are those of World War II and the socialist state after 1945. First, our aim is to present recent Slovenian history, as we strongly believe that the key to understanding contemporary Slovenia lies in understanding its colourful history. Second, we emphasise the corporatist features of the Slovenian political system and argue that these are in fact legacies of earlier political systems and the still ubiquitous socialist lines of modern political reality. Finally, we will pay close attention to the administrative reforms pursuant to the EU accession processes, another key feature for understanding Slovenian state building and politico-administrative relations. Based on classical politico-administrative divisions, we present the main hypothesis, which posits that in the case of a fairly young democracy like Slovenia, politicians are in charge of policy-making and are ranked above top-echelon civil servants, who are implementers of policy.

HISTORICAL LEGACIES AND THE DEMOCRATISATION PROCESS

We would argue that in the single party system era (before 1989), Slovenia differed in two ways from other CEE ex-communist countries: as a republic of the Yugoslav Federation, it was very different from other socialist counties, yet it also differed from the seven other Yugoslav republics (Miheljak & Toš 2002, 5). Slovenia is today a sovereign state, albeit with very little democratic continuity (von Bayme 1994, 144). Except for a deficient state-building tradition, Slovenia's characteristics as a transition state were, as mentioned, mainly positive. Slovenia had three major comparative advantages over other transitional countries in the CEE. The first was that Slovenia was (and still is) the only former Yugoslav republic with a high level of national homogeneity;[1] given the developments in other less homogenous republics (Croatia, Bosnia, Macedonia, Kosovo), this surely contributed to a less traumatic transition to democracy and independence. The second Slovenian advantage was – in view of the circumstances in Central and Eastern Europe – a high level of economic development, a favourable industrial structure, and close contacts with Western economic markets. In the Yugoslav era, Slovenia enjoyed a huge and undemanding market for all those products that could not be sold in Western markets. Here the economic advantage over the other Yugoslav republics only increased,[2] even though the federation had invested massive amounts of so-called 'solidarity money' in underdeveloped areas. The third great Slovenian advantage was the simple fact that its borders were more or less open and that two neighbouring states were (and still are, of course) democratic Western European countries (Italy to the west and Austria to the north). This basic fact made for high levels of mobility and, consequently, informational and technological modernity. These special grounds enabled Slovenia to carry out the process of democratic transition in different circumstances than the other CEE post-communist countries. The democratic changes in Slovenia did not open up its borders for the first time in many years, and Slovenians did not for the first time look with amazement at the new and fantastic Western world. Thus, the Slovenian case of democratic transition and consolidation is quite atypical because the actual transitional development had already begun a few years after Tito died (and perhaps even before that) as resistance had formed towards those tendencies in the decaying Yugoslav society that blocked the emerging democratic potential (Miheljak & Toš 2002, 12).

What is significant is Slovenia's unique historical development, and it is the key to understanding contemporary politics since history and historical divisions (all too) often reflect and influence modern political issues and developments. The focus on an analysis of contemporary corporatist features and relations between politics and the administration requires that we begin with the World War II period. The struggle for national liberation was organised by the National Liberation Front, which was made up of the Communist Party (which took it upon itself to play the decisive role), parts of various pre-war

---

1   Offe (1994, 140) defines a homogeneous nation-state as one in which more than 90 per cent of the citizens are members of a titular nation.

2   GDP Index relationships for the Yugoslav republics (1987): Yugoslavia as a whole (100), Bosnia and Herzegovina (68), Montenegro (75), Croatia (127), Macedonia (67), Slovenia (202), Serbia (99), Kosovo (27) and Vojvodina (118).

political parties and movements, and the intelligentsia. At the same time, in a concerted effort to split the partisans and the liberation movement the clerical bloc established special military units known as the Home Guard, which collaborated with the occupying forces. Supported by partisan units, the National Liberation movement expanded to cover the entire territory of Slovenia; the new people's authority led by the National Liberation Council took power and was included in formulating the constitutional foundations of the new Yugoslav state (1943). The end of the war signalled the beginning of socialism in Slovenia. Agrarian reform was undertaken and property was nationalised. Power was concentrated and centralised in federal executive organs and in the organs of the Communist Party of Yugoslavia, which directed the development of the entire country. In addition, there were various (today highly politicised and sometimes even crucial in political debates and divisions) acts of revenge against those who had collaborated with the occupying forces and those considered enemies of the working classes. More than 10,000 people lost their lives without the benefit of legal proceedings after the war ended. Further, there were instances of repression of opponents of the new regime and suppression of religious and political freedoms, etc. Many fled the country (Lukšič 2001, 3). In 1948 Yugoslavia ended what had hitherto been a close relationship with the Soviet Union, and slowly the pendulum swung the other way, bringing some level of decentralisation, a self-management system and a certain degree of autonomy.

Slovenia gradually strengthened its status within the federation, and with the promulgation of the 1974 Constitution and the introduction of an integral self-management system Yugoslavia acquired a limited selection of confederal features. The 1974 Yugoslav Constitution established a delegate system, a system of associated labour and autonomy for the republics. These new systems contained strong elements of corporatism (Lukšič 2003, 511), which was hailed as a new form of politico-economic organisation that, like socialism, involved a high level of state activity. The 1974 Yugoslav Constitution captures the spirit of an era when corporatism seemed a possible solution to the clash between capitalism and socialism, representing something viewed by Yugoslav leaders of that time as the third way.[3] Political power was so strongly controlled that it was considered safe to introduce corporatism in a relatively pure form (ibidem).[4]

A network of socio-political organisations was established with the com-

---

3   Also known as the Movement of Non-aligned Nations.

4   In contrast, Western democratic systems changed their pro-corporatist direction after the economic and political crises in the early 1970s and particularly the 1974 oil crises, reverting to neo-liberalism combined with pluralist ideas. In the early 1980s, corporatism was recognised as a variety of pluralism — to be distinguished from a more disaggregated competitive variety of pluralism at one extreme and a state-controlled variety at the other (Almond in Lukšič 2003, 511).

munist party (officially labelled the League of Communists) playing the leading role. The Socialist Alliance of Working People was the umbrella organisation that included all socio-political, professional and interest organisations. The 1974 Constitution called for self-management communities for all vital interests in society: education, culture, social security, health care, etc. Each of these components participated in matters within its competence in parliamentary sessions of the so-called fourth chamber. Thus, all vital interests were organised (at least at the official level) and included in the political system. At the same time, a delegate system was developed that provided for representation of the actual, authentic interests of working people. Assemblies were formed not based on general elections but on self-management elections (Lukšič 2003, 512). Three chambers comprised the assemblies of individual Yugoslav republics: the socio-political assembly consisting of delegates[5] from socio-political organisations; the chamber of municipalities[6] with representatives from all communes; and the chamber of associated labour with representatives from all branches of the economy and social services. These self-management agreements and social compacts between enterprises, organised working people and communities were intended to replace both market forces and state interventionism. The idea was to create a self-managing society that included civil society and the state based on the perception of a village community and common property (ibidem). Communes were recognised as the basis of the state, as places where all people's basic needs would be filled, while the communes sent delegates to the republic (chamber of communes) and federal assemblies (federal chamber). This was in fact an attempt to create a participatory political culture encompassing all working people in the various forms of political and social activities.

In the second half of the 1980s, just a few years after President Tito died, Yugoslavia experienced a severe political crisis exacerbated by the movement for greater Serbian hegemony, which was an attempt to transform the Federal Republic of Yugoslavia into a centralised state. Set in motion by new social movements, slogans seeking real and not just proclaimed democracy, political pluralism and free elections were accompanied by demands for Slovenian independence. From this point forward, the Slovenian democratic process was unstoppable.

Democratisation evolved in parallel with the Slovenian non-party opposition and the reform-oriented League of Slovenian Communists. The origins of the first parties – the Farmers' Party, the Slovenian Democratic Party, etc. – date back to that period as well. The first democratic elections were made possible

---

5   Although intended as a form of people's representation, it had little to do with representative democracy.

6   Municipalities in the Yugoslav republics were called communes and constituted the lowest level of the state bureaucracy; there was no real local self-government.

by amendments to the Constitution adopted and declared by the Slovenian legislative body at the end of September 1989. A non-party opposition had already been formed, the Democratic Opposition of Slovenia (hereafter called DEMOS), and other parties (the Socialist Party, etc.) were formally established when the electoral law was passed on 27 December 1989. The year 1990 saw the final creation of DEMOS, a coalition of the most important new parties, the Slovenian Democratic Union, the Social Democratic Union of Slovenia, the Slovenian Christian Democrats, the Slovenian Farmers' Association and the Greens of Slovenia. At political meetings, DEMOS presented a declaration on Slovenian self-determination in which, among other things, they committed themselves to a plebiscite.

In 1990, elections were held in all the Yugoslav republics and wrought far-reaching political changes. Only the Serbian entrenched political powers survived. On 8 April 1990, the first post-war direct multi-party elections were held in Slovenia. In addition to electing the President, the most interesting aspect was the elections for the Socio-political Chamber of Slovenia. In the democratic elections for the Slovenian parliament in April 1990, the DEMOS coalition secured victory with 55 per cent of the vote, while the remaining votes went to the three parties considered heirs to the previous system, even though they too had declared themselves in favour of a market economy and political democracy. DEMOS won 126 of 240 seats in the Slovenian tri-cameral legislative body. The DEMOS government was headed by Lojze Peterle, president of the Slovenian Christian Democrats, the strongest coalition party. The new government was elected in a joint session of all three chambers on 16 May 1990. Milan Kučan was elected President of the Republic (58.6 per cent of the vote). On 9 May 1990, a new leadership was elected in a joint session of all three chambers of the National Assembly.

The newly elected leaders of the Yugoslav republics began discussions of the long-term future of Yugoslavia. By late spring 1990, all Slovenian parties in the new democratically constituted government had agreed on a platform of national and governmental Slovenian independence within a Yugoslav confederation, and were resolved to settle Slovenia's relationship with this union in a peaceful and democratic way through mutual agreements as soon as practicable. But neither the central government, nor the Presidency of Yugoslavia or the Federal Assembly was ready for serious negotiations. It was soon clear that most of the republics saw independence and disbandment of the federal entity as the most viable solution. The citizens of Slovenia overwhelmingly approved this decision in the December 1990 independence plebiscite. On 25 June 1991, the new Republic of Slovenia officially declared its independence from the Federal Republic of Yugoslavia. A 10-day war commenced during which Slovenian territorial troops repelled incursions by the Yugoslav National Army. In January 1992, the European Community recognised the new Slovenian republic, followed by the United States on 7 April of that year. Slovenia was formally accepted as a member of the United Nations in May 1992.

Political life in the first fifteen years of the republic's independence was – and remains – dominated by several political parties elected under the proportional system of representation, and they have formed coalition governments of varying ideological stripe. It should be noted here, however, that political parties in their pure form have never been fully accepted in Slovenia. Only for two very short periods were parties at the centre of public interest: at the beginning of the 20th century (formation of a new state) and the beginning of the 1990s (formation of another new state). To Slovenians, politics has always been perceived as something bad, remote, even sordid. They have been active in politics only when compelled to for reasons involving their very existence. Political parties have generally been perceived as conflict-generating entities run by a small, manipulative and corrupt elite. Slovenians learned this lesson at the beginning of the 20th century. During the 20th century, party criticism and anti-party sentiments were far stronger than allegiance to the party system (Lukšič 2002, 515).

Despite the vast potential for fragility, governments and politics have remained remarkably stable. The dominant role (1992-2004) was played by the centre-left Liberal Democracy of Slovenia party (LDS) of former Prime Minister Drnovšek and the centre-right Slovenian Democratic Party (SDP) of current Prime Minister Janša, who was an immensely popular defence minister during the brief armed conflict with Yugoslav forces in 1991. Before the 2004 elections, there were repeated demands to put an end to the twelve-year rule of the centre-left coalitions led by the Liberal Democracy of Slovenia party – understandably mainly from the centre-right. These demands were substantiated with repeated – and what seemed at the time to be at least partly accurate – accusations of clientelism, corruption, an ongoing process of centralisation and usurpation of power.

There were especially persistent calls for a thorough decentralisation process as the Liberal Democracy of Slovenia government had failed to implement several important reforms. It did not begin the regionalisation process,[7] could not decide what to do with the 'unicameral or bicameral parliament issue', mainly ignored questions of administrative decentralisation, and so on. But perhaps the call for decentralisation was just a convenient political strategy for undermining the position and influence of what appeared to be the hegemonic and unbeatable Liberal Democracy of Slovenia party.[8] It is really quite

---

7   Slovenia only has a one-tier local self-government system and lacks any wider local self-government units such as regions.

8   The argument for this statement is simple: the current ruling centre-right coalition did not manage to initiate any of the mentioned reforms that had been so frequently referred to before the election.

paradoxical because the Liberal Democracy of Slovenia party did occasionally command (with other coalition partners) the two-thirds majority in parliament[9] needed to make the most difficult decisions and amend the Constitution, and yet it completely failed on these reform issues. The current ruling coalition, which managed to come to power after the elections of 3 October 2004, is a centre-right coalition led by the Slovenian Democratic Party and includes the Slovenian People's Party, the New Slovenia – Christian Democratic Party and the Pensioners' Party. This coalition now controls 49 of the 90 seats in the Slovenian National Assembly.

CORPORATISM AND DIVISION OF POWER

We may assume that two political cultures were present in the communist era. At the level of declaration and manifests, there was the dominant self-management culture, and then there was the traditional culture that existed before the communist revolution but did not function as a counter-culture because it was forcibly suppressed (Brezovšek, Haček & Zver 2007). Based on this presumption we can draw a couple of structure-political parallels. One is clearly the idea of corporatism (Zver 2002). In the 1920s and the 1930s, corporatism spread in Slovenia across three special structural fields.

In the social field, it advocated the idea of an ordered class society and harmony among the classes. It was also very critical of capitalist society, which favours egoistic individuals. The guiding principle was solidarity. Corporatism introduced a nation-based economy – a closed protectionist system based on the institutional integration of labour, capital and the state (assembly system). The roles of the market and free entrepreneurship are limited.

Corporative political ordinance was supposed to resolve the crisis of parliamentary democracy in the 1920s and 1930s. Political corporatism sought to change the existing democracy by introducing corporate assemblies – the professional augmentation of a political parliament with legislative competencies, the introduction of the principle of delegates, affirmation of associations of classes and professions in a political system, the introduction of self-management, etc. (Zver 1992).

Discussions in the late 1980s about a new Slovenian constitution often revolved around the issue of whether parliament should be unicameral or bicameral. Advocates of bicameralism felt that the political will of each Slovenian region should be institutionalised in a separate chamber because of the tradition of respecting regional identities. They pointed out that a bicameral

---

9   For instance, in the 2000-2004 mandate, the ruling coalition led by the Liberal Democracy
     of Slovenia party held 59 of the 90 seats, but also had a special co-operation agreement with
     the Youth Party, which had four seats.

system would provide partially corporative functions. The advocates of uni-cameralism, on the other hand, argued that political representation via the party system would flourish fully in a single chamber. In their opinion, the second chamber would be identical to the first one in political terms (Lukšič 2001, 17). Two versions of the parliamentary system were prepared, the first a bicameral system whose two chambers had equal rights and powers, and the second a similarly bicameral system, but with greatly circumscribed powers for the second chamber. The second version won the day.[10]

The corporative National Council was to reflect the social structure in that it is a representative body of social, economic, professional and local interests. Its forty members consist of four employers' representatives; four employee representatives; four members representing farmers, crafts, trades and independent professions; six from non-commercial fields; and, finally, twenty-two local-interest representatives. Its role is to advise and intervene in legislative issues, although it cannot actually vote on these issues. According to its drafters, this uniquely Slovenian system represents an effort to advance beyond the solely quantitative principles that dominated the positivist concept (Lukšič 2001, 17; Bučar 2001); it is an attempt to legitimise and accord respon-sibility to a number of informal processes, influences and lobbies that exist in all parliamentary systems around the globe. This chamber includes several elements from the previous system, specifically the Chamber of Communes, the Chamber of Associated Labour, and some of the Self-Management Com-munities. The Council represents a reference point for the corporatisation of interest groups (Lukšič 1994, 207), and is unique in the political systems of Western democracies. It was intended to reflect the structural composition of Slovenian society. Three principal factors influenced the introduction of the National Council into the Slovenian political system: the tradition of representing collective functional interests, the tradition of a three-chamber parliament, and the desire to emulate the model of the legislative system of the Free State of Bavaria (Lukšič 2003, 516). Councillors are elected indirectly by and within the interest organisations or local communities that they rep-resent. According to the principle of a relative majority, the candidate with the most votes wins. The electoral assembly elects 18 members of the National

---

10 The first chamber, the National Assembly, is the representative chamber of parliament and the only entity in the state that can pass laws. There are 90 members; the Italian and Hungarian minorities have one representative each. MPs are elected representatives of the people and do not derive their authority from any specific instructions. Their term of office is four years and they have parliamentary immunity. If a deputy becomes a minister, another representative from the same party takes his or her place in the National Assembly for the remainder of the election period. The National Assembly has electoral, legislative and supervisory functions. See also Lukšič (2001).

Council – representatives of functional interests. The local communities elect 22 people.

The creation of the National Council was discussed intensely and many experts hoped it would not survive for more than a few years; but it is still there. However, the corporative tradition has always played an important role in Slovenian political life. For much of the country's history, interest groups and professional associations preceded political parties, the community preceded the market, and individuals came before the notion of the abstract citizen. The National Council embodies this uniquely Slovenian interpretation of political life (Lukšič 2003, 517-518).

The issue of whether to establish a unicameral or a bicameral parliament was first debated by the constitutional committee of the Republic of Slovenia, and since its decision in 1991 the debate has never quite ceased. Back in the 1990s, the vision of an essentially unicameral parliament supplemented by a second chamber with an advisory role finally got the support of the majority. Over the years, the National Council has not managed to live up to the expectations of major political actors or political science experts. The launch of the regionalisation process[11] revived the debate over the role and function of the second chamber. There are various ideas about just how Slovenia could go about transforming its unicameral and semi-cameral system into a fully bicameral one, turning the existing National Council into an autonomous political body consisting of regional interest representatives.

The laws regulating public television and radio broadcasting in Slovenia (RTVS) also reflect the corporatist element of Slovenian political culture, even though the RTVS is not part of the political system. The Council of the RTVS has 29 members, 16 of them appointed by the National Assembly upon the proposal of TV viewers and various groups in society (trade unions, churches, employers' associations etc.).[12] The principal idea behind the composition of such a body was no different from the idea that led to the creation of the National Council: interest groups were the best representatives of the public will and civil society, not political parties.

Corporatist features are also characteristic of the system of professional chambers. Three large associations of employers are the main constituent parts

---

11 Slovenia reinstated its local self-government system in 1994 with the establishment of 147 middle-sized but autonomous municipalities. But political will to establish autonomous regions has never materialised because of the diversity of interests among political forces. Accession to the EU and access to the EU cohesion and structural funds provided the incentive for serious attempts to establish regional self-government, and in 2006 the constitutional changes needed to establish regions as wider units of local self-government were finally accepted in the national parliament.

12 The Law on Radio and Television Slovenia (RTVS), which came into force on 15 July 2006.

of the social partnership system: the chamber of commerce, the association of employers and the trade chamber. Until recently, membership of the Chamber of Commerce and Industry was compulsory for every enterprise in the country. The chambers system was created to reflect certain vital professional interests. It is still partly organised[13] on the basis of compulsory membership. Some of the member organisations existed before the democratic changes got underway (such as the Medical Chamber, the Chamber of Lawyers, the Chamber of Social Service, the Chamber of Agriculture and Forestry, the Chamber of Medical Nurses), and most of their competencies remain intact.

The corporate character of Slovenian politics was evident during the transition period, during which many key players from the communist political establishment retained their positions as part of the political elite. Even today they continue to occupy important positions. Slovenia's unique system of pluralist corporatism has also meant that no single power base from the past – be it socialism or the Catholic Church – has been able to play a dominant role in the system. Both have had to coexist on an equal basis (Lukšič 2003, 524). In contemporary Slovenia, various forms of corporatism are embodied in the National Council, in the system of professional chambers, the system of social partnership and the RTVS Council. It is also present in certain elements of the political culture, for instance in the fact that a partnership is valued over competition and community over the individual.

THE MODERNISATION PROCESSES OF THE SLOVENIAN STATE ADMINISTRATION

The democratisation of society after the first free elections (in 1990 and independence in 1991) also marked the beginning of the transformation of the Slovenian public (state) administration, initially on a non-systemic basis, but with the adoption of a government strategy for transforming the public administration (in November 1997) on a broad scale. The main lesson learned by actors involved in development of the public (state) administration reform from the experiences of the past several years was that overly ambitious short-term planning does not bring about substantial results. Based on this realisation, a project called 'reform of the public (state) administration' was reformulated using the more descriptive phrases 'modernisation of the administration' or 'development of the administration', and is now looked upon as a continuous development process. As it is part of the social system, the public (state) administration reform now appears to be an ongoing story, but within a firm

---

13 The current government began a gradual change of this system in late 2005, when a new law regulating the Chamber of Commerce and Industry was passed that abolished obligatory membership.

framework and the complex of budget periods. Modernisation of the public administration focuses on augmenting and improving the public administrative system.[14] The essence of the reform processes is to improve the functioning of Slovenian public (state) administration, which involves working towards greater professionalism, political neutrality, transparency, efficiency and increased focus on the users of public services.

The process of reforming the state administration is also one of the very few large-scale reforms that the ruling centre-left coalition under the leadership of the Liberal Democratic Party managed to at least initiate and (in part) implement during their long 1992-2004 rule. One might also ask about the impact of the European Union accession process[15] on the administrative reform process. Both processes (accession and administrative reform) were launched in the early stages of Slovenian independence, in the 1992-1996 mandate of 'the great coalition', when all three major political parties of the time[16] united to form a government that had to confront the massive reforms ahead. Both reform processes were seen as being of crucial importance for the future of

---

14 As to reform measures introduced from 1997 on, the European Commission has primarily acknowledged the progress made in the formation of administrative institutions, that is, the strengthening of administrative professionalism. In comparison the general assessment of progress in the public administration reform was not entirely positive because some of the most significant laws have yet to be fully implemented. For example, the law on public sector wages, which was adopted in 2004, has not been implemented because of the inability of the social partners to reach the agreement required to start implementing the law.

15 The EU officially recognised Slovenia as an independent state in January 1992, and a formal co-operation agreement came into force in September 1993. Since independence, Slovenian politics has focused on EU accession. An Association Agreement signed in 1996 covered trade issues, political dialogue and co-operation in a number of areas. An Interim Agreement implementing the trade provisions of the Europe Agreement came into force in January 1997. And there was the Europe Agreement in February 1999. Slovenia applied for EU membership in June 1996 and became a full member on 1 May 2004. The Commission's opinion was issued in 1997 and negotiations commenced in March 1998. The EC has provided substantial assistance for reforms and for accession preparations. A referendum on EU accession was held on 23 March 2003, in which 90 per cent voted in favour (60 per cent turnout). In a simultaneous referendum on NATO membership 66 per cent voted in favour. Accession to the EU on 1 May 2004 is seen as a great success and recognition for Slovenia, especially in view of the relatively short period since independence. Slovenia was also the first ex-communist country to adopt the Euro on 1 January 2007. Membership of the EU and NATO and adoption of the Euro were the only Slovenian political projects that have gained the support of all major political forces and the majority of the population.

16 The centre Liberal Democratic Party, the left-wing United List of Social Democrats (the former Communist Party) and the right-wing Christian Democrats.

Slovenia as an independent state, so initially they ran in parallel, but more or less independently of each other. When Slovenia signed an Association Agreement with the European Union in 1996 and almost immediately applied for full membership, the state administration reform process and EU accession became increasingly intertwined because the Slovenian reform process from 1997 followed existing trends in the EU and the rest of the world. This encompassed five fundamental and interdependent areas: 1) functional and organisational reform adopted by the legislation; 2) inclusion of the system of public officers; 3) abolition of administrative barriers; 4) introduction of quality in administration and electronic administration; and, finally, 5) targeted training in management and European affairs. The goal of the public (state) administration reform, at home and abroad, was to become a modern, efficient and user-friendly service backed by modern information technology. The package of systemic legislation (public servants, state administration, public agencies and the audit act) prioritises an apolitical, professional, transparent and efficient public administration.

It should be pointed out that the legalistic approach was (and still is) of course supplemented by a series of practical policies and activities in order to concretise the public (state) administration reform. The practical strategies employed to modernise the administration include activities that complement and solidify the normative framework, for instance the introduction of quality standards in the administration, educating public employees, electronic administration and the abolition of administrative barriers. All these initiatives were set in motion by a competent government board. The primary goal of the last project that has been implemented in specific short-term measures is to erase key anachronisms of the Slovenian state, leftovers from the old communist regime like the rigidity of human (staff) resource management, standardisation and modernisation of procedures in relation to clients, lack of co-ordination, lack of efficiency indicators/measures etc. Among other things, the programme was designed to help eliminate administrative barriers in the economic field and stimulate investments, to simplify construction permits and residence permits for foreigners, and to introduce a simpler system of diplomas. The globalisation processes were taken into account as well, with the aim of improving the competitive position of the Slovenian national economy (by overcoming administrative obstacles to enterprises/entrepreneurship).

The quality of public (state) administration is mainly ensured by certification according to quality standards. Quality is measured using a complex list of indicators, and does not manifest itself only through (dis)satisfied customers, as some might express it in simpler terms. It is also measured via financial indicators, employee satisfaction, statistics on case decision making, assessment of various forms of control, continuous progress and so on. The quality policy of the state administration adopted by the Slovenian government in October

1996 binds state employees in a relation system that is ethical, partner-like, in harmony with European standards, norms and legislature, oriented towards education and training, linked to other administrative bodies, efficiency in budget spending, and developing possibilities for improving the quality of work and the lives of its citizens. Quality is a complex concept, and can only be captured in complex mechanisms such as the European model of professional excellence, which, by evaluating individual measures in over 50 per cent of measures, stresses the importance of people (public-service clients and public employees). In the field of quality, we are among the first in Europe to use the Common Assessment Framework (CAF) model, which encourages increasing compatibility with the European administrative area. The second example of innovative Slovenian spirit is found in the field of E-government, where much energy was initially put into intergovernmental relations like exchanging data from official records and relations with citizens and legal entities (government to citizens/business).

In terms of content and time, the transformation of the administrative paradigm was a demanding task that was undertaken to realise a complete reform of the public administration. The goals of the Slovenian reform mostly corresponded to the concepts of new public management. The reform of the administration was adapted to the changing role of the state from a repressive to a service-oriented one. This involved decentralisation of decision making and of organisational structures. It also implied increased emphasis on professionalisation of the administration. These reforms are intended to lead to the abolition of, or at least to help diminish, the most pressing issues besetting the administrative system, such as the lack of vertical and horizontal co-ordination, the unregulated status of para-state organisations, and insufficient connections to the (state) budget. They should also lead to a more well-defined division of power between parliament and the government, and the work of the public administration, inducing greater political support for the reform processes. The key issues in the development of the Slovenian public administration were (and still are, because the reform has not yet been fully implemented) the democratisation of society and the public administration, human resource management, public administration efficiency, 'public administration' in the information society, and professional training of public employees. The democratisation of the administration primarily requires a reorientation towards people, clients and its own employees. This is a reference to the introduction of the 'notice and comment' system, i.e. the right of citizens to participate in the creation and execution of rules/regulations, and their right to demand a systematic analysis of the influence of regulation on society, thereby bringing Slovenia even closer to the concept of the contemporary state and public administration.

SLOVENIAN POLITICO-ADMINISTRATIVE
RELATIONS: WHO HOLDS THE KEYS?

We now turn to selected aspects of politico-administrative relations, which are in fact highly significant for contemporary political reality and reflect some of the features of corporatism discussed above. We will begin with classical writers on politico-administrative relations (Aberbach et al. 1981; Peters 1988), who basically claimed that the basic model is a formal (or Weberian) model in which the role of the civil servant is limited to implementing the orders of the politician, and the civil servant does not participate in the political process (policy-making, interest articulation etc.). Throughout the process of democratic transition, public administration in Central and Eastern European countries has been marked by the need for rapid de-politicisation involving the development of legal instruments to safeguard civil servants against political abuse. The civil service system is also marked by significant dependence on legalism and the application of employment legislation without regard to the specifics of the civil service (Verheijen 1999, 2-3), all of which also characterise the formal model.[17] Based on classical politico-administrative divisions, the newly consolidated democracy and the fact that the Slovenian public (state) administration is a somewhat recent institution, one would expect the politicians to be in charge of policy-making and to dominate over high-ranking civil servants, who are supposedly mere technical implementers of policy. The most intriguing part of the analysis, however, will be to see – from the perspective of the corporatist tendencies discussed earlier – what roles these actors actually play and what is the impact of various pressure groups in society on politicians and especially on civil servants. We will use empirical data from our own study (Haček 2006), which included high-ranking civil servants and politicians at the national level.[18]

---

17 In the formal model, politicians always win in the political process, given that civil servants are only the technical implementers of the orders given them. Another major characteristic of the formal model is legalism (people with law degrees prevail in public administration), and a relatively large number of politicians with their own advisers or expert staff (Peters 1988).

18 There were 469 high-ranking civil servants, all secretaries-general of ministries and all undersecretaries. Under the Civil Servants Act (2002: Article 80), these two groups occupy the highest positions in the Slovenian civil service system. The group of politicians consisted of 228 people; 90 were employed in the legislative and 138 in the executive branch of government. For two reasons we were mainly interested in the executive branch: first, because it also employs high-ranking civil servants, and second, because research into the relationship between high-ranking civil servants and politicians usually focuses on this branch (Peters, 1988). The survey was conducted in 2004 via questionnaires. The response rate (numbers

First, we must analyse Slovenia's administrative and political elite and their role focus.[19] Are there differences between the two groups of actors? The answer is yes. Politicians tend to focus more on the roles of advocate, broker, promoter, partisan and policy-maker, while high-ranking civil servants are more likely to adopt the role of legalist. These findings confirm that politicians assign the greatest importance to their representative and political functions. One quite surprising finding is the proportion of members of Slovenia's administrative and political elite who attach significant importance to the role of advocate (fighting for or representing the interests of broad social groups). Further, the group of politicians is not homogeneous. Quite a large proportion see themselves as technicians, while a comparatively small proportion describe themselves as partisan politicians. Further, the situation is similar for high-ranking civil servants. A comparatively large proportion see themselves as legalists,[20] and comparatively few as policy-makers. High-ranking Slovenian civil servants see their role as one of fighting for or representing the interests of a broad social group (72 per cent),[21] solving technical problems (69 per cent), representing the state (65 per cent), and being responsible for legal matters (61 per cent). Slovenian politicians, on the other hand, see their role as also representing the interests of broad social groups (93 per cent) and policy-making (76 per cent). More politicians (76 per cent) than high-ranking civil servants (58 per cent) emphasise the role of policy-maker, but the real comparative difference is that in Western Europe more civil servants than politicians emphasise their role in policy-making.

Our second finding is that while politicians do not a priori oppose the idea of high-ranking civil servants participating in the policy-making process, they do not think that is a particularly important role for them to play. In their jobs, 76 per cent and 58 per cent of Slovenian politicians and high-ranking civil servants, respectively, participate in policy-making (Haček 2006, 182). Both groups are almost unanimous when asked what attributes are desirable in high-ranking civil servants. They were not quite as unanimous in their response to

---

in brackets) was very good. We received 342 completed questionnaires (49.1 per cent), 233 of them from high-ranking civil servants (49.7 per cent), 64 from politicians in the executive branch (46.4 per cent), and 45 from politicians employed in the legislative branch of government (50.0 per cent).

19 Measurement of the perceptions people have of the role(s) they play in their job.

20 What is interesting is that in the same study we found that legal specialists do not prevail among members of Slovenia's administrative and political elite: with 24 per cent, they only come in third, after those educated in the social (42 per cent) and natural sciences (25 per cent).

21 In six Western European states the average response rate of high-ranking civil servants to this question was just 24 per cent (see Aberbach et al. 1981).

the statement that the policy-making process should be the exclusive domain of politicians who have been given a mandate by their constituencies. Less than half the members of the administrative and political elite at the national level agreed with this statement. High-ranking civil servants, however, were in the majority (46 per cent) compared to politicians (39 per cent). Based on these findings, we can conclude that the key role of Slovenian high-ranking civil servants is to solve technical and legal problems, to apply specialised knowledge, and – occasionally – to involve themselves policy-making, which should not be the exclusive domain of politicians.

According to Aberbach et al. (1981, 206), the world of civil servants is a fairly isolated one where the basic reference point in interactions with various political and societal actors is one hierarchical level up or down; a civil servant should have very limited interactions with various pressure or interest groups. The world of the civil servant is not marked by a host of demands and pressure from political parties, interest groups, voters and organised civil society groups; that is the world of the politician (Aberbach et al. 1981, 210). As shown in Table 1, interactions between civil servants and interest group representatives are rare.[22]

TABLE 1: COMPARISON OF THE FREQUENCY OF INTERACTIONS BETWEEN SLOVENIAN HIGH-RANKING CIVIL SERVANTS AND POLITICIANS WITH VARIOUS ACTORS IN SOCIETY

ACTORS	POLITICIANS	HIGH-RANKING CIVIL SERVANTS
COMMON CITIZENS	2.67	3.17
MINISTERS IN GOVERNMENT	3.00	3.60/5.02*
LOCAL GOVERNMENT REPRESENTATIVES	3.98	4.80
INTEREST GROUP REPRESENTATIVES	3.61	4.73
MPS	3.39	4.90

Source: Haček (2004).

* *ministers outside their own ministry.*

Average value according to the scale: 1 – 'many times a week', 2 – 'once a week', 3 – 'regularly, but not every week', 4 – 'at times', 5 – 'rarely', 6 – 'never'.

Various influence groups in society do not think it is worthwhile to try to influence Slovenian civil servants, but even more surprisingly, the politicians are seen as being much the same. These findings confirm the conclusions above that much of Slovenian politics goes on outside regular and official

---

22 Much rarer than in Western states, where the average value for high-ranking civil servants and politicians in Great Britain, Germany, France, Italy, the Netherlands, the USA and Sweden was 2.81 and 3.31 per cent, respectively, on the same scale (Aberbach et al. 1981, 215).

channels and that the real power brokers are neither elected politicians nor civil servants, but informal actors hidden behind civil society movements, interest groups and economic lobbies. To summarise, the administrative and political elite members perceive their responsibilities in different ways, and yet they are all quite heavily influenced by the deeply held belief that they should fight for or at least represent the interests of civil society groups. There is a division of labour between the two groups of actors, but it is less clear in Slovenia than in some Western states. This fact notwithstanding, we cannot say that a formal model describes the relationship between bureaucrats and politicians. On the contrary, the empirically verified differences correspond more to the second image of Aberbach et al. (1981), which represents a more complex view in which politicians and bureaucrats alike are seen to exert some degree of political influence.

CONCLUSION

There is little doubt that Slovenia is one of the most successful ex-communist countries, if not the most successful one. Its legacy and historical path towards independence were quite different from those of other ex-communist countries in Eastern Europe and the former Soviet Union. It must be stressed that Slovenian communism was of a very different nature than that of the Soviet Union; it was far more adaptable, was based on different ideas (economic openness, self-management, independent movement), and closer to Western thought. In Slovenia the clientelistic interests of the former socialist elite survived both politically (at least until defeated at the national elections in 2004) and even more so in the economy, as the privatisation process has never quite been finished. The state still owns a substantial part of the economy.

However, the focus here is the two key features of the contemporary Slovenian political system: corporatism and administrative reform combined with the EU accession processes. The corporate character of Slovenian politics remains evident as many individual and corporative players from the old socialist political establishment are still part of the political and/or economic elite and even today exert great influence on political and societal reality. There is no doubt that the communist ideologists consciously copied some systemic solutions from the Catholic corporatism of the pre-war era. They radically upgraded the familiar structure and added a new ideology. However, various elements that may be regarded as value-directed have retained their similarity, for example the renunciation of democracy, parliamentarianism, party pluralism, etc. While it is difficult to prove cultural-political continuity from the pre-war era, the question remains just how half a century of communist rule affected the cultural and political orientations of contemporary Slovenia. Alas, a clear answer is not forthcoming due to the mixed cultural-political legacy.

Slovenian political parties are still not accepted as integral parts of the democratic system, and trust in these parties is as low as it can get – only a small fraction of the population express at least moderate trust in political parties. This is also evident from the results of the recent local elections in October 2006, in which all political parties suffered defeat for the first time. The winners were independent candidates and candidates put forward by groups of citizens. Of course, questions about the nature of so-called independent candidates arise in that some of them are clearly not very independent, as was evident in the capital city of Ljubljana, where the former CEO[23] of the state-owned Mercator company won a vast majority of the votes in the mayoral elections as an independent candidate.

It seems that in Slovenia, we do indeed have a political phone booth[24] with two revolving doors, one used once in a while by elected politicians and the other a little less frequently by civil servants. Alas, the main prize – the phone – is still beyond the reach of civil servants and elected politicians alike. In fact, there is (as yet) no phone in the phone booth.

References

Aberbach, D.J., R.D. Putnam & B.A. Rockman 1981. Cambridge, Mass.: Harvard University Press.

Bayme, K. von 1994. 'Ansätze zu Einer Theorie der Transformation der Ex-Sozialistischen Länder Osteuropas'. In: Markel W. (ed.), *Bureaucrats and politicians in Western democracies.* Systemwechsel I: Theorien, Ansätze und Konzeptionen. Opladen: Leske und Budrich, 141-171.

Brezovšek, M., M. Haček & M. Zver 2007. *Democratic praxis in Slovenia.* Plzen: Faculty of Philosophy, Bohemia University of Plzen.

Bučar, F. 2001. 'Ustava kot političen projekt' (The Constitution as a political project). In: Drago Zajc (ed.), *Slovenska država ob deseti obletnici.* Ljubljana: Slovenian Political Science Association.

---

23 Zoran Jankovic is also a member of Forum 21, a civil society movement that incorporates some of the most influential people in the country, including a number of managers and former managers of state-owned companies; he is also a personal friend of the former president and last leader of the Communist Party, Milan Kučan.

24 The symbolism of Slovenia's 'political phone booth' was first presented by Lars Johannsen on Slovenian national TV on 9 October 2006 on the Studio City programme, although he was talking in a different context.

Haček, M. 2004. *Dihotomija uprava – politika: odnosi med javnimi uslužbenci in politici̇nimi funkcionarji v slovenski javni upravi* (The politico-administrative dichotomy: relations between politicians and civil servants in the Slovenian PA). Ljubljana: Faculty of Social Sciences.

Haček, M. 2006. *Politika birokracije* (Politics of bureaucracy). Ljubljana: Modrijan.

Lukšič, I. 2001. *The political system of the Republic of Slovenia*. Ljubljana: Znanstveno in publicistično središče.

Lukšič, I. 2003. 'Corporatism packed in pluralist ideology: the case of Slovenia', *Communist and Post-Communist Studies*, 36, 509-525.

Miheljak, V. & N. Toš 2002. 'Pogled nazaj' (A look back). In N. Toš & I. Bernik (eds.) 2002. *Demokracija v Sloveniji*. Ljubljana: Faculty of Social Sciences.

National Assembly 1991. Constitution of the Republic of Slovenia. Ljubljana.

Offe, C. 1994. *Der Tunnel am Ende des Lichts*. Frankfurt am Main: Campus Verlag.

Peters, B.G. 1988. *Comparing public bureaucracies: Problems of theory and method*. Tuscaloosa: The University of Alabama Press.

Verheijen, T. (ed.) 1999. *Civil service systems in Central and Eastern Europe*. Cheltenham: Edward Elgar.

Zver, M. 1992. 'Korporativizem v slovenski politični misli v 20. in 30. letih' (Corporatism in Slovenian political thought in 1920s and 1930s), *Časopis za kritiko znanosti*, 20(148/149).

Zver, M. 2002. *Demokracija v klasični slovenski politični misli* (Democracy in classical Slovenian political thought). Ljubljana: Orbis.

CHAPTER 6

Democracy or deficiency?

Czech politics in the context of the consequences of its party system

Rick Fawn

The preceding version of this chapter, written about six years ago, concluded:

> Czech politics will almost certainly continue to hinge on coalition building. The game will be more complicated than in some two- or three-party Western political systems. But that also provides for more diversity and potentially for more political renewal. (Fawn 2004).

The nature of the political party system and the resulting necessity of coalition-building has continued to be the fundamental element of Czech politics in practice. Until 2006 every government in the life of the Czech Republic was a type of coalition, some of them resting on a majority of a single seat.

The 2006 election produced a complete deadlock. The previously ruling Social Democratic Party (ČSSD) lost both power and its plurality of votes, coming second behind the Civic Democratic Party (ODS), and with a parliamentary balance of seats that was perfectly split between center-left and center-right parties. The final outcome, months in the making, was yet another coalition government that was formed in January 2007, partly because of the defection of two members of parliament. It also involved the Green party in government for the first time, a party that had existed since 1990 but had never secured enough votes to sit in parliament until 2006.

This chapter addresses the nature and impact of party politics in the Czech Republic. It does so by giving an analytical overview of electoral outcomes and party deals throughout the life of the Czech Republic. The chapter broadens its discussion beyond relations between political parties to 'civil society'. It does so in order to suggest that civil society, including the media, remains relatively weak and neither provides a strong contrast to political parties for political influence nor a sufficient check on the power of political parties. The chapter cannot, however seek to explain *why* Czech politics produces such divided results. Part of the answer may rest in political culture.[1] But this is a different and important issue that requires consideration in another venue.

THE FRAMEWORK FOR PARTY POLITICS

The starting point for analysing Czech politics must be structural. The country's Lower House of Parliament, requires each political party to secure five per cent of the popular vote in order to sit in the Lower House. The threshold increases to eight per cent for two parties running together, and to ten per cent for three parties. This system means that significant numbers of votes may be unrepresented in parliament. Thus, for example, while eight parties received a sufficient percentage to sit in parliament in the 1992 elections, 21 per cent of all of the votes cast received no parliamentary representation. The pressure for parties to get in parliament and for the electorate to make votes count may account for the amalgamation or elimination of smaller parties – in the 1996 election 6 parties entered parliament and the unrepresented votes fell to 10 per cent of those cast. By 2006, even though 20 parties ran, 95 per cent of the votes cast were represented in parliament.

The number of parties has ensured that no political party has been able to govern alone. This is arguably a political tradition dating back to the interwar period, when a broad political party system existed (so broad that Czechoslovakia was the only Central European state in which the Communist Party was legal throughout the interwar period). But governance worked on the basis of consensus in the *Pětka* (or 'Five'), which meant that for almost all the years of the First Republic coalition governments ruled. Such consensus is absent from the post-communist political system, and direct comparison is unhelpful, if not misleading.

Indeed, by contrast in the Czech Republic, the combination of a fragmented political party system and a lack of cross-party consensus (or, simply, good will), has made governance difficult but possible. This came to a head (perhaps by inevitable logic) in 2006, when no government could be formed immediately after the elections. The government that did eventually emerge was short-lived, unable to fulfil the constitutionally required vote of confidence.

Some history is illustrative of the centrality of coalitions to Czech politics. The first governments, following the 1992 and 1996 elections, were coalitions of centre-right parties. The Social Democratic government that emerged from the 1998 elections lacked an outright majority and was forced to secure an 'opposition agreement' with Václav Klaus's Civic Democrats to allow it to survive its

---

1 Work is lacking on this subject. One comparative study, now dated, of Czech and Slovak voting preferences in terms of 'political culture' and rational choice, concluded against the importance of the former and strongly in favour of the latter (Whitefield & Evans 1999).

term. This agreement was certainly curious and instrumental: Klaus retained political prominence by becoming the Chairman of Parliament and retaining life-or-death control over the Social Democratic government while having no responsibility for their policies.

In terms of the party system, the opposition agreement had the effect of prompting four other parties to form a coalition in September 1999. Called the 'Four-Party Coalition', this grouping consisted of the Freedom Union, Christian Democrats, Democratic Union and the Civic Democratic Alliance. But this logical strategy (some ideological and policy differences notwithstanding) still faced the adversity of the electoral threshold. As magazine editor Václav Žak commented, 'We are maybe the only country in the world where coalitions must have an additional quorum, which means the Four-Party Coalition would need 20 per cent in the elections, so it could be dangerous for them' (Radio Prague 24 January 2002). The result was that the Freedom Union, itself a break-away group from the ODS, as discussed below, absorbed the Democratic Union, reducing the coalition to three, although together they still required 15 per cent of the popular vote to sit in parliament. And as if that was not enough, the financial insolvency of the Civic Democratic Alliance provoked an unresolved dispute among the four in 2002 which spelled the end of the coalition.

The Czech political party system is moderately fluid: some parties have been created; others have disappeared; and still others have experienced remarkable shifts in their electoral performance. This section first considers major political parties to show the development of political preferences and fluidity in the political party system. It then discusses the mechanics of forming and running government.

The ideologies of Czech political parties extend across the spectrum. Until 2001 the far right was represented by the Republican Party, which was established in the month following the November 1989 revolution but was declared bankrupt in 2001. In its heyday, it pandered to racist and xenophobic feelings towards such minorities as the Roma, and to anti-German sentiments in issues of foreign policy and wartime reparations. It was also irredentist towards Carpathia, which post-war Czechoslovakia ceded to the Soviet Union, and hostile to major foreign policy initiatives, including membership of NATO. The party's political significance was partly due to the fact that it held up to 10 per cent of the popular vote and had representatives in the 1992 and 1996 Czech parliaments. It failed to receive enough votes in the 1998 election to sit in the Lower House, and despite attempts by its leader, Miroslav Sládek, to attempt to retain public attention, it continued to lose popularity. The party was reconstituted under Sládek in 2002, and now goes by the name of its leader, although its prospects remain marginal. Some of its popularity, arguably, has been absorbed by the Communists and even by the centre-right Civic Democratic Party, whose prominent leader Klaus has played upon threats to

Czech sovereignty from foreign policy issues, including Western institutional accession. The Party remains opposed to integration into Westerns institutions and is overtly hostile to immigration into the Czech Republic. While migration may remain something of an issue, integration is a *fait accompli* and any platform firmly based on total opposition to it will be anachronistic.

The centre-right of the spectrum has been the most fluid and home to the largest number of parties. Its foremost organisation is the Civic Democratic Party (ODS). One of the two key parties in the governance of the Czech Republic, this centre-right party emerged from the February 1991 split of the 1989 revolution umbrella grouping Civic Forum. It argued for thorough, prompt market liberalisation and became the most popular political party in the Czech lands in 1991 and 1992, winning over 29 per cent of the popular vote in the June 1992 elections. Consequently, it led the coalition government from the June 1992 elections until 1997. Under its leader, the economist Václav Klaus, the ODS presented itself as the party of both transition and stability. Its 1996 electoral platform was 'Freedom and Prosperity, Stability and Continuity and the Non-Revolutionary Solving of Problems', and it won 68 seats in the Chamber of Deputies and held 30 in the Senate.

Electoral success, however, did not prevent internal dissension. Klaus was seen as the party's 'guiding light', but his strict control of the party brewed resentment. The ODS fractured in late 1997 and early 1998, when other leading members left it to form the rival Freedom Union. Undeterred, Klaus was re-elected leader of the ODS and led it to second place in the June 1998 elections with 27.7 per cent of the vote and 63 parliamentary seats. While out of formal power, he orchestrated the aforemeotioned 'oppositional agreement' with his staunch rival Miloš Zeman, leader of the leftist Social Democratic Party, following which Klaus became Chairman of the Chamber of Deputies.

Klaus continued to lead the ODS in the 2002 elections, in which the party secured 24 per cent of the popular vote, nearly four per cent less than in 1998. The loss of further seats, quite apart from not gaining an outright victory, solidified feelings in the party that Klaus's chairmanship should end. Klaus stepped down as party leader in December 2002, an act that also freed him to stand for president in 2003, and was replaced by Miroslav (Mirek) Topolánek. Topolánek said later in December that Klaus had lost the ability to drive the party and failed to present it as a centre-right alternative to the centre-left Social Democratic Party.

Fluidity on the centre-right of the Czech spectrum was increased by dissatisfaction with Klaus's rule over the ODS. The Freedom Union (US) emerged when dissenting members split from the ODS. In the 1998 elections the US won under 9 per cent and 19 seats, but this was enough to affect the ODS's electoral fortunes. The Union later merged with another small party, becoming the Freedom Union-Democratic Union. The party later joined forces with

TABLE 1. LOWER HOUSE ELECTIONS RESULTS FOR MAJOR POLITICAL PARTIES

POLITICAL PARTY (CZECH ABBREVIATION)	PARTY ORIENTATION	1992 SEATS	1992 % OF VOTES	1996 SEATS	1996 % OF VOTES	1998 SEATS	1998 % OF VOTES	2002 SEATS	2002 % OF VOTES	2006 SEATS	2006 % OF VOTES
CIVIC DEMOCRATIC PARTY (ODS)	Centre-right; associated with earlier heavy rhetoric towards free markets	76	29.7	68	29.6	63	27.7	58	24.4	81	35.38
CHRISTIAN DEMOCRATIC UNION (KDU-ČSL)	Centre-right, with religious following; formed government coalition with ODS 1992-96	15	6.3	18	8.1	20	9.0	*	*	13	7.22
CIVIC DEMOCRATIC ALLIANCE (ODA)	Centre-right;	14	5.9	13	6.4	-	-	-	-	-	-
SOCIAL DEMOCRATIC PARTY (ČSSD)	Centre-left; long historical origins; supports social welfare	16	6.5	61	26.4	74	32.2	70	30.2	74	32.32
FREEDOM UNION (US)	Centre-right 'defectors' from ODS in 1998	-	-	-	-	19	8.6	*	*	-	0.30
KDU-ČSL & US COALITION *								31	14.3	n/a	n/a
COMMUNIST PARTY (KSČM)	Far-left, largely unreconstructed successor to communist-era ruling party	35	14.0	22	10.3	24	11.0	41	18.5	26	12.81
REPUBLICAN PARTY (SPR-RSČ)	Far-right, nationalist and xenophobic	14	6.0	18	8	0	3.9	0**	0.97**	-	-
GREEN PARTY								***	***	6	6.29

(compiled from Czech media and www.volby.cz)

* The two parties fought the election together.

** As the 'Republikani Miroslava Sladka'.

*** The Green Party contested the European Parliamentary elections of 2004, the Senate elections of 2002 and various regional and local elections.

the centre-right Christian Democratic Union, and together they entered into a coalition to form the government after the 2002 elections with the Social Democratic Party. The US, however, became electorally insignificant in 2006.

A third centre-right party is the Christian Democratic Union-Czechoslovak People's Party (KDU-ČSL). Unlike the ODS, it has a political pedigree as the heir to the inter-war centre-left Catholic People's Party and one of the four parties in the supposedly 'coalition' government of the communist era. Its popularity is somewhat circumscribed, being not only moderately right-wing but also Christian-democrat, and it has a particular constituency in southern Moravia and eastern Bohemia. In June 1992 it won just over 6 per cent of the vote and 15 parliamentary seats; in the next elections it won 18 seats in the lower house and 13 Senate seats. This performance was sufficient to secure four cabinet posts in the ensuing coalition government. It won only 9 per cent of the popular vote and 20 seats in 1998, and despite the efforts of its adept leader Josef Lux, it was not included in a government coalition. The party's coherence also suffered when Lux was forced to resign as party leader in the autumn of 1998 because he was suffering from cancer. As mentioned, the KDU-ČSL later worked with the Freedom Union, and together secured over 14 per cent and 31 seats in the 2002 elections. Unlike the US, the KDU-ČSL survived the 2006 elections, gaining 7.22 per cent and 13 seats.

A similar (but short-lived) party was the Christian Democratic Party (KDS). The Christian Democratic Party was originally headed by communist-era Christian dissident Václav Benda, and was unusual among right-wing parties for its favourable attitude to trade unions. The KDS fought the June 1992 elections with the ODS and entered the ensuing governing coalition. It then merged with the ODS in 1995, its new leader, the youthful Ivan Pilip, gaining senior ministerial posts, including that of Finance in 1997. Several members of the ODS who split from it to create the US in later 1997 and early 1998 were originally KDS members. The KDS, too, has lost political significance.

The final centre-right organisation was the Civic Democratic Alliance (ODA). The third and smallest party of the coalition that governed the Czech Republic until 1997, it emerged like the ODS from the Civic Forum and was often considered the party of intellectuals. The ODA was largely areligious but supported market reforms. While it won 13 seats in the Chamber of Deputies and 7 in the Senate, and was rewarded disproportionately well with 4 cabinet posts, its share of the popular vote subsequently slipped below the five per cent threshold. Leadership fights hampered both the operation and the respectability of the party, and it was wiped out in the 1998 elections.

From the advent of the Czech political party system to the fall of the Klaus government in 1997, the centre-right section of the political spectrum was thus well-delineated, as well as providing the parties of governance. During this period the centre-left was in opposition and in some disarray, and its prospects for government therefore seemed limited. The two centre sections of the political spectrum exchanged fates in 1997 and 1998.

For the 1992 elections a 'Left Bloc' was created of leftist parties, including the Communist Party of Bohemia and Moravia, but excluding the Social Democrats. The Left Bloc gained 14 per cent of the vote and 35 seats. But this left-wing alliance broke three ways: into the Communist Party, the Party of the Democratic Left (SDL), and another faction registering itself as a political party in August 1993 under the name Left Bloc. The left-wing parties contested the 1996 election separately. The Left Bloc and the Party of the Democratic Left each performed dismally, and were no longer players. That left one major centre-left party: the Social Democrats, with the Communist Party clearly dominating the far-left.

The Czech Social Democratic Party (ČSSD) claims a political heritage dating back to a party established in 1878 which was assimilated into the Communist Party following the 1948 seizure of power. In keeping with its interwar traditions, the ČSSD promotes state intervention in the economy and social security, including guaranteed levels of income. One of the achievements of the ČSSD was to convince many non-communist voters by the mid-1990s that the party was a distinct and viable alternative to the far left. In addition, its support for social welfare contrasted favourably with the apparently unbridled capitalist position of Klaus. While the ČSSD was relatively marginal in the 1992 elections, gaining only 6 per cent, by 1996 it more than quadrupled its popular vote to 26 per cent and held 61 seats in the Lower House and 25 seats in the newly-constituted Senate. It also received defections of MPs from the Communist Party. While the centre-right parties still cobbled together a coalition government in 1996, the ČSSD emerged as their main challenger. In the 1998 elections it won 32 per cent of the vote and 74 MPs, which was a plurality of votes. This pre-eminence allowed it to form the government after creating an 'opposition agreement' with the second-placed ODS which meant that Klaus could not scuttle the Social Democratic government.

After leading the party for one term in office, Zeman stepped down as leader and was succeeded by Vladimír Špidla. Špidla led the ČSSD to a slightly worse performance in the 2002 elections, garnering just over 30 per cent and 70 parliamentary seats. Nevertheless, this was again a plurality and the party formed a second government, this time in coalition with the centre-right Freedom Union and Christian Democratic Party. The ČSSD had become the longest governing party in the history of the Czech Republic.

As strong as the centre-left has become through the Social Democratic Party, a far-left alternative remains in the Communist Party of Bohemia and Moravia (KSČM). Unlike the far-right, which has not won seats in two consecutive parliamentary elections, the Communist Party of Bohemia and Moravia has been represented in every Czech parliament, polling to at least fourth place, and has held between 22 and 41 seats. The KSČM was formed within the federal Communist Party in 1990, and – unlike counterparts in Central Europe – persists in celebrating its rule and the achievements of communism. Indeed, it is unique in the region for retaining its name and defending its historical record. Despite or because of this, the Communist Party continues to be a force in Czech politics, although the argument has been made that this party has also been aware of the need to make itself more modern and electable (see Hanley 2001). None of the centrist parties have, however, agreed to make a coalition government with it and Havel refused to include it in discussions about forming the interim government after Klaus's resignation. Only the ČSSD, in its weakened position following the 2006 elections, appeared willing to consider a coalition with it, but this never materialised. The KSČM was also believed to have made deals with the ČSSD for the second round of Senate elections in late 2002. Despite the splintering of votes and the open attitude of most party leaders to making coalition deals, it seems unlikely that the KSČM will be included in government at the national level.

Thus, the Czech Republic can be said to have a fairly clear political party spectrum, and also one that stretches widely across ideologies. In addition, some smaller parties have been eliminated over the years. But considering that no party has won an outright majority and that all Czech governments have either been coalitions or based on an agreement with the main opposition party, the reduction of the number of parties is probably both necessary and beneficial. Furthermore, staple parties such as those for pensioners, the environment, the Moravians, or the agricultural lobby have been unable to secure enough popular vote over several elections. The ideal would therefore be that their values were subsumed by those of sympathetic, but broader-based parties, allowing parliaments to be less hamstrung by such a multiplicity of groups. Following the elections of 2006, on the one hand, it seemed that this ideal was closer than ever – 96.1 per cent of the votes cast were represented in parliament, and (only) five parties were in parliament. On the other hand, as pointed out above, the distribution of seats ensured that a coalition could not be made.

This structural arrangement may be part of the reason why the Czech Republic appears to suffer from political malaise.

POLITICAL MALAISE?

Apathy is a scourge of mature democracies. Even so, Czech public opinion polls suggest a high degree of general dissatisfaction. As many as 70 per cent of the population are dissatisfied with the policies offered by the major political parties (Pehe 2002). Voter turnout continued to decline until the 2006 election. Part of this is surely the complacency that goes with routinised politics. Part of it, however, may derive from the very high expectations of the public based on the political discourse during the first five years of the life of the new Czech Republic. It may be that dissatisfaction is increasing precisely because of the stalemate of 2006, with voters thinking that balloting actually augments deadlock. However, the malaise runs deep and draws from a well of misleading promises by senior politicians and experience of political life in general.

In 1995, Klaus proclaimed that the Czech transformation had been completed. The Czech Republic, according to Klaus and his political lieutenants, was not a post-communist country but a 'normal' country; it had graduated from the transition stage. In keeping with such thinking, the Klaus government planned not to apply, as most post-communist countries did, for membership of the EU. Instead, Klaus believed that the robust economy of the Czech Republic would mean that it would be invited to join the EU. One EU official reminded Klaus that it was not the EU that was looking to join the Czech Republic. By 1996, the invitation had not materialised and the Czech government submitted a formal application and got in line to be considered for membership.

Sentiments may have supported Czech economic exceptionalism while the Czech economy was apparently performing well – which it was until the mid-1990s. The Czech economy enjoyed substantial growth; and privatisation appeared to be liberalising the economy and creating millions of shareholders.

The Czech economy recovered from its slide in the mid- to late-1990s. Nevertheless, Martin Myant, a leading Western economist of the Czech economy, concluded his 2003 book-length study of the transformation thus: 'It appeared that backward and inefficient centrally-planned economy was transformed into [a] weak, unstable and inefficient market economy' (Myant 2003, 262). The majority of the Czech GDP is produced by the private sector, so the Czech economy is and will remain a mixed one. Whoever is in government will find it difficult not to retain considerable social-welfare spending; and finding the cash for such spending will be vexing, as it is for any government.

Regardless of the economy, the importance of dissident-era thinking potentially remained high. While some accounts have noted with sadness or cynicism the apparent passing of these values or the ascendancy of corruption, the Czech Republic still has a relatively high number of former dissidents in public life. Even those (such as Aviezer Tucker) who argue that dissidents have disappeared completely from politics (although two members of the Zeman government were signatories of the dissident document Charter 77) still see prospects for the revival of civil society (Tucker 2000), an aspect to which the chapter now turns.

CIVIL SOCIETY

Western observers have high regard for the depth and power of Czech civil society. This is undoubtedly a feature of the prominence of communist-era dissidents such as Havel and others, and of the way in which political change was effected in 1989. Czechoslovakia, after all, gave the world its new lexicographical entry for 1990 – the Velvet Revolution. Timothy Garton Ash popularised a 'fairy tale' of that revolution in which dissidents were catapulted to high office on a wave of peaceful mass protest (Garton Ash 1990, esp. 124).

The seeming importance of civil society was heightened by the public debates, or disputes, between Havel and Klaus as to the nature and meaning of civil society. Where else in the world do the holders of the two highest political offices write about civil society? And which other countries produced debates on civil society that were translated and replicated in venerable English-language publications (e.g. Havel & Klaus 1996)?

Havel contended that civil society was fundamental to Czech society as well as being the means by which it would be revitalised after communism. For him, 'civil society' consisted (this is the general interpretation) of independent organisations and associations that mediate between the state and the individual. Havel's view could be interpreted as saying that grassroots initiatives can replace state services. He envisaged a strong civil society and even called for the government to reduce its presence to allow non-governmental activities more scope. However, this is not to suggest that Havel shared Klaus's conception of the role of the state. While he was rhetorically an economic liberal, Klaus rejected decentralisation of the state and the creation of independent and non-profit organisations. His policies were criticised for making non-profit activities very difficult, including the deliberate lack of legal provision to make charitable donations tax-free. Klaus saw the market alone as a sufficient safeguard of political rights and freedoms. The call in Klaus's government was for people to enrich themselves – there was no such thing as 'dirty money'. Indeed, some commentators have charged the Klaus government with deliberately creating an environment in which independent political initiative was curtailed. Milada Anna Vachudová writes that the Klaus government undermined 'poles of opinion outside the government, such as universities, non-governmental organisations, and interest groups. Dialogue with civic groups was avoided, and a legal framework for non-governmental organisations was delayed until 1995. No effort was made to foster public discussion and few public information campaigns were attempted' (Vachudová 2001, 337).

The irony of civil society in the post-communist transition is that dissidents – who typified communist-era civil society – became or adopted the governmental structure after the fall of the communist monopoly on power. This was of course necessary because the state was the ready means by which society could be liberalised. Civil society could arguably be any entity that was outside the official, even if democratic, institutions. That might therefore include as part of 'civil society' right-wing skinhead groups that spew hatred against minorities.

The notion of civil society is of course elusive and vexing; its manifestations are many. Despite its general political-philosophical difficulties of definition and its specific question of application in the context of Czech politics, where roles have been reversed, important expressions of grassroots political activity have still occurred. Tens of thousands of Czechs demonstrated, for example, against what was seen as the political motivations behind the replacement of the director of public television (discussed below). Countless NGOs exist, active in all realms of societal issues from the environment to support for the country's Romani minority. While important expressions of civil society exist, one Czech commentator recently observed: 'Communism depoliticised Czech society. Czechs are still very cautious to socialise themselves and build up areas of communal activities, intermediary institutions and various associations, which are so vital for the actual content of democracy' (Brodský 2001, 36).

'Civil society' aside, a plurality of views and the free flow of accurate information are essential to political life. The media are vital, but their role and quality are disputed. It is worth comparing the divergent views of well-placed observers of Czech society. Zdeněk Kavan, a Czech émigré and British academic, and former dissident and public figure Martin Palouš wrote: 'The media are basically free, operating without any political control by the state, and have become a lively and politically diverse force. Criticism of the government is considered normal and desirable' (Kavan & Palouš 1999, 85). By contrast, Czech émigré media-watcher Jan Čulík commented: 'The Czech media are generally second rate. There is no authoritative, independent, investigative journalism. Czech journalists are, on the whole, afraid to stand out from the crowd... Their weakness and incompetence is accompanied by arrogance.' He also contended that such weakness of the Czech media contributed directly to the exacerbation of political and economic problems (Čulík 1999a).

A significant political crisis concerned the newsroom strike in the state-owned Czech Television that started on Christmas Eve 2000 and ran into January 2001. The strike protested against the actions of its director, Jiří Hodač, who was accused of controlling the news and dismissing staff on a political basis. Hodač had resigned earlier as news editor because of objections to his political influence, but he was nevertheless subsequently appointed director. The newsroom staff's strike then received the support of President Havel, and, most significantly for civil society, street demonstrations numbering as many as 100,000 people. It was undoubtedly the largest protest since 1989. Many participants and observers interpreted this move as a statement to politicians not to interfere with the media. At a minimum, then, the media exist in the plural and represent a range of political views, and the population seems ready to safeguard some of its political independence.

The public manifestation of opposition to the management changes at Czech Television was frequently regarded as a revitalisation of Czech civil society. But as some involved in that movement said, there was a very identifiable aim. Two other notable civic movements had either broad or unrealistic aims. One was 'Impuls 99', launched as the name suggests in 1999 and the manifesto of which invited 'a society-wide debate about the direction of society. Its name tried to invoke the famous dissident tract Charter 77, and like that group, 'Impuls' had three spokespeople: journalist Jana Šmidová, the religious figure Tomáš Halík, and the émigré political scientist and adviser to Havel, Jiří Pehe. Commentator Jan Čulík slammed the initiative as 'absurdly amateurish' and attacked the declaration for its 'turgid newspeak, full of communist-era cliches'. While this was a brutal assault on the movement's intentions, Čulík's further observation on the passivity of society may help to explain why nothing came of the initiative: 'Czech society has lost its art of self-analysis and self-communication. Face to face with their politicians, Czech society is mute and, hence, helpless' (Čulík 1999b).

That view might help explain how the 'Thank You, Now Leave' movement arose, and also how and why it was ultimately unsuccessful. On 17 November 1999, the tenth anniversary of the start of the Velvet Revolution, students issued a declaration that appreciated the achievement of democracy in the Czech Republic but that lambasted political leaders. The declaration charged: 'We feel cheated. We are face to face with arrogant political power, incapable of agreeing on a functioning form of leadership for the country, blaming us, the public, for the way we voted'. The statement also accused politicians of damaging the country's reputation abroad and of creating conditions similar to those under communism: 'Among our fellow citizens this evokes sadness and hopelessness, sealing us once again up in the so-called inward emigration we recall from communist times'. The manifesto called on citizens to assert their personal decency, and asked the current politicians to leave office (in English, see 'Thank You, Now Leave!' 1999; and Otáhal & Vaněk 1999). It is difficult to determine how much the population responded to the first call; no politicians reacted to the second. Other than calls for strikes by parts of the public sector (which is not analogous in any case), such social movements as 'Impuls' and 'Thank You, Now Leave!' have not resurfaced.

The one development in the direction of popular mobilisation can be said to be the entry of the Green Party in the 2006 parliamentary elections. This party was founded in 1990 and entered parliament in 1992 (in a coalition with two other parties). By its own admission, the party was thereafter alienated from NGOs, which 'led to a long-lasting crisis in which Greens repeatedly failed to gain seats in parliament' (see http://www.europeangreens.org/). The fragmented political party system and the necessity of coalition-building gave the Green Party the opportunity to enter government as a minority partner of the Civic Democratic Party in January 2007. How much the Green Party can balance the representation of its social base with the need to have a professional party machine will determine whether social movements have made a successful transition to mainstream political life. Otherwise, assessments of non-party activism in the Czech Republic may continue to be somewhat pessimistic.

FOREIGN POLICY AND INTERNATIONAL INFLUENCE

Unlike domestic politics, key issues in Czech foreign policy have been settled, with two principal aims having been achieved. Nevertheless, foreign or international influence continues to be a surprisingly strong and often unpredictable element in Czech political life.

The Czech Republic, with Hungary and Poland, was first among post-communist states to achieve NATO membership (in 1999). And by the end of 2002 the accession date for the country (and nine others) to the EU was set for 1 May 2004.

Perhaps the greatest legacy of Havel is in the international realm. His personal authority alone did much to elevate the status of post-communist Czechoslovakia and the Czech Republic abroad. The country's overarching aim of going 'back to Europe', however, was not entirely straightforward – partly because of Western institutional policies, and partly because of the way accession issues were used and abused in domestic Czech politics. Indeed, entry into Western institutions provides a potential paradox for Czech politics.

Perceived historical heritage is particularly relevant to the issue of entry into Western institutions. The whole slogan 'back to Europe' is indicative of a collective sense of historical and geopolitical belonging. The fact that Prague, in the Soviet bloc, is further west than 'Western' Austria was a familiar Cold War call. Despite being despised by many Czechs, Milan Kundera made it clear (at least to the Western audience) that Central Europe had been 'kidnapped' and dragged eastwards by the Soviet Union (Kundera 1983/1984). In terms of pure political-military security, a country such as Czechoslovakia that suffered the ignoble sell-out by Great Powers at Munich would surely be expected to desire membership of a democratic military alliance. US President Bill Clinton's ambassador to the UN and Secretary of State, Madeleine Albright, was Czechoslovak-born and fled the country at the onset of the Second World War. She made clear in her later political career that her outlook on international politics was that of the 'Munich Syndrome'. She was, unsurprisingly, a leading advocate for the expansion of NATO to Central European states. Not all of her former fellow-countryfolk agreed.

What, by contrast, have been Czech attitudes on NATO and EU accession?

Public opinion polls have put Czech support for membership among the lowest of candidate countries. In the Eurobarometer study conducted for 1997, the year that Czech membership of NATO was announced, Czech support for entry was 36 per cent. The average among candidate countries was 52 per cent (*Eurobarometer No. 8* 1998). To be sure, there has always been a segment of the population adamantly committed to membership of these institutions. But considering the history as briefly outlined above, would it not be reasonable to expect much greater popular support? Membership of the EU also generated much scepticism. Some outside observers faulted the Czech Republic for its lack of interest in or dismay with Western institutions, blaming the failure on the Czech elites. As one observer summarised in 2000, 'Czech leaders still have not made the case that their country's future lies with NATO and the EU. The problem lies not in Washington or Brussels, but with the most informed and active elements in Czech society' (Rhodes 2000).

As already suggested, the Klaus government took EU membership almost for granted. In 1995, before the Czech Republic had even applied for membership, his Foreign Minister Josef Zieleniec said that such membership was definite. But apart from such self-confidence about membership, the Klaus government believed it had lessons to teach Brussels. Klaus cautioned about the bureaucracy and lack of democratic accountability in the EU, and even likened it to Soviet control over Eastern Europe. Zieleniec spoke of Europe being formed of many nations, each contributing ideas. Like Klaus, he explained that one of the ideas that the Czechs could contribute was the lesson to be learned from the excessive bureaucracy of communist rule. This 'warning', Zieleniec elaborated, informed Czech discussions of the future form of the EU (Fawn 2003, 221-24). 'Eurorealism' as Klaus and his Social Democratic followers prefer to call their Euroscepticism, has remained pronounced. The practical consequences of that view, for example regarding the future of the Lisbon Treaty, became a serious issue in advance of the Czech presidency of the EU in 2009.

Strong Czech views about the EU and of that country's place therein extended throughout the accession process. It came as some surprise that the EU's first major assessment of post-communist eligibility for accession, announced in 1997 in Agenda 2000, while favourable on some aspects of the Czech transformation, was nevertheless highly critical of others, including economic legislation, the ability of the country to meet the requirements of the *acquis*, and minority rights protection.

The Social Democratic government in power since 1998 took a much more positive view of EU accession and worked quietly to complete chapters of the accession negotiations. Nevertheless, certain issues still arose, such as the Temelín nuclear power plant and the Beneš Decrees. In both of these cases, advocates in the existing EU member states of Germany and Austria sought to make its entry into the European Union conditional on certain changes in domestic Czech policies. Temelín was perhaps the more straightforward of these two issues, with the minimum demand of neighbouring Austria being that European-standard safeguards should be put in place in the plant (the preference was for it not to operate at all).

The development of regional administration within the Czech Republic has been another area in which EU policy has changed – or even created – domestic priorities. Neither socialist nor post-communist Czechoslovak governments had regional policies, preferring centralisation. But the Czech application to the EU resulted in measures by Brussels 'to introduce and nurture a set of fairly detailed regulative and constitutive norms for regional policy making in the Czech Republic' (Jacoby & Cernoch 2000, 317-8).

The Beneš Decrees were a more complicated issue than the Temelín nuclear power plant, and really showed the potential influence of international institutions on domestic affairs. These post-war declarations cover a range of issues, but are most famous for three that laid the foundation for the expulsion of Germans and Hungarians from Czechoslovakia as collaborators in Axis occupation. While the expulsions were approved by the Big Three wartime allies, expellees and their descendants have contested their legality on the presumption of collective guilt, as well as claiming that this was accompanied by brutality and deaths. Repealing the Decrees also had implications for the Czech and Slovak citizenship and property rights of the expellees. After much consternation in the Czech Republic, the EU agreed that the Decrees were not illegal. The EU nevertheless suggested that the Czech Republic should make a 'gesture' of apology to the expellees.

These cases are a strong illustration of the way in which a range of key domestic issues – from technology and governmental organisation to history – could be subjugated to external regulation. An additional illustration of the power of international bodies over Czech domestic practice concerned the fate of the Roma minority. This issue is proving difficult for all Central and East European countries, but the Czech Republic attracted particular Western criticism for its new citizenship law, which was widely seen as discriminating against the Roma by effectively denying them citizenship in the new polity (Šiklová & Mitlusaková 1998). One recent international relations publication comparing 'pathological homogenisation' across time and place in Europe, whereby rulers culturally purify their populations as part of state building, contended that the Czech Republic only just avoided being such a case on account of pressure to appeal the citizenship law (Rae 2002). Part of the Czech attitude to international criticism – from town mayors to senior cabinet ministers – was that outside bodies had questionable rights to comment on internal Czech affairs. Ultimately, however, international pressure prevailed.

The outcome of the Czech referendum on joining the EU reflected some ambivalence. Considering that 'back to Europe' had been a popular mantra since 1989 and actually joining the EU its logical manifestation, the 77.3 per cent vote in favour of membership in the referendum in June 2003 was not overwhelming. With a turnout of only 55.21 per cent (and no minimum number being required for the validity of the referendum), those proactively voting in favour amounted to just over 42 per cent of the whole population, and this was achieved after the government deliberately held the referendum after those of other countries in the region and also over two days to maximise voter turnout. Nevertheless, the numbers voting for accession are comparable to those in many other post-communist states; and are substantially higher than in others, such as Estonia.

Membership of NATO also indicated a considerable degree of ambivalence. Joining the Alliance coincided with the Kosovo war, and the Czech Republic, by default, consented to participate in that conflict. Havel was unusual among political leaders for supporting the war; others were virulently opposed, as was much of popular opinion. Czech Foreign Minister Kavan attempted, with his anti-war Greek counterpart, to stop the NATO bombing with a peace plan devised outside Alliance structures. This was rejected and the Czech Republic, by virtue of its NATO membership, continued to be at war. Kosovo showed that membership carried unforeseen obligations.

That said, the Czech government has tried to demonstrate good 'international citizenship' by contributing to international peacekeeping missions, particularly in the Balkans. Prague demonstrated solidarity with the United States in the international war on terrorism by sending specialist medical personnel to Afghanistan and combat troops to Kuwait, although the latter were not to be deployed in the absence of specific authorization under a UN Security Council resolution. Havel, however, went as far as signing the 'Letter of Eight', the controversial document by several European heads of state backing American military action against Saddam's regime. Klaus, by then in the presidential office, demanded by contrast that the United States remove the Czech Republic from the list of coalition members. Having communist-era specialisation in anti-chemical warfare (and having supplied such a unit in the 1991 Gulf War), the Czech government has offered to provide wider training in its country to NATO forces. The Czech armed forces are cash-strapped – the massive flooding in the summer of 2002 forced the government to cancel its one major military upgrade, the purchase of Gripen fighter jets. Even so, the government is attempting to demonstrate commitments to international obligations as best it can, though some of these will continue to cause controversy. Foremost among them was the government's acceptance in 2008, although not yet that of parliament, of the US plan to site radar on Czech territory as part of a larger anti-ballistic missile defense system.

CONCLUSION

The divergent paths of the Czech Republic and Slovakia in the mid-1990s are revealing. Under Vladimír Mečiar, Slovakia fell behind the successes of the Czech Republic by being denied NATO membership in 1997 and falling out of the first line of EU candidate countries. A change of government in 1998 and increased democracy and international cooperation has now reversed those fortunes; but Slovakia, as the sibling state to the Czech Republic, illustrates the point that there are no historically pre-determined outcomes, nor that the long-term political and economic results of these two sibling polities are so fundamentally different (for a comparison, see Williams 2003a). Indeed, it is now being asked how the two countries can appear to have changed roles – with reference to the Czech 'miracle' having ceased and Slovakia no longer being a black hole in Europe (Deegan-Krause 2006).

Despite difficulties and limitations, the Czech transformation has also had considerable successes. Many of its downsides are arguably little different from those endured by established democracies and market economies. Even many of those most critical of the Klausian transformation acknowledge that despite economic problems in the 1990s the economy has developed into a market economy. Degrees of political and financial corruption are, unfortunately, an apparent feature of liberal democratic life. What is necessary is robust pluralism, including a politically aware population and active, responsible media, to ensure that this kind of rot is minimised.

In terms of the game of Czech politics, a political party system is in place, and it reflects clear political preferences, giving a defined spectrum. The presidency gives an added tier for political competition, and may become a popularly elected post, although this is extremely unlikely in the next decade as Klaus can be expected to seek another term. The continued electoral successes of the ODS also means that the ODS will hold enough seats to ensure a veto on any other successor, if not guaranteeing that Klaus will have to be re-elected president. Havel, who remains active despite many bouts of bad health, has occasionally been vocal. But much of his attention has been directed towards to developments outside the Czech Republic.

As we have seen, there is still some margin for change – for parties to fragment, merge, appear and disappear. Several small centre-right parties that were previously important to the balance of power have disappeared; and the Green Party, unable to win enough votes for parliamentary seats since 1990, managed not only to secure seats in 2006 but to enter government in 2007. Whether such fluidity among parties is a sign of democracy working well, or whether it creates practical deficiencies for governance, will continue to be the huge question hanging over Czech politics.

References

Brodský, J. 2001. 'The Czech Experience of Identity'. In: P. Drulák (ed.), *National and European Identities in EU Enlargement*. Prague: Institute of International Relations, 21-38.

Brokl, L. (ed.) 1997. *Reprezentace zájmů v politickém systému české republiky*. Praha: Slon.

Čulík, J. 1999a. 'Press Freedom under Threat', *Central Europe Review*, 1, 3.

Čulík, J. 1999b. 'No Pulse 99'. *Central Europe Review*, 1, 7.

Deegan-Krause, K. 2006. *Elected Affinities: Democracy and Party Competition in Slovakia and the Czech Republic*. Stanford: Stanford University Press.

Economist Intelligence Unit (quarterly and annually). *Country Report: The Czech Republic* and *Country Profile*.

European Commission Directorate-General, Information, Culture, Audiovisual 1998. *Central and Eastern European Eurobarometer No. 8*. Brussels.

Fawn, R. 2000. *The Czech Republic: A Nation of Velvet*. London: Routledge and Harwood Academic.

Fawn, R. 2003. 'Reconstituting a National Identity: Ideologies in Czech Foreign Policy after the Split', *Journal of Communist Studies and Transition Politics*, 19, 3.

Fawn, R. 2004. 'Understanding Politics in the Czech Republic'. *Demstar Research Report* no. 20. Aarhus: Department of Political Science, University of Aarhus.

Garton Ash, T. 1990. *We the People: The Revolutions of 1989*. London: Granta.

Garton Ash, T. 1995. 'Prague: Intellectuals and Politicians', *The New York Review of Books* (12 January), 34-41.

Hanley, S. 2001. 'Towards Breakthrough or Breakdown? The Consolidation of KSČM as a Neo-Communist Successor Party in the Czech Republic', *Journal of Communist Studies and Transition Politics*, 17, 3.

Havel, V. 1995. 'Novoroční projev' [1 Jan. 1994]. In: *Havel '94*. Praha and Litomyšl: Paseka.

Havel, V. 1997. 'Senát a Poslanecká sněmovna Parlamentu České republiky'. In: *Havel '97*. Praha and Litomyšl: Paseka, 88-100.

Havel, V. & V. Klaus, with commentary by P. Pithart 1996. 'Rival Visions', *Journal of Democracy*, 7, 1, 12-22.

Husák, P. 1997. *Budování kapitalismu v Čechách: rozhovory s Tomašem Ježkem*. Praha: Volvox Globator.

Innes, A. 2001. *Czechoslovakia: The Short Goodbye*. New Haven: Yale University Press.

Jacoby, W. & P. Cernoch 2002. 'The Pivotal EU Role in the Creation of Czech Regional Policy'. In: R.H. Linden (ed.), *Norms and Nannies: The Impact of*

International Organizations on the Central and East European States. Lanham, MD: Rowman and Littlefield, 317-39.

Kavan, Z. & M. Palouš 1999. 'Democracy in the Czech Republic'. In: M. Kaldor & I. Vejvoda (eds.), *Democracy in Central and Eastern Europe.* London and New York: Continuum, 78-92.

Klíma, M. 1998. 'Consolidation and Stabilization of the Party System in the Czech Republic', *Political Studies,* 46, 492-510.

Kopecký, P. 2000. *The Czech and Slovak Parliaments.* Aldershot: Avebury.

Kroupa, A. & T. Kostelecký 1996. 'Party Organization and Structure at the National and Local Level in the Czech Republic since 1989'. In: P.G. Lewis (ed.), *Party Structure and Organization in East-Central Europe.* Cheltenham: Edward Elgar.

Kundera, M. 1983. 'Un Occident kidnappe ou la tragedie de l'Europe centrale', *Le Debat,* 27.

Kundera, M. 1984. 'The tragedy of Central Europe', *The New York Review of Books,* 26 April.

Leigh, M. 2003. 'The Czech Republic as an EU Candidate'. In: Jacques Rupnik & Jan Zielonka (eds), *The Road to the European Union: Volume 1: The Czech and Slovak Republics.* Manchester: Manchester University Press.

Matějů, P. & B. Řeháková 1997. 'Turning Left or Class Realignment? Analysis of the Changing Relationship Between Class and Party in the Czech Republic, 1992-96', *East European Politics and Societies,* 11, 3.

Musil, J. (ed.) 1995. *The End of Czechoslovakia.* Budapest: Central European University Press.

Myant, M. 2003. *The Rise and Fall of Czech Capitalism: Economic Development in the Czech Republic since 1989.* Cheltenham: Edward Elgar.

Otáhal, M. & M. Vaněk (eds.) 1999. *Sto studentských revolucí.* Praha: Nakladatelství Lidové Noviny.

Pehe, J. 2002. 'European Union Wins Czech Elections – Barely', *East European Constitutional Review,* 11, 3.

Pithart, P. 1996. 'Občanská společnost a stát'. In: Jan Kunc (ed.), *Demokracie a ústavnost.* Praha: Karolinum.

Rae, H. 2002. *State Identities and the Homogenisation of Peoples.* Cambridge: Cambridge University Press.

Reschová, J. & J. Syllová 1996. 'The Legislature of the Czech Republic'. In: D.M. Olson & P. Norton (eds.), *The New Parliaments of Central and Eastern European.* London: Frank Cass.

Rhodes, M. 2000. 'Czech Malaise and Europe', *Problems of Post-Communism,* 47, 2, 57-66.

Roberts, A. 2003. 'Demythologising the Czech Opposition Agreement', *Europe-Asia Studies,* 55, 8, 1273-1303.

Šafaříková, V. (ed.) 1996. *Transformace české společnosti 1989-1995.* Brno: nakladelství Doplněk Brno.

Shepherd, R.H.E. 2000. *Czechoslovakia: The Velvet Revolution and Beyond*. Basingstoke: Macmillan & New York: St. Martin's Press.

Šiklová, J. & M. Miklušaková 1998. 'Law as an Instrument of Discrimination: Denying Citizenship to the Czech Roma', *East European Constitutional Review*, 7, 2.

Simmons, M. 1991. *The Reluctant President*. London: Methuen.

Skilling, H.G. 1981. *Charter 77 and Human Rights in Czechoslovakia*. London: Allen & Unwin.

Skilling, H.G. 1991. 'Lions or Foxes: Heroes or Lackeys?' In: H.G. Skilling (ed.), *Czechoslovakia 1918-1988: Seventy Years from Independence*. London: Macmillan.

Stein, E. 1997. *Czecho/Slovakia*. Ann Arbor: University of Michigan Press.

Šustrová, P. 1992. 'The Lustration Controversy', *Uncaptive Minds* (Summer), 129-134.

Svejnar, J. (ed.) 1995. *The Czech Republic and Economic Transition in Eastern Europe*. San Diego: Academic Press.

Teichova, A. 1988. *The Czechoslovak Economy: 1918-1980*. London and New York: Routledge.

'Thank You, Now Leave!' 1999. 'A proclamation of former students on the tenth anniversary of November 17th 1989', at http://www.ce-review.org/99/24/ thankyou24.html

Tucker, A. 2000. *The Philosophy and Politics of Czech Dissidence from Havel to Patočka*. Pittsburgh: University of Pennsylvania Press.

Vachudová, M.A. 2001. 'The Czech Republic: The Unexpected Force of Institutional Constraints'. In: J. Zielonka & A. Pravda (eds.), *Democratic Consolidation in Central and Eastern Europe Vol. 2*. Oxford: Oxford University Press, 325-62.

Večerník, J. 1996. *Markets and People: The Czech Reform Experience in Comparative Perspective*. Aldershot: Avebury.

Wheaton, B. & Z. Kavan 1992. *The Velvet Revolution: Czechoslovakia, 1988-1991*. Boulder: Westview Press.

Whitefield, S. & G. Evans 1999. 'Political Culture Versus Rational Choice: Explaining Responses to Transition in the Czech Republic and Slovakia', *British Journal of Political Science*, 29, 129-54.

Wightman, G. (ed.) 1995. *Party Formation in East-Central Europe: Post-communist Politics in Czechoslovakia, Hungary, Poland and Bulgaria*. Aldershot: Edward Elgar.

Williams, K. 1997. 'National Myths in the New Czech Liberalism'. In: G. Hosking & G. Schöpflin (eds.), *Myths and Nationhood*. London: Hurst, 132-40.

Williams, K. 2003a. 'The Czech Republic and Slovakia'. In: S. White, J. Batt & P.G. Lewis (eds.), *Developments in Central and East European Politics 3*. Basingstoke: Palgrave, 41-56.

Williams, K. 2003b. 'Lustration as the Securitization of Democracy in Czechoslovakia and the Czech Republic', *Journal of Communist Studies and Transition Politics*, 19, 4.

Wolchik, S.L. 1991. *Czechoslovakia in Transition*. London: Pinter.

CHAPTER 7

Breaking with post-communism in Poland

Radoslaw Zubek

This chapter studies the consolidation of democracy in Poland. In doing so, it focuses on the extent to which Polish governments produce policies that maximise collective benefits to democratic majorities ('public good policies'). It argues, first, that Polish parties find it difficult to provide the leadership for such democratic responsiveness. This is because, despite some centralisation of intra-party powers, the party leaders' control is undermined by the programmatic incohesiveness of their parties, the far-reaching politicisation of the public administration, and the porous interface between politics and business. Moreover, the erosion of party controls coincides in Poland with limited inter-party cooperation. Second, the paper shows how party configurations impinge on the emergence of state structures that facilitate democratic responsiveness. In doing so, it analyses the institutional position of the executive within parliament, and institutional configurations at the centre of government. Third, I explore the way in which Poland's accession to the European Union influenced democratic consolidation in Poland, and argue that Europe has had a fairly permanent, though restricted, impact on the development of institutions that engender democratic accountability. Finally, the chapter demonstrates how such institutional hurdles contributed to a major crisis of governance in 2003-2004. It argues that the crisis acted as a catalyst, mobilising domestic political forces to propose radical institutional reforms that may move Poland farther away from post-communism.

PARTY STRUCTURES

Internal party leadership

If governments are to be responsive to the interests of the democratic majorities, party leaders must have institutional levers to mobilise individual members and control their behaviour. The emergence of strong leadership within political parties is thus a prerequisite for democratic consolidation (Cox & McCubbins 1993). The Polish party organisations that emerged after 1989 provided their leaders with a relatively high degree of institutional control. Party leaders dominated the process of candidate selection, and had a decisive voice in the formulation of party policies. The key mechanism was the overlap between the composition of party leadership and that of both the cabinet and the parliamentary club (Szczerbiak 2001, 105; Grzymala-Busse 2003, 236). The presence of party leaders in parliament and cabinet provided them with opportunities for administering selective incentives to party members and for monitoring individual actions. This was most evident in parliament, where party leaders hired whips and checked voting behaviour to ensure discipline and cohesion (ibid 257-8). Party leaders also controlled intermediate executive bodies inside their party organisations, which further reinforced their grip on the selection of party candidates to parliament and executive posts (Szczerbiak 2001, 105-6). The existence of nation-wide parliamentary party lists (until 2001) provided yet another instrument with which to mobilise individuals towards collective interests. The progressive development of intra-party controls occurred both in successor parties such as the Democratic Left Alliance (SLD) and the Polish Peasants Party (PSL), and in parties with a post-dissident lineage such as the Freedom Union (UW). The party where centralisation of leader controls was perhaps most problematic was the Solidarity Electoral Action (AWS), whose federal structure inhibited the reinforcement of its leadership.

Although Polish leaders centralised institutional controls within party organisations, three general factors simultaneously undermined their grip on party members. The first problem is that, in 1989-2005, Polish political parties aggregated less around socio-economic policy platforms and more around attitudes to the communist past (Szczerbiak 1999; Markowski & Czesnik 2002). In effect, party leaders found it difficult to use party programmes or political ideology as a coordination mechanism. The internal heterogeneity of Polish political parties was most evident in the case of the two parties that won the largest share of seats in the three parliaments between 1993 and 2005. The Democratic Left Alliance (SLD), a descendant of the Polish communist party, attracted mainly former communist apparatchiks for whom shared biographies and political survival provided the principal integrating element, while left-right identification was accorded secondary importance (Paszkiewicz 2000; Raciborski 2001). Thus, the SLD emerged as a programmatically heterogeneous organisation, marrying socialists with technocrats and market liberals (Paradowska & Baczynski 2004). A similar predicament befell the Solidarity Electoral Action (AWS). The AWS was formed in 1996 as a coalition of many post-dissident parties clustered around the Solidarity Trade Union. The key integrating principle was the ambition of the post-Solidarity forces to remove the post-communist SLD from power. In programmatic terms, however, the AWS remained a diverse amalgamate of left-wing populists, Christian democrats and liberals (Paradowska 1998; 1999; Gadomski 2000). The shaping power of the historical cleavage extended well beyond the SLD and the AWS, and affected the evolution of the entire Polish party system.

The second factor that undermined the internal control of party leaders is that Polish parties had both ample opportunities and strong incentives to politicise large parts of the state administration. These opportunities stemmed chiefly from a high degree of formal discretion embodied in the legal framework (Nunberg 1998; 1999). More importantly, lacking well funded organisations, party leaders perceived personnel policy as an attractive instrument of loyalty and party building (Paradowska 1998; Raciborski 2002; Solecka 2003). These incentives were further reinforced by a cyclical mistrust in incumbent bureaucrats as post-dissident parties took turns with post-communists to form majority governments (see Meyer-Sahling 2004). The expansion of party rule into the governmental administration put increasing strain on the party leaderships' ability to control party members. The sheer number of posts to be filled increased the likelihood that nominees would become unresponsive to party leaders. Moreover, a rich reservoir of resources appurtenant to state posts provided individual members with capacities to establish networks autonomous from party leadership (Staniszkis 2000; 2001). This effect was further reinforced by a far-reaching reliance of Polish parties on parliamentary resources. For example, it is standard practice for constituency offices to function as local party headquarters (Wiatr 2003, 187-9). Party organisations also crucially rely on financial contributions from their parliamentary deputies, who transfer part of their salary and expense allowances to the party coffers (Szczerbiak 2001, 439). This dependence of Polish parties (and their leaders) on parliamentary resources increased the autonomy of members of parliament vis-à-vis party leaders (Wiatr 2003).

The third factor contributing to the erosion of leadership control is the rotation of political elites in and out of the business environment (Staniszkis 2000, 2001). This process was initiated in 1989, when many of the communist activists, including members of secret services and youth organisations, used their own personal ties and material resources to set up private businesses (Staniszkis 1992). The emerging private sector offered them a safe haven in a world in which their political future was uncertain. Many of these people returned to politics in 1993 and 2001, the times when the SLD won parliamentary elections. A similar strategy was adopted by activists of the post-dissident right-wing parties who lost parliamentary representation in the 1993 elections but returned to power in 1997. Although originally a survival strategy, the rotation of political elites between business and politics was also driven by opportunities for financial gain (Hausner et al. 2000). This was because the state offered access to attractive sources of capital that were otherwise hard to come by in the private market place due to high interest rates (Staniszkis 2000, 198). Unsurprisingly, the memberships of both the AWS and the SLD grew considerably when the parties were heading for an electoral victory. The external push for a return to politics further coincided with a strong 'pull' from party leaderships. Private business controlled resources that helped leaders win elections. Moreover, it had the skills and the personal connections that proved useful in reinforcing the parties' influence and organisational reach after the elections (Hausner et al. 2000; Wiatr 2003). Although helpful in achieving electoral success, the rotation of elites made the task of party leaders much more difficult. The control and coordination levers available to them came under severe pressure when confronted with interest networks that extended beyond the party and the state into the private sector. As a result, the central control over the actions of party members in government and parliament was frequently less effective that the evidence of intra-party centralisation would indicate.

Coalition leadership

Internal party control is the key determinant in single-party governments. In multi-party governments it must be accompanied by mechanisms for inter-party cooperation. Significantly, in 1989-2005, all Polish majority governments depended on the support of two or more parties. The need to form coalition governments is in large part due to the proportional electoral system (Antoszewski 2002; Markowski & Czesnik 2002). If governing parties were to be responsive to the interests of the electoral majority, the leaderships of the coalition parties would have to undertake inter-party cooperation (Muller & Strom 2000; Thies 2001). Indeed, all Polish governments have sought to institutionalise mechanisms that would facilitate cooperation. For example, ever since the Suchocka government, parties concluded coalition agreements that spelled out common policy objectives (Zubek 2001; Jednaka 2004). The parties in government provided for regular or ad hoc meetings of their leaders and, at times, set up joint working groups (Zubek 2001; Dimitrov et al. 2006). It was also a common practice for coalition parties to share senior posts at the top of each ministry – if the minister came from one party, the deputy minister would come from the other coalition partner (Rydlewski 2002).

However, despite all such endeavours at inter-party cooperation, Polish governing coalitions were simultaneously subject to strong centrifugal forces that pushed them towards ministerial-type government in which individual parties wielded dominant influence over the policy profile of departments headed by their own minister. The first such factor is the programmatic incohesiveness of nearly all Polish cabinets. Governing coalitious formed according to historical rather than ideological criteria (cf. Rydlewski 2000; Jednaka 2004). The shadow of the communist past prevented parties who had their roots in the anti-communist opposition from forming coalitions with the descendants of the former communist party or its two satellite organisations. Therefore, coalition opportunities were explored only within these two families of parties, precluding the formation of minimal range coalitions or minimally connected winning coalitions. The programmatic differences within coalitions were stark. The Suchocka government was dominated by both liberals (UD, KLD, PPG) and Christian democrats (ZChN, PChD, PL). The three SLD-PSL cabinets combined the SLD's social democrats with the PSL's Christian peasant parties. The AWS-UW coalition married the UW's liberals with the AWS's Christian democrats and conservative nationalists. The SLD-PSL-UP cabinet was, again, a coalition of social democrats with a Christian peasant party (Jednaka 2004, 281).

The other factor is that the logic of party and identity building often dominated the coalition strategies adopted by Polish political parties. As already mentioned above, lacking mass membership, the party leaders tended to perceive state offices as an attractive source of funding. Most parties, for example, required their state appointees to contribute a share of their salaries to the party. Such resource extraction strategies provided a natural push towards seeking full control over specific executive agencies and ministerial departments. Perhaps more significantly, all Polish political parties, including the successor parties, wished to establish their identities in the electoral market and, in doing so, wanted to differentiate themselves from other parties. This meant that leaders had a strong predilection for realising ideal point policies in their quest to reinforce ties with their natural voter constituencies. When combined with major programmatic differences, bias against compromise policies led to frequent confrontations among coalition partners when one party's ideal policies hurt the electoral appeal of the other party. Under such conditions, parties in government rarely intended to run together in parliamentary elections, and coalitions often broke down around mid-term to allow parties to re-emphasise their identities.

STATE STRUCTURES

The position of the executive in parliament

The combination of strong party leadership and inter-party cooperation is a necessary but not sufficient condition for the consolidation of democracy. Democratic responsiveness is much greater if the executive enjoys agenda-setting powers within the parliament (Döring 1995; Döring & Hallerberg 2004). In 1998-2005, the Polish executive gained some important new institutional levers that improved its position in the lower chamber of the Polish Sejm. For example, under the 1992 constitutional amendment, the parliament lost the power to pass resolutions that were binding for the government. In budget-making the Sejm ceased to approve socio-economic guidelines for the state budget. The 1997 constitution has introduced some further changes that reinforce the executive's position in parliamentary policy-making. Perhaps most significantly, it positioned the speaker – who is normally a senior member of the largest governing party – as the key management body within the lower chamber. That change had a particular significance for the government's day-to-day control over the parliamentary agenda. It is now the speaker who decides on the plenary agenda after non-binding consultations with party caucuses, and it is he who may delay the introduction of an item for a vote for up to six months (see Kudej 2002; Kubuj 2004). Finally, in the area of fiscal policy, the parliament lost the power to increase the budget deficit proposed by the executive (see Kosinski 2001; Gluchowski 1997, 2001).

These efforts at centralisation met with strong countervailing forces, however. The key inhibiting factor was the legacy of the communist past, when parliament was accorded supreme authority while the executive was relegated to the position of a 'central administrative body'. Not without significance was the general enthusiasm for parliamentary legitimacy that prevailed in the early 1990s as well as the strong preference for parliamentary supremacy cherished by law professors who shaped the public discourse during the constitutional debate in 1991-2 and 1996-1997 (Rokita 1998). But, perhaps most importantly, any moves towards a strengthening of the executive inside parliament were blocked by the parties in government, whose leaders (rightly) feared that institutional reinforcement would reduce their ability to use parliament as an alternative arena for recouping any losses at the cabinet level. This strategy was a corollary to the programmatic incohesivenss of most Polish coalitions and of the strong penchant of governing parties to realise their ideal point policies. The parties in government thus cherished parliament as an alternative arena in which to recoup losses sustained during intra-executive policy-making.

As a result, the position of the executive in parliamentary policy-making continued to be heavily circumscribed (Zubek 2001; Goetz & Zubek 2007). Three procedural weaknesses are worth noting. First, members of parliaments have extensive powers to initiate legislation. It takes fifteen deputies to submit a new bill and draft legislation can also be proposed by committees, the Senate, the president and large citizen groups. There are no limitations on when non-executive bills may be proposed, and the government has a monopoly of initiative only with regard to the budget, public debt and state guarantee bills. All other bills, including 'money' bills (tax and spending legislation) can be submitted by non-executive actors. Second, not only do deputies and committees enjoy extensive powers to initiate legislation, but once submitted such legislation is processed according to the same rules as government-initiated legislation. Although the government can ask the parliament to apply accelerated procedure, this is very rarely done for fear of party political backlash (see Lipski 2004). In effect, the government does not have many levers to prioritise its legislation. Third and finally, parliamentary committees exercise wide-ranging agenda-setting powers (Goetz & Zubek 2007). They have the right to rewrite original bills, which means that when they report to the full chamber, the committee text has precedence over the original copy. The plenary cannot bind a committee on the general principle of a bill. Although the first reading may take place in the full house, the vote at that stage is only binding as to whether a bill lapses or is referred to committees. In any case, two in three bills on average have their first readings in committees, further reinforcing their agenda-setting powers (Osiecka-Chojnacka 2004).

The limited procedural powers within parliament made it difficult for the parties in government to develop 'public good' policies that maximise the interests of the democratic majority. Most significantly, the executive had to compete with non-executive legislation for scarce parliamentary time and resources. In the 1993-1997 and 1997-2001 parliaments, private member and committee bills accounted for 52 and 48 per cent, respectively, of all drafts considered by parliament (see Zubek 2006). Although executive bills enjoyed a higher success rate, the parliament was still responsible for initiating between 20 and 40 per cent of drafts that became law (ibid). Such non-executive bills often covered major policy issues. For example, in autumn 2004 a private-member bill opposed by the Belka government succeeded in introducing a new 50 per cent tax rate to the personal tax system. Executive bills were also substantially amended in parliament. It is widely recognised that many such amendments were driven by sectoral or other lobbies and led to legislation that was replete with legal loop-holes and that privileged narrow interests (see for example Majewski & Reszka 2002; Lukaszewicz 2004).

Core executive

Party leaders are able to ensure democratic responsiveness more effectively if they enjoy extensive procedural powers within the executive (cf. Zubek 2005; Dimitrov et al. 2006). This is because such powers enable leaders to control ministers and monitor their behaviour at departmental level. In parliamentary systems, and particularly in single-party cabinets, such procedural powers normally fall within the prerogative of the prime minister. In Poland, the prime minister's position vis-à-vis his cabinet and ministers was improved substantially between 1989 and 2004 (Zubek 2001, 2006). The new 1997 constitution placed the premier firmly at the helm of the executive power, curbing the prerogatives of the president in domestic and foreign policy. The prime minister was accorded absolute power to allocate and reshuffle portfolios among ministers. Besides such organisational competence, he acquired the power to command, coordinate and control his ministers. The prime minister may chair any of the standing cabinet committees, and may establish and chair ad hoc committees and advisory councils. He may further request information and reports on any matter from ministers and directors of executive agencies. Inside the cabinet, the premier exercises full control over which items are placed on the agenda and which are debated and for how long. Last, but not least, it is the prime minister who sums up the debate in cabinet, and his private office writes up the protocols and instructions.

While in legal terms Poland clearly experienced a growing prime minis- terialisation of the executive, the new institutional rules proved less effective in practice. In addition to the exigencies of coalition management that placed political constraints on the prime minister's manoeuvring room, most Polish premiers since 1989 enjoyed relatively weak political standings because their office was rarely supplemented by leadership of the largest majority party. This meant that even when the new formal powers had been introduced, the prime minister often lacked the political authority to exercise them. For example, Jerzy Buzek, the AWS prime minister, often refrained from using his powers because he was pressed by coalition party leaders (Zubek 2001). Political con- straints were less of a problem for Leszek Miller, prime minister from 2001 to 2004. Miller was leader of the SLD, a party that dominated parliament and the SLD-UP-PSL government. Drawing on his party and government authority, he was able to effectively enforce internal rules in the cabinet. But even Miller's ability to invoke legal powers declined as his government became increas- ingly unpopular with the electorate. However, the most serious impediment to the prime minister's ability to provide incentives and monitor ministers was the limited nature of the organisational resources available to him at the Chancellery. Despite numerous attempts at reform, the Prime Minister's Chancellery had neither the sufficient nodality nor the expertise necessary to support the control and coordinating functions of the prime minister (Zubek 2006). For example, the Chancellery had not set up mirror desks to monitor and verify ministerial compliance with overall government strategy. Neither did it establish policy departments that could provide the prime minister with advice independently from line ministries. Where such expertise was avail- able in-house – as was clearly the case in economic policy – organisational boundaries prevented the premier from having ready access to it. Lastly, the Chancellery had restricted access to policy-making arenas early in the legisla- tive process. A key factor inhibiting a change in the position of the Chancellery was open or tacit opposition from ministers and other coalition leaders. The comprehensive reforms by Wieslaw Walendziak were frustrated in 1998 by fierce opposition from the Freedom Union leader and some powerful leaders within the AWS (Zubek 2006). Under Miller, a major additional disincentive was the premier's personal penchant for relying on personalised party-based lines of accountability.

Democratic responsiveness is facilitated if institutional rules exist that require cabinet ministers to make decisions as a group. In parliamentary governments such rules usually mandate the existence of committee-type structures (cf. Baylis 1989; Andeweg 1997; 2000). Committees help overcome democratic unresponsiveness because they encourage ministers to act as monitors or competitive agenda-setters for one another, and to consider the impact of individual actions on their collective interest. In 1989-2004 many such collective decision-making mechanisms were institutionalised within the Polish executive (Zubek 2001; 2006). For one thing, the organisation of the cabinet itself was streamlined. The number of full ministers was reduced from 25 under the Suchocka government to 14 under the first Miller cabinet, and non-ministerial and other external participants were denied cabinet standing. In the early 1990s, two cabinet committees for social and economic affairs were granted formal status and all cabinet submissions were routed through these committees. By the end of the decade, the number of ministerial-level committees stood at four under the Buzek government. The Miller government, however, decided to replace them with a single cabinet committee at junior minister level. Last, another form of collectivity-enhancing mechanism was conciliation conferences held when a draft policy was considered controversial. The centre was also populated with other standing or ad hoc task forces, working groups, councils and special committees.

The system of cabinet committees and other joint working groups clearly offered ministers and civil servants the opportunities to consider and decide on policy choices as a group. This said, there were three factors that undermined the effectiveness of cabinet committees in ensuring better democratic responsiveness. The first factor was that most cabinet committees were simply too large to engender a common understanding of problems and to seek compromise solutions. Their membership normally stood at 15-16 ministers, and the sessions were attended by two or three junior assistants per minister. As such, committees frequently turned into weekly or monthly debriefings on individual ministerial positions, and had little capacity for practical decision making. The second (and closely related) factor is that owing to their composition, committees provided only limited room for political coordination. Rather, they frequently dealt with technical and administrative detail, leaving most political decisions to the full cabinet. The attempt to harness *cabinets ministeriel* to provide political horizontal coordination proved largely unsuccessful (Zubek 2006). Finally, many committees and other working groups were vulnerable to capture by narrow sectoral interests because their chairs were recruited from among sectoral ministers of economics, social affairs or defence. Such chairs had little incentive to uphold the collective interest of the cabinet, and often transformed their committees into ministerial or party fiefdoms. The constant in-fighting between cabinet committees was a key motive behind Prime Minister Miller's decision to set up a single cabinet committee under the chairmanship of the finance minister.

IMPACT OF EUROPEANISATION

Institutional misfit

After Poland applied for EU membership in the early 1990s, the domestic party and state institutions began to come under increasing adaptational pressures, which culminated when accession negotiations commenced in March 1998. The key institutional misfit was that while during pre-accession the EU-related policy alignment required that public good policies be produced (maximising benefits to the electoral majority rather than the interests of individual voter constituencies), the party and state structures were in many cases poorly equipped to handle that process.

The assumption that domestic adaptation was a 'public good' policy rests on two observations (see Zubek 2005; 2008). First, Polish legislators were likely to expect the implementation of EU legislation to bring largely diffuse benefits. This was because the largest gain from domestic alignment – moving closer to EU membership – accrued to the government as a whole, regardless of whether a given executive or parliamentary legislator contributed or not. Perhaps more importantly, lacking experience in policy formulation, Polish decision-makers were uncertain about the precise benefit distribution of EU-related adaptation. In effect, they were likely to perceive it mainly through the lens of policy modernisation and EU accession. Even when they were able to identify concentrated private benefits, they expected such benefits to materialise only after enlargement.

The other observation is that domestic policy alignment required joint legislative action from most, if not all, Polish ministries and parliamentary committees. The collective production of legal adaptation was necessary because the Community's *acquis* contained several thousand legal measures that spanned almost the entire policy spectrum. The Polish ministries and parliamentary committees had to transpose more than two thousand directives covering various policy fields. More importantly, many of the Community measures dealt with horizontal, cross-cutting policy problems that required the collaboration of many different ministries and committees for full transposition.

The misfit with the domestic institutional configuration was most evident at the intra-coalition level. In 1998, the programmatic incohesiveness of the AWS-UW cabinet made it impossible for the coalition parties to develop a compromise policy on EU-related domestic alignment. Although both the Solidarity Electoral Action and the Freedom Union were committed to European integration in principle, major differences persisted at the level of practical policy choices. The AWS opted for gradual alignment sensitive to the interests of large state enterprises and lent a sympathetic ear to reports from socio-economic interests about difficulties in complying with EU requirements. The UW was much more euro-enthusiastic, advocating a much quicker alignment that would benefit the emerging small and medium-sized private sector. These major policy differences prevented the coalition parties from agreeing on a joint approach and undermined the political resolve of the government in that area. The policy conflict took on an institutional dimension when Prime Minister Buzek caved in to his party's pressure to appoint a eurosceptic member of the AWS to the position of chairman of the Committee for European Integration (KIE), a central body coordinating EU affairs within the executive. A full cabinet member, the KIE chair attempted to realise his ideal policy preferences in clear opposition to the standpoint of a more enthusiastic UW-nominated foreign minister. In effect, the Buzek cabinet quickly reached a point where progress in domestic alignment stalled due to the lack of inter-party control and coordination.

Besides party-based mechanisms, the internal coalition deadlock impinged on the functioning and development of state structures that could facilitate the production of 'public good' policies (Zubek 2005; 2008). Inside the executive, the standing of the key collectivity-enhancing mechanism – the KIE committee – was substantially downgraded. The KIE lost competence to process EU-related legislation, which was now to be routed through the standard interministerial channels instead. It met infrequently and was dominated by formal presentations of reports and documents rather than real decision making. Moreover, the KIE chair and his office (UKIE) failed to develop mechanisms for administering selective incentives and monitoring for line ministries. Other than a reactive EU compatibility assessment, the UKIE staff were rarely involved in policy-making at the operational level of inter-ministerial committees. Furthermore, legal alignment was not subject to monitoring procedures that could mobilise ministerial officials on a regular basis. The KIE chair also commanded a limited number of institutional levers to sanction noncompliance if adaptation delays were detected. Inside parliament, EU-related laws were processed according to the same procedure as domestic legislation, and the executive had very few instruments to prioritise the process. Nor did it have a monopoly on legislative initiative in EU adaptation, and in some cases it was parliament that initiated legal adaptation drafts. Last but not least, the deputies continued to enjoy far-reaching amending powers and frequently rewrote government bills to an extent that rendered them incompatible with the EU law.

EU pressures and domestic mobilisation

The institutional misfit between the challenges of Europeanisation and the domestic institutional set-up caused serious delays in Poland's alignment to EU requirements. In 1998-1999, the Polish government implemented on average only one in four of its adaptation commitments, while parliament often took up to two years to process EU-related legislation (see Buras & Cichocki 2000;

Zubek 2005). The evidence of major delays began to reach both the political elites and the general public already in late 1998. But it was the European Union that played a key role in forcing EU adaptation high on the agenda of the AWS-UW coalition. It did so by placing more emphasis on policy adaptation as a measure for assessing Poland's progress towards accession. The decisive moment came when, in April 1999, the European Commission clearly stated that unless Poland improved its adaptation record, it would not be admitted in the first round of enlargement. In response to these threats, the AWS-UW government first attempted to achieve progress through the existing framework, but soon realised that a major improvement would not be feasible without institutional change (Zubek 2005; 2008). From mid-1999 it began to introduce rules that would facilitate domestic adaptation. Such institution-building was by no means unproblematic because internal coalition disputes over which part of the Polish executive should coordinate EU adaptation militated against the development of stable and lasting institutions in the short term. In the event, the provisional cover was provided by the cabinet's parliamentary secretary in the Prime Minister's Office (KPRM), who harnessed his personal authority and organisational resources to facilitate the production of 'public good' policies.

From mid-2000, however, a series of quick reforms institutionalised a more stable set of state structures. The change was eased by an impending accession crisis that made the Freedom Union drop its objections to key KIE appointments. Over the next several months, the KIE and the UKIE were reorganised into effective mechanisms for administering incentives and monitoring inside the executive. The KIE committee was transformed into a dedicated cabinet committee to work on EU-related legislation. It started to meet every week and the prime minister chaired its sessions. The KIE was shadowed by ad hoc conferences at lower levels at which the UKIE staff played a key role. The KIE chair and its secretary closely monitored the legislative actions of the line ministers, and a comprehensive list of all outstanding commitments was reviewed at each KIE and cabinet session. Close monitoring was combined with strict enforcement by the prime minister and the KIE secretary. Finally, the UKIE's legal department facilitated the process of policy adaptation by extending substantive assistance to line departments. The UKIE lawyers became closely involved in developing alternative policy choices and guiding the transposition process in methodological terms.

A similar change occurred within parliament, where the executive exploited the newly emerging consensus among coalition parties to win new prerogatives in EU-related policy-making (cf. Jaskiernia 1999; Laskowska 2004). The executive was granted the right to submit 'omnibus' bills, thereby reducing the time required for parliamentary passage. A special European Law Committee was established in the Sejm for the exclusive purpose of dealing with transposing legislation, and the executive was granted a monopoly on legislative initiative in this committee. The deputies' rights to propose amendments were heavily constrained. It took as many as three deputies to submit an amendment in a committee, and the number was increased to five in plenary sessions. The executive also won strong representation within the committee. All its sessions were attended by a junior UKIE minister for legal adaptation, who was empowered to intervene whenever he thought that the committee ran the risk of adopting provisions incompatible with EU law. Finally, the new committee's bylaws provided for a reduction of most procedural time limits. For example, the second reading had to be held immediately at the next parliamentary session after the committee submitted its report.

Most of these institutional innovations were left intact under the next SLD-UP-PSL government headed by Prime Minister Leszek Miller. If anything, the core executive's grip on EU-related policy-making was tightened as the KIE secretary established strong institutional links with undersecretaries of state in line ministries, while the rolling catalogues of outstanding commitments became more and more detailed. In parliament, the passage of transposing legislation continued to benefit from special procedures. The institutional changes to state institutions proved fairly permanent. The enhanced position of the core executive was retained after Poland's accession, though Miller's attempts to further strengthen the executive failed. This said, the political cooperation unravelled quickly after accession. It is rather telling that one of the first decisions of Prime Minister Miller after EU accession had been assured was to eject the PSL from his governing coalition. Besides its mixed durability, the 'Europeanisation effect' proved rather limited in scope, affecting only those state structures that tackle EU legislation. The remainder of the executive and parliament were not affected. The centre of government continued to have a weak position, while the executive lacked the levers needed to gain the upper hand in parliament.

TOWARDS ENHANCED DEMOCRATIC GOVERNANCE?

This chapter has argued that the democratisation in Poland was inhibited by institutional incentives encouraging political actors to underproduce 'public good' policies. These opportunities have arisen from weak party political leadership; limited inter-party cooperation inside coalitions; an under-resourced centre of government; and parliamentary dominance over the executive in policy-making. What are the prospects for dealing with these problems? EU accession has contributed to enhancing democratic governance, but its overall impact has been limited. Perhaps a more transformative development has been the domestic crisis of governance in 2003-4, when the Polish media exposed an unprecedented series of corruption scandals (Krasnodebski 2003; Wnuk-Lipinski 2003; Staniszkis & Kutz 2004). These affairs featured bribery by Miller cabinet officials and members of parliament, legislative corruption, clientelistic party-business ties, and illegal party funding. The parliament set up two enquiry commissions, the first such move in Polish political history after 1989. Established consecutively in 2003 and 2004, the commissions subpoenaed political and business leaders who testified in publicly televised hearings.

The public exposure of serious irregularities within the Miller government led to the resignation of the prime minister and the collapse of the SLD-UP cabinet in May 2004. The SLD party split in mid-2004 and suffered a humiliating defeat in the 2005 parliamentary and presidential elections. The elections were won by two reformist right-wing parties – the Law and Justice Party (PiS) and the Civic Platform (PO). Both parties advocated radical changes to address democratisation deficits, including the overhaul of the constitutional system. The PiS pushed for a reinforced presidency, a new lustration law and tough anti-corruption measures. The PO wanted to switch from a proportional to a majoritarian electoral system to enhance government stability. Unfortunately, the PiS and the PO failed to form a coalition, not least because the presidential elections pitted the two parties against each other. In effect, the PiS decided to join forces with two small extremist parties. In the months after the elections this governing coalition turned out to be rather prone to internal crisis, which undermined its effectiveness. It thus remains to be seen if the 2003-4 governance crisis will indeed contribute to moving Poland farther away from post-communism.

References

Andeweg, R. 1997. 'Collegiality and Collectivity: Cabinets, Cabinet Committees and Cabinet Ministers'. In: P. Weller, H. Bakvis & R.A.W. Rhodes (eds.), *Hollow Crown; Countervailing Trends in Core Executives*. Macmillan Press.

Andeweg, R. 2000. 'Ministers as Double Agents? The Delegation Process Between Cabinets and Ministers', *European Journal of Political Research*, 37, 377-395.

Antoszewski 2002. 'Ewolucja polskiego systemu partyjnego'. In: Antoszewski (ed.), *Demokratyzacja w III Rzeczpospolitej*. Wroclaw: Wydawnictwo Uniwersytetu Wroclawskiego.

Baylis, T.A. 1989. *Governing by Committee: Collegial Leadership in Advanced Societies*. New York: State University of New York Press.

Buras, P. & M.A. Cichocki 2000. *Harmonizacja polskiego prawa z prawem UE a sytuacja polityczna rzadu po powolaniu rządu mniejszosciowego*. Warsaw: Centre for International Relations.

Cox, G.W. & M.D. McCubbins 1993. *Legislative Leviathan. Party Government in the House*. Berkeley: University of California Press.

Dimitrov, V.T., K.H. Goetz & H. Wollmann 2006. *Governing After Communism: Institutions and Policy-making*. Lanham: Rowman and Littlefield.

Döring, H. 1995. *Parliaments and Majority Rule in Western Europe*. Mannheim: Mannheim Centre for European Social Research.

Döring, H. & M. Hallerberg (eds.) 2004. *Patterns of Parliamentary Behavior: Passage of Legislation Across Western Europe*. London: Ashgate.

Gadomski, W. 2000. *Smialy slaby rzad*. Gazeta Wyborcza, 135, 10-11 June 2000.

Gluchowski, J. 1997. *Uchwalanie budzetu panstwa*. Warszawa: Wydawnictwo Sejmowe.

Gluchowski, J. 2001. *Budżet i procedura budzetowa*. Warszawa: Wydawnictwo Sejmowe.

Goetz, K.H. & R. Zubek (2007) 'Government, Parliament and Lawmaking in Poland', *Journal of Legislative Studies*, vol. 13, no. 4, pp. 517-538.

Grzymala-Busse, A. 2003. 'Political Competition and the Politicization of the State in East Central Europe', *Comparative Political Studies*, 36, 10, 1123-1147.

Hausner, J., M. Marody, J. Szlachta, J. Wilkin, A. Wojtyna & M. Zirk-Sadowski 2000. *The Quality of Governannce: Poland Closer to the European Union?* Warsaw: Friedrich Ebert Foundation.

Jaskiemia, J. 1999. 'Badanie zgodności ustaw z prawem Unii Europejskiej w sejmowym postępowaniu ustawodawczum', *Państwo i Prawo*, 7, 19-33, Polska Akademia Nauk, Komitet Nauk Prawnych.

Jednaka, W. 2004. *Gabinety koalicyjne w III RP*. Wroclaw: Wydawnictwo Uniwersytetu Wroclawskiego.

Kosinski, E. 2001. *Procedura budzetowa a deficyt: zagadnienia prawne na tle porownawczym*. Warszawa: Wydawnictwo Sejmowe.

Krasnodebski, Z. 2003. *Demokracja peryferii*. Warszawa: slowo/obraz terytoria.

Kubuj, K. 2004. 'Rola Marszalka Sejmu w postepowaniu ustawodawczym', *Przeglad Legislacyjny*, 42, 12-35.

Kudej, M. 2002. *Postępowanie ustawodawcze w Sejmie RP*. Warszawa: Wydawnictwo Sejmowe.

Laskowska, M. 2004. 'Procedura dostosowywania ustawodawstwa polskiego do prawa Unii Europejskiej', *Przeglad Legislacyjny*, 11, 1, 41.

Lipski, J. 2004. *Analiza ilościowa projektów wniesionych do Sejmu IV kadencji w toku pierwszych dwóch lat jego działalności*, Raport nr. 221, Kancelaria Sejmu, Biuro Studiów i Ekspertyz.

Lukaszewicz, A. 2004. *Gorliwe psucie prawa*. Warszwa: Rzeczpospolita.

Majewski, M. & P. Reszka 2002. *Wojna o biopaliwa, czyli lobbing po polsku*. Warszwa: Rzeczpospolita.

Markowski & Czesnik 2002. 'System partyjny po wyborach 2001 roku', *Studia Polityczne*, 13.

Meyer-Sahling, Jan-Hinrik 2004. 'Civil Service Reform in Post-Communist Europe: The Bumpy Road to Depolitisation', *West European Politics*, 27, 1, 71-103.

Muller, W.C. & K. Strom 2000. *Coalition Governments in Western Europe*. Oxford: Oxford University Press.

Nunberg, B. 1998. 'Breaking Administrative Deadlock in Poland: Internal Obstacles and External Incentives'. In: B. Nunberg, L. Barbone & H.-U. Derlien (eds.), *The State After Communism: Administrative Transitions in Central and Eastern Europe*. Washington, D.C.: The World Bank.

Nunberg, B. 1999. *Public Administration Development in the EU Accession Context*, internal document. Washington, D.C.: The World Bank.

Osiecka-Chojnacka, J. 2004. *Analiza ilosciowa prac komisji sejmowych nad projektami ustaw wniesionymi do Sejmu IV kadencji w latach 2001-2003*, Raport no. 222, Kancelaria Sejmu, Biuro Studiow i Ekspertyz, Warszawa.

Paradowska, J. 1998. 'Mily premier, slaby rzad', *Polityka*, 17.

Paradowska, J. 1999. 'Sila odpychania: rozmowa z Waldemarem Kuczynskim, doradca premiera ds. gospodarczych', *Polityka*, 42.

Paradowska, J. & J. Baczynski 2004. 'Wyborcy bez wyboru', *Polityka*, 17.

Paszkiewicz, K.A. 2000. *Partie i koalicje polityczne III Rzeczpospolitej*. Wroclaw: Wydawnictwo Uniwersytetu Wroclawskiego.

Raciborski, J. 2001. 'Tajemnica sukcesu SLD', *Rzeczpospolita*, 82.

Raciborski, J. 2002. 'Widmo partyjnego panstwa', *Rzeczpospolita*, 95.

Rokita, J.M. 1998. 'Batalia o rzad, w Nelicki, A.', *O Naprawe Rzeczpospolitej*. Krakow: Platan/Instytu Spraw Publicznych.

Rydlewski, G. 2000. *Rzadzenie koalicyjne w Polsce*. Warsaw: Elipsa.

Rydlewski, G. 2002. *Rzadowy system decyzyjny w Polsce: studium politologiczne okresu transformacji*. Warsaw: Elipsa.

Sejm 2004. 'Raport komisji śledczej do zbadania ujawnionych w mediach zarzutów dotyczących przypadków korupcji podczas prac nad nowelizacją ustawy o radiofonii i telewizji', przyjęty przez Sejm RP w dniu 28 maja 2004, Warszawa.

Solecka, M. 2003. 'Grupa trzymajaca fundusz', *Rzeczpospolita*, 26 May 2003.

Staniszkis, J. 1992. *The Dynamics of Breakthrough in Eastern Europe*. Berkeley: University of California Press.

Staniszkis, J. 2000. 'The Post-Communist State: In Search of a Paradigm', *Polish Sociological Review*, 2, 193-214.

Staniszkis, J. 2001. *Post-komunism proba opisu*. Gdansk: slowo/obraz terytoria.

Staniszkis, J. & K. Kutz 2004. *To nie to... nie tak mialo być: Jadwiga Staniszkis i Kazimierz Kutz w rozmowie z Jerzym S. Macem*. Warszawa: Dom Wydawniczy Ergo.

Szczerbiak, A. 1999. 'Interests and Values: Polish Parties and their Electorates', *Europe-Asia Studies*, 51, 8, 1401-1432.

Szczerbiak, A. 2001. 'Party Structure and Organizational Development in Post-communist Poland', *Journal of Communist Studies and Transition Politics*, 17, 2, 94-130.

Thies, M.F. 2001. 'Keeping Tabs on Partners: The Logic of Delegation in Coalition Governments', *American Journal of Political Science*, 45, 3, 580-598.

Wiatr, J.J. 2003. 'Narodziny i przemiany systemu wielopartyjnego'. In: J.J. Wiatr, J. Raciborski, J. Bartkowski, B. Fratczak-Rudnicka & J. Kilias (eds.), *Demokracja Polska 1989-2003*. Warsaw: Scholar.

Wnuk-Lipinski, E. 2003. *Granice wolnosci: pamietnik polskiej transformacji*. Warszawa: Scholar.

Zubek, R. 2001. 'A Core in Check: The Transformation of the Polish Core Executive', *Journal of European Public Policy*, 8, 5.

Zubek, R. 2005. 'Complying with Transposition Commitments in Poland: Collective Dilemmas, Core Executive and Legislative Outcomes', *West European Politics*, 28, 3.

Zubek, R. 2006. 'Poland: A Core Ascendant?' In: V.T. Dimitrov, K.H. Goetz & H. Wollmann (eds.), *Governing After Communism: Institutions and Policymaking*. Lanham: Rowman and Littlefield.

Zubek, R. 2008. *Core Executive and Europeanization in Central Europe*. Basingstoke: Palgrave Macmillan.

CHAPTER 8

Keys to transition and paths leading beyond

Lars Johannsen and Karin Hilmer Pedersen

The preceding chapters reflect a microcosm of post-communism in a collection covering countries from within and outside the former Soviet Union, Slovenia representing a Yugoslav variant. Politically, the selection spans authoritarianism or, at best, defective democracy, and more or less consolidated democracies with minor deficiencies. Economically, there is variation not only in economic wealth but also in economic reform models. Institutionally, statebuilding processes vary a great deal between countries that have had to build modern states and new institutions to suit their newly won independence, and countries facing the challenge of reforming a communist state apparatus because of their heritage. On the ethnic dimension some of the countries belong to the nation-state category, whereas others more or less successfully strive to build a nation or political community on a foundation of ethnic heterogeneity. Finally, in the international arena some of our countries have close connections to the European Union, while others manoeuvre between the two global powers, Russia and the USA. More than that, all these tasks have been carried out simultaneously but, admittedly, with varying levels of attention and choices by policymakers.

As discussed in chapter 1, our case selection underscores the striking variance in the post-communist world, both with respect to initial inherited conditions and the outcomes of the processes unleashed by the implosion of communism within each country. To critics eager to point out that we are comparing the incomparable and that prudent methodological considerations require 'that differences be joined with similarities; otherwise, too much is in motion to trace relationships and to draw meaningful conclusions' (Bunce, 1995;119), we say: granted, our unit of investigation may initially be based on the political and economic development in individual countries, but we are comparing along the parameters of the quadruple challenge given the international context, searching for patterns or paths of transition. If we picture each case study as a square chocolate bar, the contributors have identified the type and flavour of each bar, while our task is to break up each bar along the prepressed lines, forming a puzzle we can then use to make new brands.

In the final part of this chapter we will argue that a fruitful new 'brand' is *political stabilisation,* understood as a combination of *consensus* and *inclusion.* Consensus is about the direction of policy and institutions, while inclusion relates to the extent to which different interests are included in policy decision making. The concept of *political stabilisation* takes us back to classical insights formulated by Huntington (1968) and Lijphart (1977). These insights, in turn, can revitalise the more recent debate over consolidation.

Before turning to *political stabilisation,* however, we discuss the core aspects of the cases under scrutiny. We assign a 'key' to each case, attempting to draw meaningful conclusions from the case studies, and thus, to follow a strategy of comparable cases consisting of parameters that, when combined, reveal the paths that lead beyond transition.

A POCKETFUL OF KEYS

The following discussion of the core aspects of the political and economic transformations and the challenges of building nations and developing modern states is not one we have asked the individual authors to carry out. As a first step we boiled down the discussion of each contributor to a number of keywords describing each of the four transitions. As a second step we assigned a 'key' to each case. We believe these 'keys' are central to understanding each case as reflected in our headlines.

Coping with heterogeneity: Kazakhstan

Political developments in Kazakhstan are shaped by the heterogeneous character of the country, in which both multi-ethnic and sub-ethnic elites have played essential roles. When it gained independence Kazakhstan was a multiethnic state in which the titular nationality accounted for less than half the citizens. Moreover, the Kazakhs themselves are traditionally divided into three groupings known as hordes. However, a horde does not necessarily control the territory ruled by the khan, a fact that rendered internal command weak and ineffective. The heterogeneity of Kazakhstan has been exacerbated by economic differences. While the northern parts remain economically integrated into the Russian economy, the southern and eastern parts are still predominantly rural, effectively making for a decentralised and poorly integrated economy.

In constituting a Kazakh state, this setting of heterogeneity has been a great challenge. When Nazarbaev transformed himself from First Secretary of the Communist Party into president of independent Kazakhstan in 1991 (first elected president by the Supreme Soviet in 1990), he solved this challenge by manoeuvring carefully between the different groups. First a unitary state was established in order to retain control over the territory and reject secessionist claims by the Russian population, which by then was almost in the majority.

Deprived of a ready-made identity that would have provided legitimacy for the newborn state, this choice is quite remarkable as a federate structure would have accommodated the Russians, who instead responded in kind by emigrating on a massive scale. The result was that ethnic Kazakhs gained the numerical upper hand, and as a concession to the Russians, who were now clearly in the minority, the Russian language was accorded the status of an official language in the 1995 constitution. Second, Nazarbaev consolidated his authoritarian rule in Kazakhstan by striking a delicate balance of power between the numerous clans and groups through clientelistic networks and careful division of power in politics, the economy and the state apparatus. His grip on power did not go unchallenged, but was furthered by orchestrated elections, constitutional engineering, regime repression and laws limiting opposition activities as well as monopolisation of the state media.

Nazarbaev's authoritarian rule was facilitated by vast natural resources. Increasing revenues accruing from foreign direct investments and trade with natural resources aggravated corrupt practices. However, increased international attention served to minimise the problem in two ways. First, Kazakh dependence on natural resources and contact with international actors made inclusion in the global economy mandatory and facilitated the development of pockets of reliable business infrastructure, most notably in banking and foreign investment. However, this was only a partial success as it was accompanied by an informal sector in which the rules of the game are not the same for all participants. Second, international influence is evident in the Kazakhi attempts to build a state apparatus on meritocratic principles even though personal loyalties continued to be decisive.

By coping with heterogeneous elites a foundation was established for Nazarbaev's increasing power, which by 2007 became de facto authoritarian. At the same time, Nazarbaev has managed to construct a political system that functions on dual principles that in the long term may prove to be unstable once he has to resign the presidency.

Flexible clientelism or 'Absurdity Fair': Georgia

The background for the Georgian 'Absurdity Fair' was the chaos unleashed by secessionism, derailed economic and political reforms, and the erratic rule of the first post-communist president, *Zviad Gamsakhurdia*. This led to a coup d'etat in late 1991 and the return of the former Minister of Foreign Affairs in the USSR, Eduard Shevardnadze, as the leader of Georgia in early 1992. Gradually some order was built up in which the incumbent elite was able to reproduce and then use its hold on power to exploit the spoils of half-baked reforms through clientelism and flexibility. But Georgian developments in no way resembled the clientelism and flexibility we know from the literature on predatory states. The Georgian version of clientelism and flexibility degenerated into an absurdity where rules were made only to be broken, thereby tightening control over people through mutual understanding in the form of *kompromats*. Compared to Georgia, the traditional forms of predatory regimes seem quite structured and well organised. But it was by setting up this *Absurdity Fair* that Shevardnadze co-opted and balanced different groups against each other.

Nation building was a bone of contention from the outset, causing two secessionist wars. Never really working to solve this issue, Shevardnadze instead chose to instil strong nationalist feelings among ethnic elites. Moreover, in order to avoid new ethnic conflicts Shevardnadze accepted that tolls collected on the border with Turkey and oil transit revenues from the port of Batumi were kept by the autonomous region of Adjara, thus adding to the absurdity. In contrast to nation building, the Georgian statebuilding process was marked by clientelist networks using corruption as a means to impose discipline on subordinate agents in the state and local administrations. Thus, the Georgian *Absurdity Fair* was an administrative state upheld through mutual agreement to be entitled to bribes from the public at all levels.

The *Absurdity Fair* was exacerbated by incomplete political and economic reforms. The political system landed somewhere between democracy and authoritarian rule, and Shevardnadze groomed the Civic Union to become the organisational vehicle and elite hub. Thus, until 2001 the executive consisted not of party members but of representatives of rival personal networks carefully balanced by the core elite. Elections were held, but they were never free and fair. Moreover, it was a system without a distinct leading political ideology or mission. It was merely an authoritarian system built on the desire to live off the spoils wherever and however they could be found. In the economic system market reforms ground to a halt on the core issue of ownership transformation. Thus, the extensive system of state-owned industry prolonged elite control over resources and distribution. Access to and control over resources together with generous inputs of foreign aid further fuelled the fire. Consequently, after 1995, when Georgia's relations with the international community began to calm down and privatisation schemes were forced through in 2003, Shevardnadze was unable to retain the loyalty of his numerous clients and his regime broke down during the Rose Revolution in 2005.

The tutelary elite (or a 'dual' society): Estonia

In Estonia a strong consensus among the titular nationality to negate Soviet rule and secure independence, market economy and democracy served to create a tutelary elite. The concept of a 'tutelary elite' highlights the elite's capacity and willingness to make longstanding and comprehensive reform policies, focusing on what they perceived to be the long-term interests of society, albeit with limited inclusion of not only the Russian minority but the population at large, thus forming a strongly divided 'dual' society.

A tutelary elite as a key to understanding Estonian developments was especially evident in the nationbuilding process. The need to rebuild the nation and secure independence after the Soviet occupation during World War II strengthened an elite consensus to refrain from granting citizenship to Soviet-era immigrants and their descendants – that is, primarily Russians. This step effectively barred a sizeable part of the population from political influence, which may or may not have politicised the elite's reform goals. A consequence of the nationbuilding policy towards ethnic Russians was that the sole official language in the state apparatus was to be Estonian. This decision had an immense impact on state building. The majority of public servants were used to Russian as the official language, and many had never learned Estonian. These people were summarily dismissed and younger Estonian personnel were employed, people who either had an education from abroad or were eager to seek out qualifications and alternative models through assistance programmes from the EU and the US.

From the very beginning of the transition period, the renewed state administration diligently oversaw the implementation of the tutelary elite's imperatives in economic policies. Following a strategy of extreme liberalism, a flat-rate tax system and an independent new currency were introduced as early as 1992. There was also early implementation of large-scale privatisation, housing privatisation and restitution, as well as trade liberalisation based on low import and export taxes. Although these policies strictly adhered to neo-liberal recommendations, they did impose heavy economic burdens on parts of the population.

With respect to political developments, elite consensus contributed to an emerging cartelisation among the multiple political parties, which narrowed competition and favoured older and larger parties over newcomers. The tutelary character of the Estonian elites was especially evident in the fact that although governments frequently changed, confirming that multi-party systems such as that of Estonia are often associated with cabinet instability, a change of government in reality had few consequences. So even though the population was increasingly divided with respect to living standards, there were never any real political conflicts over economic policy.

Working corporatism – reinforced consensus: Slovenia

Understanding Slovenian polity and politics requires a careful look into the specifics of Slovenian history and how it has shaped the interests of a small nation determined to unite all aspects of society into consensual policy making. The key to understanding Slovenian history is the many centuries of foreign domination, supplemented by more recent experiences with Tito's Yugoslavia, where self-management and inclusion of vital interests were the main organising principles of the ruling Communist Party in its attempts to maintain order within a heterogeneous nation. Although the corporatist character of Tito's regime was largely formal and it remains a question just how much real influence other interests had, it seems that the successor regime is based on de facto *working corporatism*. Moreover, in terms of nation building the main lesson of Slovenian history has been the survival of a small ethnically homogeneous population. Slovenia has therefore avoided the challenge of the fourth transition.

The domination of the corporatist idea in Slovenia means that various sectors of society are well represented in the political system, the economy and the state administration. With respect to the political system inclusiveness was written into the Constitution, which calls for a bicameral system consisting of an upper chamber, the National Council, which reflects the structural composition of Slovenian society by including representatives of collective functional interests, i.e. economic interests (labour, industry, farmers, etc.), the professions (higher and lower education, culture, sports, etc.) and the regions. Although the National Council is only accorded an advisory role, giving the first chamber, the parliament, the decisive role in determining Slovenian politics, it nevertheless controls a strand of policy direction, and the council has used its veto power.

Inclusiveness in the Slovenian political system is evident in the almost fifteen years of domination by a centre-left government in which the reformed socialist party, the Liberal Democratic Party, served as the backbone. The survival of the elite of the old system together with the principle of including social interests via the National Council has delayed some economic reforms. Despite considerable economic success in achieving one of the highest GDPs per capita in the region, Slovenia has maintained a high level of taxation and strong state interests in the economy, paving the way for clientelism and corruption, but has nevertheless kept a tolerable level in comparison with other post communist countries.

The policy of inclusiveness inherent in the term *working corporatism* is also evident in the extensive use of tripartite negotiations that determine socio-economic policy directions. However, the Slovenian process of state building suffers from a lack of capacity to make in-depth changes in the administration, especially in terms of effectuating decentralisation and regional self-management.

Contested consensus: The Czech Republic

The key factors in understanding political developments in the Czech Republic concentrate on a fragmented political party system in combination with a lack of cross-party consensus. Taken together, these two factors constitute a key that we have labelled *contested consensus*, a label which, although a contradiction in terms, describes Czech politics in the quadruple transition.

In terms of nation building, the Czech Republic was constituted after the *velvet divorce* from Slovakia in 1992. The relatively homogeneous population furthered the Constitutional choice to institute 'citizenship' rights and not ethnicity or nationality as the tenets of citizenship. While this choice formally put an end to the question of nation building, the small Republican Party managed until 2001 to pander to racist and xenophobic feelings towards minorities such as the Roma, as well as to anti-German sentiments. Thus, while the Czech Republic has had no serious problems regarding nation building, the issue has not been undisputed and unchallenged.

Contested consensus is also seen in the functioning of the political system. First, the Constitution – in part because of federal conservatism – called for a bicameral system. However, the Senate was not assembled until 1996 because of resistance by Prime Minister Václav Klaus. Second, the largely unreconstructed successor to the ruling party of the communist era, The Communist Party of Bohemia and Moravia (KSČM), has continued to play a prominent role. Winning from 26 per cent of the vote in 1996 to 12 per cent in 2006 and deemed unfit as a coalition partner, the party's position in parliament has compelled parties to form odd coalitions.

In the economic sphere Václav Klaus' reforms are known as *unbridged capitalism*. His neo-liberal approach was never uncontested, however. First, despite the rhetoric real privatisation was never actually realised, and the economic market therefore did not become efficient. Second, although voucher privatisation created many individual shareholders, the economic crises of the mid-1990s eradicated the positive effect. And finally, when the Social Democratic Party entered government in 1998 their majority was ensured only by an 'opposition agreement' with Václav Klaus's party, keeping them from making substantial changes in the direction of economic policy.

The international arena has played a significant role in Czech developments. But once again, even though membership of NATO and the EU were officially the most salient foreign policy goals, they were pursued in an unpredictable manner. This was in particular evident in Klaus's politics regarding EU accession, in which he held that the EU should invite the Czech Republic to become a full member, not the other way around. Consequently, the Czech Republic did not apply for EU membership until 1995, when it finally dawned on Klaus that this was how the game had to be played.

Reluctance with regard to EU membership also played a role in matters of state building. First, when dismantling the former federalist structure with Slovakia the focus was on creating a centralised state administration. This policy directly rejected the EU requirements for regional decentralisation. Second, in contravention of EU requirements civil society organisations were deliberately not included in policy making or deliberation – as seen by the merely formal dialogue with business and labour organisations in tripartite committees.

Institutional reform as policy response: Poland

Blessed with a largely homogeneous population, the question of nation build-ing never really became an issue in the Polish transition. Nor did anyone on the political scene feel called upon to ask questions about the Polish diaspora living in bordering countries. However, a consensus was never really reached on the direction of policies. Instead the rule of the game became an ongoing search for new institutional arrangements in response to persistent problems.

First, the institutional response was characteristic of the way the new politi-cal system was formed. While it took its point of departure in the negotiations between Solidarity and the Communist Party in 1989, paving the way for a specific institutional agreement that distributed parliamentary seats such that a fixed number of seats was reserved for the Communist Party, it resulted in an interim 'Small Constitution' agreed upon in 1992 that had to be amended in 1997 following a new political constellation in parliament.

Second, the ongoing institutional responses were made to solve problems at hand, improving the capacity of Polish governments to make political deci-sions. Three factors were at play. First, the long shadow of the communist past made ideological criteria more salient than party programmes based on socio-economic policies. Second, a proportional electoral system made coali-tion governments imperative and required institutional arrangements such as coalition agreements and complex checks and balances systems between ministers and vice-ministers. This, however, was complicated by the first fac-tor and intensified by weak party leadership, despite numerous attempts to centralise intra-party power. A third factor was that in terms of agenda-setting power the executive was quite weak in relation to parliament.

Third, in the economic sphere Poland is often referred to as *the* example of a post-communist transition where radical liberal market reforms were intro-duced early in 1989-1991 by a strongly autocratic, autonomous and internally very coherent 'change team' that was relatively insulated from social actors and made extensive use of foreign expertise. This change team took advantage of the 'window of opportunity', the time of 'extraordinary politics' characterised by the absence of political parties and nearly unequivocal public support for political and economic reforms (Balcerowicz 1992). Although Poland was con-sidered the frontrunner in market reform, it had been lagging behind in actual privatisation of major industrial assets. This delayed privatisation afforded the elite ample opportunities to play a 'two-level' game, switching between the political and economic arenas depending on which was the most profitable at the time. This elite instability has contributed to an already fragmented party system in which parties have often been led by 'party owners' with little or no substantial link to their constituencies.

The continuous institutional reform needed to modernise and democratise Poland was pushed by European Union conditionality. In late 1999, the Euro-

pean Commission stated that if Poland did not transpose EU-related legislation at a greater pace, it would be barred from participating in the first round
of enlargement. No consensus existed in any policy area other than Polish
EU membership. Thus, an improved adaptation record and the concomitant
institutional reform were completed. This international context supported and
secured the changes in institutional arrangements necessary to improve decision-making capacity and create a more effective market economy, and it was
all accomplished primarily by enhancing the powers vested in a core executive.

COMBINING ELITE KEYS TO UNDERSTANDING
TRANSITIONS – CONSENSUS AND INCLUSIVENESS

Having chosen to maximise variation, it is obvious that the issue is not whether
there are differences but rather what precisely the differences are and how
simplifying assumptions about elite characteristics can improve our understanding of the dynamics of transition processes. Turning to the outcome in
terms of political development, our cases vary from countries that have actually
turned away from a clear path to democratisation, and others who – partly
due to EU membership – have upheld the virtues of democratic institutions.
Thus, when looking at political developments we find the expected variation in
the dependent variable. However, a more fruitful concept when discussing the
final target for elite choices in the quadruple transition that post-communist
countries have faced is *political stabilisation*.

The choice of political stabilisation as the dependent variable is based on
insights from the contributions of two prominent researchers to democracy
and democratisation literature. First, Samuel Huntington (1968) contends that
when it comes to political development, the essence is found in the concrete
outcome of *order* defined as the relation between the development of political
institutions and the mobilisation of social forces into politics. Second, Arend
Lijphart (1977) argues that when it comes to pluralistic societies and democratic
regimes, it is essential to look not only at the achievements of democratic government but also at its maintenance. These two insights prompt us to look not
at political development in terms of democratisation, but to establish a typol-
ogy that can help demonstrate how elite choices lead to more or less stabilised
political systems that are either authoritarian or democratic. We suggest that a
common denominator crucial to regime stability is the character of consensus
among elites and the degree of inclusion of interests in society. To paraphrase
Huntington, the important distinction among countries is not their form *but
their degree of consensus and inclusion*,[1] because those are two dimensions

---

1 "The most important political distinction among countries concerns not their form of
   government but their degree of government." (Huntington, 1968; 1).

required to *stabilise* a political system. Consequently, the more the elite contest the end goal of political decisions and the less different societal interests are included in political decision making, the more fragile the political system. That is not to say that democratic states may turn to authoritarianism. It is to posit that if there is insufficient consensus on the end goals and if different interests find themselves excluded, democratic states will be fragile in terms of future policy direction. Thus, consensus and inclusion also add depth to the story of state capacity and how capable states have been in meeting the quadruple challenge of transition. Before elaborating on this with respect to the six cases in this book, we briefly define our two dimensions.

Consensus describes a commonly shared agreement among the elites about where the road of the transition ends. This consensus can assume many different forms. Consensus in Estonia, for example, is closely connected to a rejection of the Soviet past and a clear and coherent foreign policy goal leading towards NATO and EU membership; while in Kazakhstan consensus mainly concerns economic and administrative reforms that can attract the foreign direct investments required to extract natural resources.

Inclusion means the extent to which different elites and/or the population at large are included in deciding policy and how to reach common goals. Like *consensus, inclusion* can take different forms. It is important that inclusion in our terms does not necessarily refer to electoral participation. Electoral participation may lead to inclusion, but can also reflect regimented voting by force or habit. In our case selection Slovenia is at the one extreme, with a reinforced working corporatism in which virtually all interests can have a say at different points; and Georgia is at the other extreme, where a true *Absurdity Fair* has barred elite oppositions as well as the population from participating in actual decision making.

Figure 1 illustrates how we would place our six cases on the two dimensions. The expected variation is obvious, but it does not follow a variation we would expect if we only looked at political development. Slovenia, Estonia and Georgia are located in three different 'extreme' corners, whereas Poland, the Czech Republic and Kazakhstan show mixed characteristics.

Starting with Georgia, the transition away from a Soviet system has resulted in the least stabilised political system among our cases. *Absurdity Fair* as the key is manifest in two ways. First, fundamental questions of political direction – even ongoing border disputes and ethnic unrest – are still contested; and second, political decisions have been evaded by playing different actors off against each other, creating a system devoid of inclusiveness. Although the 2005 Rose Revolution has given new hope for stabilisation, it fails to demonstrate whether and how the new regime will manage to dismantle *Absurdity Fair* and thus set a new course towards more consensus and inclusiveness. The war with Russia in August 2008 and the two ethnic

FIGURE 1: COMBINING CONSENSUS AND INCLUSION

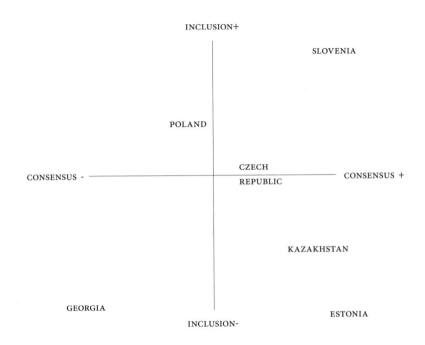

provinces' demands for independence clearly call political stabilisation into question.

At the diametrically opposite point of our figure we find Slovenia, perhaps the best stabilised political system. Although Ernst B. Hass did not have Slovenia in mind when he described the 'typical democracy', the Slovenian choices do in fact resemble his description: 'the continuous participation of *all major voluntary groups* in European society through elaborate systems of committees and councils. … Permanent negotiation and occasional conciliation tend to replace active confrontation, doctrinaire discussion and class warfare' (Haas, 1964; 68, 70. Italics as in Lijphart, 1977; 106-107). Thus, because of its *working corporatism* Slovenia shows a profound consensus on the policy direction of the country, in part due to an extreme level of inclusion of all societal interests through corporate institutions, making for a very stable system.

Conversely, we find Estonia to the lower right. Despite scoring high on the Freedom House index of democracies and the fact that the Estonian elite is characterised by a high degree of consensus about the goals of society, Estonian society is essentially more fragile. Estonians vote in regular elections but are otherwise not included. The high level of consensus among the elite has been used in a tutelary way, and was thus achieved at the expense not only of an excluded Russian minority, but also following the exclusion of a large segment of the population who do not feel that their interests are being looked after. It is exactly the character of the Estonian elite as *tutelary* and the *dual society* it created that brings in a destabilising element and a characterisation of Estonia as a democracy with deficiencies. In terms of stability, the challenge facing the democratic regime in Estonia is inclusion to broaden the base of democracy.

Turning to the mixed countries, Kazakhstan stands out as potentially more stable than the other two simply because it has not taken a path to democracy but has reinstated authoritarianism instead. Moreover, Kazakh authoritarianism is built on skilful *management of its heterogeneous population*. This process has required a high level of consensus among the elites and a good deal of inclusiveness. The potential threat to stability comes from the fact that consensus is essentially only about the reforms required to extract natural resources to pay off various loyal social interest groups, thus establishing a form of legitimacy of the system. Kazakhstan is therefore seen as more inclusive than both Georgia and Estonia, which is a stabilising factor. Being non-democratic, however, the lack of inclusion of all interests constitutes a potentially destabilising factor. Kazakhstan may be capable of controlling its economic transition and building a nation and state, but unfortunately this may be at the cost of democracy.

In Poland and the Czech Republic political stability is questionable on two grounds. In Poland continuous *institutional reforms* resulted in very little consensus among the elite and poor inclusiveness of different societal interests. Poland is therefore less stable than it ought to be, and politically it is not a completely reliable partner in the international context. The recent Polish attempts to achieve opt-outs in connection with the Lisbon Treaty of the European Union are very illustrative in terms of how the Polish elite contests agreed institutional choices and tries to renegotiate whenever a new political problem crops up. In the Czech Republic it is *contested consensus* that makes the country fragile. Although there is some level of elite consensus about the political direction in terms of institutions and economic policy, this consensus is not uncontested, in part because of the relative exclusiveness of the Czech system expressed by a semi-loyal opposition that leans on the unreformed Communist Party of Bohemia and Moravia. Thus, as Linz (1978) makes clear in his analysis of democratic breakdown, semi-loyal oppositions may endanger stability if they are attracted to anti-system parties. Worse than this, however, not having 'Koalitionsfähigkeit' makes it difficult to form governments, potentially making governance unstable.

Consensus and inclusiveness shed new light on the developmental paths taken by various countries after communism. It helps us understand how these countries cope with the challenges and how they manage the massive transition in all aspects of their societies: a transition that redefines the position of every citizen, from work identities to understanding one's own role within the political system; a transition that redefines who the 'others' are by creating new friends and foes in the international arena; and not least a transition that redistributes wealth. Huntington (1968) saw that modernisation created new identities and unleashed political mobility and participation which, if unchecked, would lead to instability. We suggest that the quadruple challenge does the same in the post-communist countries. Consequently, if the elites try to handle this challenge without consensus and inclusion, these countries risk being unable to steer through and beyond transition.

References

Bunce, V. (1995). 'Should Transitologists Be Grounded?', *Slavic Review*, Vol. 54, No. 1, pp. 111-127.

Haas, E.B. (1964). 'Technocracy, Pluralism and the New Europe'. In Stephen R. Graubard (ed). *A New Europe?* Boston: Houghton Mifflin.

Huntington, S.P. (1968). *Political Order in Changing Societies*, Yale University Press, New Haven and London.

Lijpart, A. (1977). *Democracy in Plural Societies. A Comparative Exploration*, Yale University Press, New Haven and London.

Biographies

SALLY N. CUMMINGS teaches in the School of International Relations, University of St Andrews, UK. Her research interests in Central Asia date from 1992, and have included several years of residence in the region. She researches topics related to political science, political communication, culture and identity. Her book publications include: *Kazakhstan: Power and the Elite* (IB Tauris 2005); *Oil, Transition and Security in Central Asia* (London and New York: Routledge, 2003); *Power and Change in Central Asia* (author and editor, London and New York: Routledge, 2002); *Kosovo: Perceptions of War and its Aftermath* (co-editor, London and New York: Continuum, 2001); and *Kazakhstan: Centre-Periphery Relations* (Washington, DC: Brookings Institution and London: Royal Institute of International Affairs, 2000). Contact information: snc@st-andrews.ac.uk, School of International Relations, University of St Andrews, UK KY16 9AX.

NINA DADALAURI is a PhD student at the Department of Political Science, Aarhus University, Denmark. Her publications include: 'Transnationalization and Georgian State: Myth or reality?' forthcoming in *The transnationalization of states, economies, and civil societies: The new challenges for governance in Europe,* edited by Laszlo Burst and Ronald Holzhacker; and 'Political Corruption in Georgia' pp. 155-167, in *Corruption and Development: The Anti-Corruption Campaigns,* edited by Sarah Bracking (2007), London: Palgrave Macmillan. Contact information: dadalauri@ps.au.dk, Department of Political Science, Aarhus University, Bartholin Allé, DK-8000 Aarhus C, Denmark.

RICK FAWN is a Senior Lecturer in International Relations at the University of St Andrews. He has published several books, including *Globalising the Regional, Regionalising the Global* (as editor, Cambridge University Press, 2009); *The Iraq War: Causes and Consequences* (as co-editor, Lynne Rienner Publishers, 2006); *The Czech Republic: A Nation of Velvet* (as author, Routledge, 2000); and numerous book chapters and journal articles, some of which have appeared recently in such journals as *Cambridge Review of International Affairs, Communist and Post-Communist Studies, Europe-Asia Studies,* and *International Affairs.* Contact information: rick.fawn@st-andrews.ac.uk, School of International Relations, University of St Andrews, St Andrews, UK.

MIRO HAČEK is an Associate Professor at the Faculty of Social Sciences, University of Ljubljana. His recent publications include *Upravljavska sposobnost in koalicijsko povezovanje v slovenskih občinah* (Administrative capacity and coalition building in Slovenian municipalities), FSS Publishing House, Ljubljana (2008), co-authored with Marjan Brezovšek and Irena Bačlija; *Organizacija oblasti v Sloveniji* (Organisation of government in Slovenia), FSS Publishing House, Ljubljana (2008), co-authored with Marjan Brezovšek and Milan Zver; 'Separation of powers in Slovenian political system: problems and solutions', *Journal of comparative politics* 1, 1: 5-33, (2008), co-authored with Marjan Brezovšek; *Sodobni uslužbenski sistemi* (Contemporary civil service systems), FSS Publishing House, Ljubljana (2007), co-authored with Irena Bačlija; 'Limited opportunities for political participation: a case-study of Roma local councillors in Slovenia', *Romani studies* 17, 2: 155-179 (2007), co-authored with Irena Bačlija; 'Positive discrimination of the Roma minority', *Ethnicities* 8, 2: 227-250 (2008), co-authored with Irena Bačlija and Marjan Brezovšek; and 'The relationship between civil servants and politicians in a post-communist country: a case of Slovenia', *Public Administration* 84, 1: 165-184 (2006). Contact information: miro.hacek@fdv.uni-lj.si; Miro Hacek, University of Ljubljana, Faculty of Social Sciences, Kardeljeva ploscad 5, 1000 Ljubljana, Slovenia.

LARS JOHANNSEN is an Associate Professor of Comparative Politics at the Department of Political Science, Aarhus University, Denmark. His research interests include political development, administrative reform and corruption in post-communist countries. Among his recent publications are 'The Responsive State: Openness and Inclusion in the Policy Process' in A.A. Dani & A. de Haan (eds.), *Inclusive States: Social Policy and Structural Inequalities*, The International Bank for Reconstruction and Development, Washington, D.C. The World Bank: 73-95 (2008 with Karin Hilmer Pedersen); 'Europeizacija i implementacija politika u Sloveniji, Republici Češkoj, Mađarskoj i Poljskoj', *Anali* 3: 247-259 (2007); 'Corruption: Commonality, Causes and Consequences in Fifteen Post-communist Countries' in A. Rosenbaum & J. Nemec (eds.), *Democratic Governance in Central and Eastern European Countries*, NISPAcee, Bratislava: 311-336 (2006 with Karin Hilmer Pedersen); and *Från Sovetunionen till Europeiska unionen: De baltiske ländernes fremgångssaga*, BBS, Kalmar (2005 with Sebastian Stålfors). Contact information: johannsen@ps.au.dk, Department of Political Science, Aarhus University, Bartholin Allé, DK-8000 Aarhus C, Denmark.

KARIN HILMER PEDERSEN is an Associate Professor of Comparative Politics at the Department of Political Science, Aarhus University, Denmark. She has a Master's degree in Political Science and a PhD in the Sociology of Law. Her research interests include developments in the EU and its member states, policy transfer, and political, economic, judicial and administrative changes. Issues of research cover corruption, climate and environmental policies. Among her recent publications are 'The Responsive State: Openness and Inclusion in the Policy Process' in A.A. Dani & A. de Haan (eds.), *Inclusive States: Social Policy and Structural Inequalities*, The International Bank for Reconstruction and Development, Washington D.C., The World Bank: 73-95 (2008 with Lars Johannsen); 'The Talk of the Town: Comparing Corruption in the Baltic States and Poland', in M.-B. Schartau, S. Berglund, S. & B. Henningsen (eds.), *Political Culture: Values and Identities in the Baltic Sea Region*, Berlin: Berliner Wissenschafts-Verlag: 117-134 (with Lars Johannsen); and 'Ret og kultur – dilemmaer i Tjekkiets omstilling til en demokratisk retsstat' (Law and culture – dilemmas in the Czech transition to a democratic *rechtsstat*) in O.B. Nielsen & K.H. Pedersen (eds.) *Om ret og kultur*, (On law and culture), Copenhagen: Jurist- og Økonomforbundets Forlag: 103-124. Contact information: khp@ps.au.dk, Department of Political Science, Aarhus University, Bartholin Allé, DK-8000 Aarhus C, Denmark.

VELLO PETTAI is Professor of Comparative Politics at the University of Tartu, Estonia, where he has been working since 1995. He received his PhD in Political Science from Columbia University and did undergraduate work in Russian and Political Science at Middlebury College. His research interests are in democratic transition, ethnopolitics and party development. He has published on Estonia in *Nations and Nationalism, European Journal of Political Research, World Politics, Europe-Asia Studies, Journal of Legislative Studies* and *Journal of Baltic Studies*. Contact information: vello.pettai@ut.ee, Institute of Government and Politics, University of Tartu, 50090 Tartu, Estonia.

RADOSLAW ZUBEK is a postdoctoral Research Fellow in the European Institute at the London School of Economics and Political Science. He holds a PhD in Government (LSE) and an MSc in European Studies (LSE). He is the author of *Core Executive and Europeanization in Central Europe* (Palgrave Macmillan 2008), and has published in the *Journal of European Public Policy, West European Politics, Journal of Legislative Studies, Communist and Post-communist Studies,* and various edited volumes. He has also worked as a consultant to many private and public organisations, including Ernst & Young, OECD-SIGMA, and the Polish Ombudsman Office. Contact information: r.zubek@lse.ac.uk.